OCT 23 '74			

REPRESENTATION

N O M O S

I Authority 1958 (*out of print*)

II Community 1959 (*out of print*)

III Responsibility 1960 (*out of print*)

IV Liberty 1962

V The Public Interest 1962

VI Justice 1963

VII Rational Decision 1964

VIII Revolution 1966

IX Equality 1967

X Representation 1968

NOMOS X

REPRE

SENTATION

Yearbook of the American Society for Political and Legal Philosophy

Edited by J. ROLAND PENNOCK
Swarthmore College

and JOHN W. CHAPMAN
University of Pittsburgh

A T H E R T O N P R E S S · New York · 1968

REPRESENTATION: Nomos X
J. Roland Pennock and John W. Chapman, editors

Address all inquiries to:
Atherton Press, Inc.
70 Fifth Avenue, New York 10011

Library of Congress Catalog Card Number 68-16404

FIRST EDITION

Manufactured in the United States of America

PREFACE

Whether the concept of representation may be usefully employed in political theory and analysis has been questioned, for, as in the case of many terms in our vocabulary, scrutiny quickly reveals its meaning to be vague and ambiguous. Such a concept is bound to arouse the suspicion of those bent upon the achievement of scientific precision. Would we not be better off without it? Could we not rely upon some more operational equivalent? Or does the way to greater clarity run through linguistic and theoretical refinement? The latter course is pursued in this volume; and at least two considerations, one practical and the other philosophical, suggest that our appreciation of the nature of political activity will thereby deepen.

In the first place, whether we like it or no, the concept of representation will probably remain in use for some time to come. The United States Supreme Court's decision in *Baker* v. *Carr* and in others that have followed—especially *Gray* v. *Sanders*[1] in its enunciation of the "one-man, one-vote" standard for the determination of what is fair and constitutional representation—have assured the concept a continuingly prominent place in the literature of political and legal theory. An important, though incidental and unintended, consequence of that line of judicial decision has been a revival, in the United States and elsewhere, of thought and discussion about representation. This volume, and the 1965 meetings of the American Society for Political and Legal Philosophy that gave rise to it, at least point in this direction. It is also worth noting that new concepts, such as "contestation," invented for the purpose of analyzing political relations in more imperfectly representative systems, take on their meaning by way of reflection from the concept of representation: we would seem to have in it one of those peculiarly practical forms of abstraction that A. D. Lindsay called "operative ideals."

In the second place, one is inclined to look beneath mundane usage and usefulness for roots in philosophic vitality. Here the notion of "plastic control," introduced by Karl Popper to describe the relation between two interacting and indeterministic systems, offers an analogy that helps to account both for the difficulties encountered in rendering the concept of representation more precise and for its operational capacities.[2] A society does not determine the actions of its representatives; a representative system does not determine the shape and growth of its society. But between the two a relation of mutual or "plastic" control does exist. It is this relation, into which enter elements of both freedom and rationality, that this volume, in part, seeks to elucidate.

Like its predecessors in this series, this collection of essays does not pretend to completeness of coverage nor to sustained argument throughout. Rather, we have aspired, in soliciting essays in addition to those that were prepared for the meetings, to secure some analysis of aspects of the subject that could not be dealt with on that occasion and, at the same time, to maintain as much unity as practicable.

We note, with appreciation and thanks to Joel Feinberg, Professor of Philosophy at the University of California at Los Angeles,

[1] 372 U.S. 368 (1963).

[2] See Karl Popper, *Of Clouds and Clocks: an Approach to the Problem of Rationality and the Freedom of Man* (St. Louis: Washington University, 1966).

who served as Chairman of the Program Committee, that the contributions by Professors Black, Brown, Cohen, Diggs, Dixon, Novak, Pitkin, Riker and Shapley, and Stokes are lineal descendants, if not replicas, of papers presented by these authors at the annual meetings of the Society.

J. Roland Pennock
John W. Chapman

CONTENTS

Preface vii

THE CONCEPT OF REPRESENTATION

1 Political Representation: An Overview
J. ROLAND PENNOCK 3

2 Practical Representation
B. J. DIGGS 28

3 Commentary: The Paradox of Representation
HANNA PITKIN 38

4 Commentary: Representation and the Problem of Identity
JULIUS COHEN 43

5 Two Notes on Representation
WILLIAM K. FRANKENA 49

HISTORICAL DISCUSSION

6 Modern and Medieval Representation
HARVEY C. MANSFIELD, JR. 55

7 An Augustan Debate: Notes on the History of the Idea of Representation
ISAAC KRAMNICK 83

THE THEORY OF REPRESENTATION

8 Electors and Representatives: A Contribution to the Theory of Representation
MAREK SOBOLEWSKI 95

9 Representation, Governmental Stability, and Decisional Effectiveness
ERIC A. NORDLINGER 108

CONSTITUTIONAL DECISIONS AND THE THEORY OF REPRESENTATION

10 Representation in Law and Equity
CHARLES L. BLACK, JR. 131

11 Black on Representation: A Question
STUART M. BROWN, JR. 144

12 Political Parties in the Normative Theory of Representation
DONALD E. STOKES 150

13 Standards for Representative Selection and Apportionment
LEWIS A. DEXTER 155

14 Representation Values and Reapportionment Practice: The Eschatology of "One-Man, One-Vote"
ROBERT G. DIXON, JR. 167

WEIGHTED VOTING AND THE THEORY OF REPRESENTATION

15 Weighted Voting: A Mathematical Analysis for Instrumental Judgments
WILLIAM H. RIKER and LLOYD S. SHAPLEY 199

16 Weighted Voting and "One-Man, One-Vote"
ROBERT NOZICK 217

EXTRA-ELECTIVE REPRESENTATION

17 The Bureaucracy as Representatives
JOSEPH P. WITHERSPOON 229

REPRESENTATION UNDER NONCOMPETITIVE PARTY SYSTEMS

18 The Mechanism of Popular Activity in the Exercise of State Authority in People's Poland
WITOLD ZAKRZEWSKI 259

19 Notes for a Theory of Nondemocratic Representation
DAVID E. APTER 278

CONTRIBUTORS

DAVID E. APTER
Political Science, University of California, Berkeley

CHARLES L. BLACK, JR.
Law, Yale University

STUART M. BROWN, JR.
Philosophy, Cornell University

JULIUS COHEN
Law, Rutgers, The State University

LEWIS A. DEXTER
Political Science, Belmont, Massachusetts

B. J. DIGGS
Philosophy, University of Illinois

ROBERT G. DIXON, JR.
Law, The George Washington University

WILLIAM K. FRANKENA
Philosophy, The University of Michigan

ISAAC KRAMNICK
Political Science, Brandeis University

HARVEY C. MANSFIELD, JR.
Political Science, Harvard University

ERIC A. NORDLINGER
Political Science, Brandeis University

ROBERT NOZICK
Philosophy, The Rockefeller University

J. ROLAND PENNOCK
Political Science, Swarthmore College

HANNA PITKIN
Political Science, University of California, Berkeley

WILLIAM H. RIKER
Political Science, University of Rochester

MAREK SOBOLEWSKI
Political Science, University of Cracow, Poland

LLOYD S. SHAPLEY
Mathematics, The Rand Corporation

DONALD E. STOKES
Political Science, The University of Michigan

JOSEPH P. WITHERSPOON
Law, The University of Texas

WITOLD ZAKRZEWSKI
Political Science, Jagellonian University, Cracow, Poland

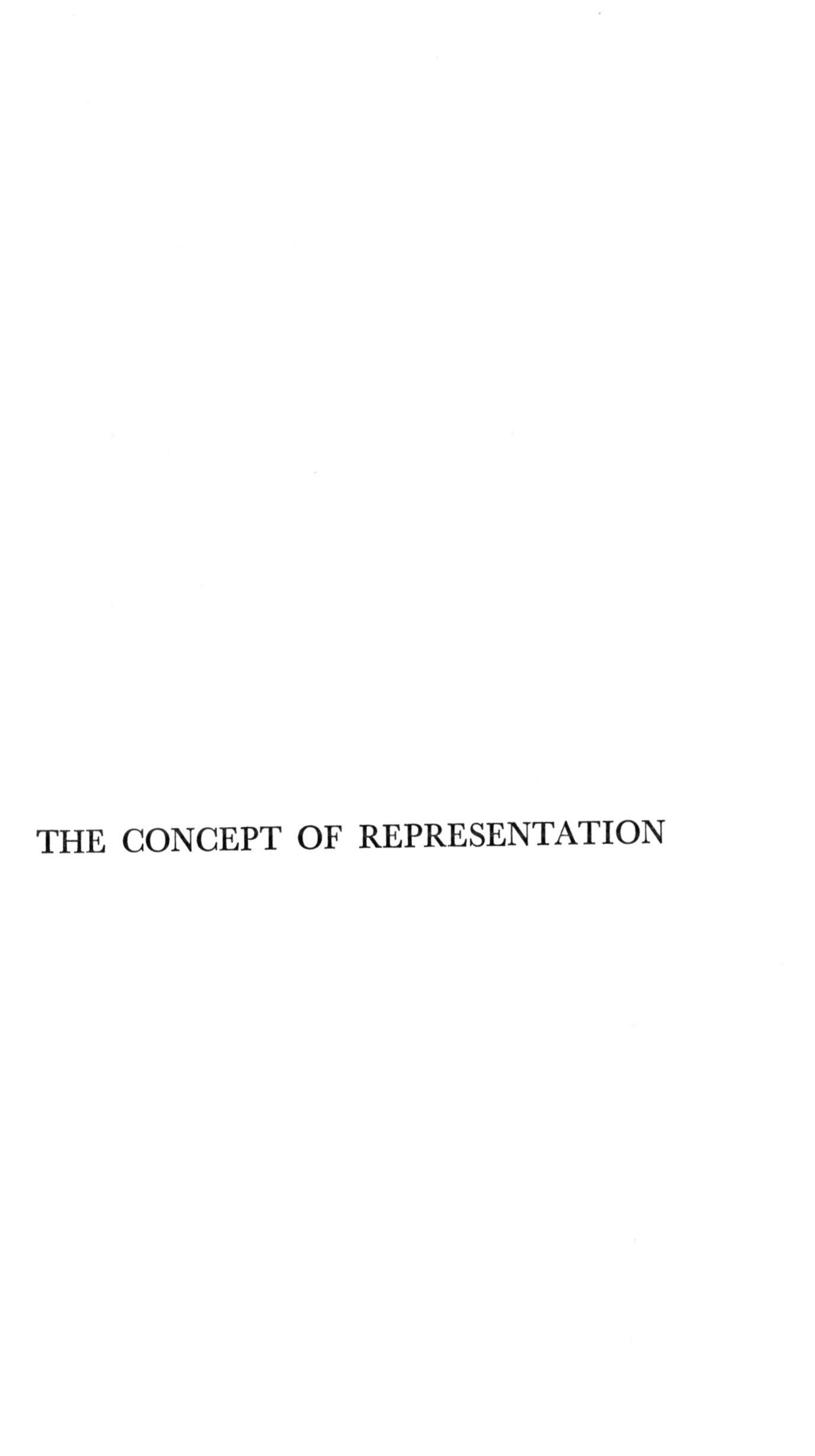

THE CONCEPT OF REPRESENTATION

1

POLITICAL REPRESENTATION: AN OVERVIEW

J. ROLAND PENNOCK

"Our common conceptions of representation are obsolete."[1] So declared Heinz Eulau at a recent meeting of the American Political Science Association. He argued that both Burkean analysis and the attempt to deal with the concept of representation primarily in terms of responsiveness and responsibility were inadequate. He noted also that the literature concerning the new nations contains very slight references to representation and suggested that this fact provided further evidence of the obsolescence of the term.[2]

I am indebted to my co-editor and to Professor Robert F. Lyke of Bryn Mawr College, as well as to members of Dr. Brian Barry's Politics Group at Nuffield College, Oxford, for helpful comments on an earlier draft of this chapter.

1 "Legislators and Magistrates," mimeographed; paper delivered at the meetings of the American Political Science Association, September 1966.

2 How much it takes to exceed "very slight references" is a matter of

A few years ago, H. B. Mayo reached a similar conclusion. "Democratic theory," he wrote, "has little to gain from talking the language of representation, since everything necessary to the theory may be put in terms of (a) legislators (or decision-makers) who are (b) legitimated or authorized to enact public policies, and who are (c) subject or responsible to public control at free elections. The difficulties of policy-makers are practical," he continued, "and there is no need to confuse democratic politics by a theory that makes the difficulties appear to be metaphysical or logical within the concept of representation."[3]

Statements like these, coming from both empirical and theoretical directions, might well give pause to anyone who would give further serious consideration to the subject. At the very least they call for a justification of the present enterprise, which this introductory chapter aims to supply.[4]

My argument will proceed along two lines. The first will point out that parts of the government other than elected representatives (members of the legislature) serve representative functions and that the concept of representation then links or relates to each other these various carriers of representative roles.[5] The second point will be that even the personnel more specifically thought of as "representatives," i.e., members of an elective legislature, have various roles from which frequently emerge conflicting directives that can be reconciled only by reference to some superior set of norms. It is suggested here

---

judgment. Lucian Pye, in his general summary of the theory and practice of political development, makes numerous references, and in more than incidental fashion, to political representation. See Lucian W. Pye, *Aspects of Political Development* (Boston: Little, Brown, 1966), pp. 20, 21, 26, and 81. See also Samuel P. Huntington, "Political Development and Political Decay," *World Politics,* 17 (April 1965), 386–430, at 414; and his "Political Modernization: America vs. Europe," *World Politics*, 18 (April 1966), 378–414, at 412–13. A third instance is provided by Edward Shils, "Opposition in the New States of Asia and Africa," *Government and Opposition,* 1 (January–April 1966), 175–204, at 201.

[3] H. B. Mayo, *An Introduction to Democratic Theory* (New York: Oxford University Press, 1960), p. 103.

[4] Of course, the subject of elective legislatures would lose none of its present importance no matter what happened to the concept of representation; hence, many of the chapters in this volume would emerge unscathed from any attack on that concept.

[5] An even broader concept of representation than that presented here, and one that stresses more than I do the two-way flow of information and influence, will be found in the final chapter in this volume by Professor David Apter.

that, in some measure, the concept of representation, *considered in the specific contexts in which it is applied,* provides this superior set of norms. Much that would be hopelessly vague considered in the abstract becomes more precise in actual application. In making this second point I shall give some indication of the relation between the theory of representation and certain analyses and empirical studies of legislative roles.[6]

To guard against misconceptions, certain explanatory notes are in order here. In the first place, I assume that the word "representation" may not always have had the same meaning and that it may not always mean the same thing today in different countries. Where the context does not indicate otherwise, I am speaking of Anglo-American usage in the twentieth century.[7]

Second, while I shall deal mainly with the "concept" of representation, I shall refer also to various "theories" of representation. The two may be kept mutually distinct, but they tend to merge; and just where the line is to be drawn between them is in a measure arbitrary. For instance, if the word meant—as it does not—that a "representative" was a person who should do what and only what his constituents demanded of him, one would not need a "theory" about his proper role. The substance of such a theory would have been incorporated into the definition. If, on the other hand, the word meant that a representative was a person empowered to do whatever he chose on behalf of those whom he represented, and this was all it meant, then only a theory about how representatives should behave could supply such a normative element.[8] In other words, in default of general agreement upon a single theory, no theory would become part of the definition, but the latter would tend to be supplemented by two or more alternative theories. Incidentally, this explains why I said above that representation "may" not always have had the same meaning. Whether the meaning of the term itself

[6] In this connection I have in mind especially the extensive and valuable study of *The Legislative System* by John C. Wahlke, Heinz Eulau, William Buchanan, and LeRoy C. Ferguson (New York: Wiley, 1962).

[7] Most of what I shall have to say relates primarily to the American situation, being rendered not wrong but largely irrelevant by the strength of party commitment in Britain. See pp. 23–24.

[8] A "theory" of representation may relate to how representatives do in fact behave (descriptive theory) or it may be some sort of prescriptive or normative theory, relating to how representatives believe they should behave, or to how their constituents believe they should behave. It is the latter with which this essay will be mainly concerned.

varied depends upon how much of the attendant theory one tries to pack into the definition.

Finally, as has been already implied, it will not be argued that all elements of vagueness can be eliminated from the term. Nor is vagueness always a vice; indeed, in moderation, it may be a virtue! Ponder that popular (and useful) term in modern political science, "consensus"; or consider "power," "liberty," "cleavage," or "the public interest." Imprecise terms, in this case terms that lay down a standard (as contrasted with a rule) of conduct, often have the virtue of holding together, before the mind's eye, related though distinct ideas. They show linkages and continuities that might otherwise be overlooked. Synthesis as well as analysis has its uses in contributing to the understanding of systems of all kinds, including political systems. As the use of the word "standards" may suggest, terms with some element of vagueness are especially likely to be required where norms are involved, but the examples of "power," "consensus," and "cleavage" show that not only normative terms are difficult to render precise.

POLITICAL REPRESENTATION NOT CONFINED TO THE DEMOCRATIC STATE

In considering political representation in its broadest sense, we should remember that the idea of political representation is by no means modern or confined to the democratic state.[9] In a proper

[9] I do not speak here of symbolic representation, referred to in Professor Diggs' essay (Chapter 2), for it is hardly "political representation," at least in the restricted sense in which that term is being used here. The flag, for instance, is a political symbol, and in a sense it stands for, or represents, the nation. Its function is to make present in the minds of the viewers the idea of the nation. An individual, too, a monarch or a president, may be the vehicle for symbolic representation, as various heads of state, or their deputies, represented their countries at the funerals of President Kennedy and Konrad Adenauer. But presidents who are more than ceremonial figures are also "political representatives" in the sense in which that term is used here. Yet it would be easy to overdo the distinction. It is probably not more than a matter of degree. The substance of representation varies with the context. For certain purposes, the kind of representation that is called for is purely formal; it has nothing to do with policy; it may even be performed by an inanimate object. It is this kind of passive and completely "mindless" representation that I am excluding from discussion here. For a fascinating and illuminating treatise on this kind of representation, see E. H. Kantorowicz, *The King's Two Bodies: a Study in Medieval Political Theology* (Princeton: Princeton University Press, 1957).

use of the word, all legitimate governments are "representative." Thus medieval kings were thought to be made legitimate not only by hereditary right and divine ordination but also by the acclaim of the nobles. They owed their authority also, at least in some dim past, to the people more generally, or so it was widely held. It was part of their office as well to see that justice was done, "to protect the poor as well as the rich in the enjoyment of their rights."[10] Even that great apostle of Divine Right, James I, considered himself trustee for the realm, though accountable to no one but God for the execution of that trust.

Thomas Hobbes, absolutist of a different sort, insisted that his sovereign was representative of the polity, having been authorized to rule by the unanimous voices of the citizenry. While, as Hanna Pitkin says, this was "formal" rather than "substantive" representation,[11] and is an example of the opposite of the delegate theory of representation, yet Hobbes' sovereign, like James I, had a duty to maintain justice and serve the interest of the people, it being understood (as far as Hobbes is concerned) that their primary interest was security.[12] Finally, it will do no harm to remind ourselves that even the modern totalitarian dictator, even Hitler, sought legitimacy by claiming to represent the people. Ultimate power and final responsibility were his, said the Führer, because through him the true spirit of the German people found expression. He also sought to authenticate his legitimacy by claiming the constitutional legality of his regime and by subsequent reliance upon plebiscites. And of course he was recognized by the governments of other states as the authorized spokesman, the representative, of the German people.

It will be noted that the two main claims of monarchs and dictators from which their legitimacy appears to have derived were (1) the contention that they stood for, gave expression to, and supported the interests (and, we should add, ideals and aspirations) of their people; and (2) the argument that they were in some fashion

[10] R. W. and A. J. Carlyle, *Medieval Political Theory* (Edinburgh & London: William Blackwood & Sons, 1915), III, 33.

[11] Hanna Pitkin, *The Concept of Representation* (Berkeley: University of California Press, forthcoming).

[12] It is perhaps worth emphasizing that Hobbes' theory that, since the sovereign had, in his view, been authorized by the people to speak and act for them, therefore each subject was the "author" of all the sovereign's commands, was in certain respects less far removed from medieval theory than is commonly recognized.

authorized to act (generally within variously stated or implied limits) in their behalf. All this is not of mere historical interest, nor applicable only to nondemocratic states. *All* regimes obtain legitimacy by being in some degree representative or at least convincing their subjects that they are. One of the traditional arguments for absolute monarchy has been that the monarch could have no interest that conflicted with that of the welfare of the realm, since his greatness varied directly with its greatness.

As certain elements of the realm became dissatisfied with the operation of this theory, they demanded a more responsive form of representation, one over which they had control.[13] Thus today the man in the street tends to think of elected officers and especially of the elected legislature as *the* representative body and of its members as *the* representatives. Elections are thought of as providing the great sanction for assuring representative behavior. Above all else, they supply the element of authorization, keeping it current. It is reasonable to believe that they tend to secure governmental action in the interest of those whom they are supposed to represent, both by enforcing accountability and by giving some indication of what the people consider their interests to be.[14]

THE BUREAUCRACY AND REPRESENTATION

Yet it would be a great mistake to assume that elections are the only means by which persons in positions of authority are encouraged to act representatively, even today, or that elected officers

[13] Of course, this is schematized history at best. In England, for instance, elected representatives were first created at the king's instance (although it is doubtful that they had legislative power); but the statement is valid for a later period. This distinction, it may be noted, is compatible with Mansfield's contention (see Chapter 6) that modern representative government did not come about as a gradual development from medieval representation; but it is in no way dependent upon his particular theory of what happened.

[14] Hard data on such questions of causation are difficult to secure. It was V. O. Key's cautious conclusion, after surveying the data, that constituency opinion is one of the factors influencing the votes of legislators. He also concluded that legislators frequently have considerable freedom of choice (freedom from constituency pressure) and that they tend to exercise this choice in a way that suggests a relation between the votes they cast and the characteristics of the constituency (as revealed by demographic data). V. O. Key, Jr., *Public Opinion and American Democracy* (New York: Knopf, 1961), pp. 486–87.

are the only ones whose behavior is in a measure representative. Members of the bureaucracy, even though they may be practically immune from even indirect elective pressure, are expected to exercise their discretionary authority subject at least to some guidance by the norms of representation.[15] This point, treated at length by Joseph Witherspoon in Chapter 17, need not be elaborated here. However, in one of its meanings, the concept of representation is normative in the ethical sense; and like all such norms, it has a certain force of its own, without reliance upon externally imposed sanctions. This, of course, is not to deny that the discretionary powers delegated to administrative officials may not in some cases be so great that internalized norms (either of a representational or of a professional variety) are an inedequate assurance of representative behavior, as Professor Witherspoon argues.

In arguing that administrators, especially those having broad discretionary powers or exercising great influence on the making of policy, are acting in a representative role, I do not mean that this is the only role they play or even that the role in this context calls for the same behavior as it would in a legislative context. The circumstances associated with the establishment of the authority in question, especially the terms of the basic legislation, may indicate that the wishes of a particular segment of the polity, perhaps a particular industry, are to be given exceptional weight in the exercise of this authority. Or they may suggest that representation in this case should veer sharply away from the responsiveness-to-desire pole toward that of estimation of public interest.[16] Naturally, the first type of situation might be expected to prevail where the powers to be exercised have their major impact on the section of the public in question and where the issues are such that this public would normally have the most relevant information or expertise. The

[15] It is at least an arguable position to contend that, as the policy role of bureaucracies in both England and the United States has increased, and as this role has become more widely recognized, the ideal of administrative "neutrality" has weakened and the demand to strengthen popular control over those administrators who in fact make policy in important matters has grown. One thinks, for example, of Britain's recently created specialized select committees for the supervision of administration. It should be noted that what is discussed in this chapter as "administrative representation" or "representation through the bureaucracy" is dealt with by David Apter, in Chapter 19, under the heading of "functional" representation.

[16] The distinction between "desire" and "interest" will be discussed later.

powers of the United States Department of Agriculture over acreage allotments, under the Agricultural Adjustment Act, would be a good example.

A rather different situation, which also frequently leads to the demand for a more "representative" bureaucracy, is found where a new policy has been established, let us say for the benefit of some group deemed to be especially in need of governmental assistance. This demand may result in the creation of a new agency, independent of other departments and staffed as far as possible by personnel who are highly sympathetic with the new policy. They may therefore be expected to be especially concerned to find out the desires and interests (particularly the "needs") of the group in question. The "poverty program" and its Office of Economic Opportunity provide an obvious example.

One may note a certain similarity between this analysis and that of Don Price in his discussion of the relations among what he calls the new "estates": (1) the scientific, (2) the professional, (3) the administrative, and (4) the political. He suggests two principles to govern the delegation of authority to these groups: "(1) the closer the estate is to the end of the spectrum that is concerned solely with truth, the more it is entitled to freedom and self-government; and (2) the closer it gets to the exercise of power, the less it is permitted to organize itself as a corporate entity, and the more it is required to submit itself to the test of political responsibility, in the sense of submitting to the ultimate decision of the electorate."[17] For our purposes the contrast is not so much between freedom and responsibility (or accountability) as it is between judgment of public interest and response to demand (desires).

ELECTED REPRESENTATIVES: GENERAL THEORY

Let me turn to my second theme, elected representatives, which has already been briefly introduced. First, in speaking of "elected representatives" I am referring to members of a legislature with power, collectively, to make laws and determine national policy. In principle, elected representatives need have no such power. They might be simply advisory or expressive. Thus a modern

[17] Don K. Price, *The Scientific Estate* (Cambridge: Harvard University Press, 1965), pp. 135–48. (The quotation is from p. 137.)

elective legislator—at least in the Anglo-American tradition—is not simply a representative. He has powers that do not necessarily adhere to representing. But whatever else he may be, whatever roles he may play, he is a representative and therefore should act representatively, subject to the norms of representation, whatever they may be.[18] In the United States, the same is true of the President: he performs his functions as President in a representative capacity, subject therefore to the norms attached to this concept as they apply in the context of his office.

Whether leadership is to be considered as an aspect of representing, as entailed by it, or as a necessary means to performing the

[18] Professor A. Phillips Griffiths has argued that political representation is a variety of ascriptive representation in his article "How Can One Person Represent Another?" *Aristotelian Society,* Suppl. Vol. XXXIV (1960), 182–208. An ascriptive representative is one who has authority to act for and commit those whom he represents. At best, this theory seems to me to place the emphasis in the wrong place—on the powers of the representative rather than on his responsibilities. Further, I am not sure in what sense political representatives *can* always "commit" those whom they represent. If my representative votes unsuccessfully for a bill, I am in no way committed by his action. Likewise, if he makes a speech condemning the President, or libeling someone, it would appear to be not the representative who has the power to commit me but the body of which he is a member. Even then I am "committed" only in the sense that I am legally bound to obey duly enacted legislation, as I might be—perhaps less strongly—even in the absence of "representative" government.

Two other concepts of representation discussed by Griffiths should also be mentioned. He disposes effectively of the idea of "descriptive" representation—representation by persons who as nearly as possible reflect the complexion of the constituency. As he says, no one would argue that morons should be represented by morons. Insofar as it is felt desirable to have a given group represented by members of that group, it is surely as a means to the end of getting the point of view of that group expressed and its interests advanced. In any given case, descriptive representation may or may not be the best way to accomplish those purposes.

Griffiths' final category, representation of interests, would not today find many supporters as a theory pertaining to members of a legislature. Interests pertain to people. It is true that geographically selected representatives may by themselves give inadequate attention to certain important interests. This is the justification for the extensive operations of pressure groups. But to incorporate the representation of interests as such into the legislative body creates problems that have never been solved—problems of selection and of the weighting of interests. Consequently, in the Anglo-American tradition at least, countries have come to consider interest representation on the one hand as one aspect of how representatives selected by geographically defined constituencies do and should behave, and on the other hand as the basis for representative devices supplementary to the more formal, legislative representatives. (The role played by representation of interests in developing countries is discussed by David Apter in Chapter 19.)

representative function, is of no real importance; but a discussion of representation without reference to leadership would lack an important element. Those who seek to represent large numbers of people are bound to find that consensus, even majority opinion, is often lacking. Likewise they may be convinced that what their constituents seem to desire and what is in their real interest or in the national interest, as the case may be, are far apart. In either case, the optimal performance of their function calls for leadership, for forming or re-forming public opinion, and for building consensus, thus easing the task of representation by lessening the tension between its frequently conflicting norms of reflecting constituency desires and pursuing constituency and national interest. That is to say, the very fact that representatives are severally related to distinct localities strongly implies that they have a special obligation to look after the desires and interests of the people in those localities (or the national interest as seen by the voters in those localities). Clearly, at least in the United States, this is the accepted theory. The difference between the United States and Great Britain will be discussed later on.

When we were talking about a monarch or dictator professing to represent a realm, with no authorized intermediary spokesmen, the question of whose view of the national interest should be considered did not arise. But now that attention has shifted to a group of elected intermediaries, close enough to their constituents that it is possible for them to know the views of the majority on a few issues, that question does arise. We now have the outlines of four distinct theories about the duty of a representative. These theories may be stated in the following propositions:

1. The representative should act in support of what he believes an effective majority of his constituency desires.[19]

2. The representative should act in support of what he believes is in the constituency's interest.

3. The representative should act in support of what he believes the nation (or an effective majority of it) desires.

[19] Desires, of course, need not be self-regarding; they may relate to the realization of ideals. This theory is variously known as the "delegate theory" or, in Professor Sobolewski's terms, the theory of "imperative mandate." (See Chapter 8). The term "effective majority," though not uncommon in the literature of political science, is vague. It is used here simply to indicate that the notion of representation, as I believe it is properly understood, includes weighing the intensity of opinions as well as counting them.

4. The representative should act in support of what he believes is in the nation's interest. (Sobolewski's "free mandate."[20])

It will be observed that these theories rely heavily upon the distinction between "interest" and "desire." Because the first of these terms, in particular, is notoriously ambiguous or vague, I must digress to discuss the meaning intended here. I believe that for present purposes the word's ambiguities can be confined within reasonable limits. When I speak of the "interest" of a person, or a constituency, or a nation, I mean "advantage." An action, policy, law, or institution is in the interest of a person if it increases his opportunity to get what he desires, including the realization of his aspirations and ideals.[21] To spell this out a little further, the distinction I am intending to make between "desire" and "interest" is the distinction between what is immediately demanded and what in the long run, with the benefit of hindsight, would have been preferred or would have contributed to the development of the individual into a person capable of making responsible decisions.

If, after the representative has done his best to form an enlightened opinion, he believes that a given measure would in fact improve, for example, the economic or educational level of his constituency, other things being equal he would be entitled to conclude that it is in their interest. Of course, most of the time he will be making the kind of judgments that involve weighing an advantage against a disadvantage (both being incurred by the same

[20] The analysis by Wahlke, Eulau, *et al.* of the roles of a representative is much more detailed than the set of four theories enumerated here. They speak of representational "styles" and representational "focuses." Under the former heading, they identify "delegates," "trustees," and "politicos" (an intermediate category), corresponding closely to the analysis given here; but under the heading of "focus" they consider such "clientele roles" as the "party role," the "areal role," the "pressure group role," and the "administrative role." (Wahlke *et al., op. cit.*, p. 14 and Ch. 12.) It seems clear that these various roles impose conflicting demands upon the legislator and that they all relate to his role as representative. It is one contention of this essay that the concept of representation considered in the context of particular situations can be of some assistance in solving this problem.

[21] See Brian M. Barry, "The Use and Abuse of 'The Public Interest,' " in Carl J. Friedrich, ed., *The Public Interest,* Nomos V (New York: Atherton, 1964), 191–204; also Brian Barry, *Political Argument* London: Routledge & Kegan Paul, 1965), p. 176. See also, especially for what follows in the text above, S. I. Benn, " 'Interests' in Politics," *Proceedings of the Aristotelian Society* 1959/60, 122–40, at 139. On the terms "interest" and "public interest," see as well Richard E. Flathman, *The Public Interest* (New York: Wiley, 1966), Chap. 2.

course of action), just as an individual tries to decide whether something is in his interest. All that can be demanded is that the representative make this kind of judgment as wisely and impartially as he can. In most cases the standard will not be more vague than the one we all must use for our private choices. The same will be true when a decision must be made between what is judged to be a great advantage for a sizable minority and a lesser advantage for a bare majority. All this must be within the framework of what the society in question has established (whether or not in the form of a written constitution) as proper for the state to do—i.e., it must respect recognized rights.

To return now from definitional digression to our discussion of theories of representation, it is well known that American legislators do not all adopt the same theory. At least, when they are asked about how they view their roles, some stress the delegate concept, while others say they consider themselves trustees; some are constituency-oriented, while others take a more Burkean view.[22] The thesis that will be advanced here, however, is that, regardless of what they may say, legislators in fact do not have this wide a choice.[23] It will be argued further that the common understanding of representation itself, shaped partly by the circumstances, provides guidance, even though the area of "common understanding" is not complete.

DELEGATE VERSUS TRUSTEE

Among these theories, it is probably safe to say that the dichotomy between acting as a delegate and acting as a trusteee is most fundamental. It also seems clear that neither pole of this dichotomy is adequate to explain democratic representation in the

[22] See Wahlke *et al.*, *op. cit.*, especially Chap. 12, and Frank J. Sorauf, *Party and Representation* (New York: Atherton, 1963), Chap. 6.

[23] As V. O. Key, Jr., put it: "Most of the time the elegant prose spilled over the question whether a legislator should be a man and vote his mature convictions or a mouse and bow abjectly to the parochial demands of his constituents is irrelevant to the realities." Key, *op. cit.*, p. 482. Of course, it is by no means my contention that legislators have no discretion. Nor would I deny that legislators may differ somewhat among themselves as to how they in fact interpret their roles. My colleague, Charles E. Gilbert, has written very perceptively about certain traditional types of political theory as they affect doctrines of representation. See his "Operative Theories of Representation," *American Political Science Review,* 57 (September 1963), 604–18. Insofar as these theories might affect the actual behavior of representatives (a subject not discussed by Gilbert), it would appear to be largely, but

modern Anglo-American tradition. For a representative to act purely and simply as a delegate would be to make him functionless most, if not all, of the time, for it is seldom clear precisely what a constituency, or even its majority, wishes. Most of the individuals who compose it either do not know enough or do not care enough (or both) about the issues on which their representatives must vote to have clear opinions of their own; and even when opinions are formed, a majority is likely to be lacking. Representing a constituency is not like representing a client, whose wishes, on a single issue at least, are presumably unitary. A constituency, on the contrary, is rarely unified, even on a single question. Of course, in some cases a clear majority has a definite view on an issue. It might be argued that in such cases the representative should act as a delegate, supporting the majority's desires even though he believes these desires are contrary to their own interests. Thinking for himself and deliberating on the basis of discussion with others, in other words, should be reserved for cases where no clear majority opinion unopposed by an intense minority exists. This is, to be sure, a logically possible position. My own view is that it would not be held by many thoughtful people who consider the implication of the legislative situation, with its opportunties for discussion, deliberation, and obtaining information. In any case, the burden of proof under these circumstances would certainly be on the legislator to justify voting contrary to the majority will.

Similarly, in other ways, what "representation" entails is affected by the context of the office of elected legislator. For instance, if the general attitude of the people in a given constituency were, let us say, anti-French, one would properly say that a person who held that attitude was, other things being equal, "representative" of the constituency. It would not follow, however, that a representative elected by this constituency should vote for anti-French policies, regardless of other considerations. Interests would also need to be taken into account.

But the interest pole of the desire-interest axis is also untenable. Even Burke did not contend that it was the proper function of a representative to act without any consideration of the desires of those whom he represented.[24] In fact, it appears to be generally

---

not entirely, a matter of whether they took a narrow or broad (including ideals) view of "interest."

[24] In his Bristol address, referring to his constituents, he said, "their wishes

agreed that representation in a democratic context makes the satisfaction of popular desire itself a legitimate interest, thus blunting the sharpness of the contrast between representation of desires and representation of interests. It seems clear, then, that the proper role of a political representative today is generally believed to fall somewhere between these poles, as several contributors to this volume maintain. Thus, it is argued here, the prevailing concept of political representation itself gives some guidance for the reconciliation of these conflicts.

Let us consider the delegate-trustee issue in the light of a series of examples illustrating various combinations of strong or weak (and positive or negative) majority desires, strong or weak (and positive or negative) minority desires, and strong or weak (and positive or negative) convictions on the part of the representative as to the constituency's real interest. Suppose it is a question of whether funds should be spent on a fish hatchery and a research institute to study certain diseases that have been limiting the local fish supply, or whether they should be spent on improving the roads. Assuming that motorists outnumber anglers by a staggering ratio, it is not unlikely that a majority, while not feeling very strongly about the matter, might oppose the hatchery, whereas only the minority would have very strong feelings about it and support it. Suppose also that the legislator's own study convinced him that the hatchery and research institute were, on balance, more in the public interest than the additional funds for roads (perhaps partly because of a putative lift to the tourist industry and, through it, to the economy as a whole). Under these circumstances a vote for the fishermen would seem to be in order. If, however, his informed judgment was clearly in the contrary direction, he should vote for the roads. But what if it seemed to him a toss-up? Should he follow the rather passive majority or the relatively small but demanding minority? To this question no pat answer is available. If electoral considerations point in one direction or the other, that fact in itself would be significant and it would be right to allow them to govern.

Now take a proposal to fluoridate the water supply. Polls reveal that 45 per cent of the electorate are mildly in favor of the plan, 40

---

ought to have great weight with [their representative]; their opinion high respect; their business unremitting attention." *The Works of the Right Honorable Edmund Burke* (The World's Classics, Vol. LXXXI [London and New York: Oxford University Press, 1906]), Vol. II, p. 164.

per cent are indifferent, and 15 per cent are violently opposed and strongly organized. (The medical association, comprising about 0.5 per cent of the population, is on record as strongly favoring the proposal.) The representative in question, having read the literature submitted to him by the medical association and by the antifluoridation society, as well as that supplied by the public health authorities (cf. Wahlke's "administration" role), is firmly convinced that the fears expressed by the "antis" are groundless and that in the long run fluoridation would be of great advantage to all members of the society. Here again the duty of the representative seems clear enough: to vote for fluoridation. Suppose, however, that the campaign of the "antis" has been highly successful. Opinion polls show the following distribution:

Strongly pro	10%
Weakly pro	20%
Indifferent	10%
Weakly anti	30%
Strongly anti	30%

How should the legislator "represent" his constituents in this situation, still assuming that he is convinced that no harm to health or the security of the country, and a great deal of good, will come of the move? It would appear that we are now in a gray zone where the norms of representation are at best ambiguous. A strong majority will oppose a strong general interest. He might argue (to himself) that, while the satisfaction of desire is always a good in itself and exerts a claim upon the representative, the claim is weakened when the desire is clearly based upon a misconception of the facts. Such a weakened claim might be overridden by the strong claim based upon the enlightened view of interest. This would be my conclusion on the facts as stated.

As another example, let us consider proposed anti-closed-shop ("right-to-work") legislation. We shall assume a widespread popular prejudice against the closed shop, while the pressure groups of business and organized labor (the latter being considerably the larger but a minority of the electorate) line up, respectively, pro and con. This case is in some ways similar to the preceding one; but the question of "interest" here is much less susceptible to objective determination, and opinion among the experts is more sharply divided. Assuming that the vote must be "yes" or "no," the presumption would appear to be for following the legislator's own instructed judgment of what was in the constituency's interest.

But now suppose that a substantial segment of business sided with labor on the issue (finding that the closed shop made for greater stability of labor relations). In this situation, even though the two made up only a sizable minority of the electorate, there would be a strong argument that representation of the people (a weighted amalgam of their desires and their interests) called for siding with the minority, unless the legislator's own instructed judgment of constituency interest pointed strongly in the opposite direction.[25]

The very way in which these hypothetical cases have been discussed indicates that the concept of representation, while giving a fairly clear answer to some of the dilemmas created by the multiple roles that a democratic legislator must play, is bound to leave large gray areas. Two devices for narrowing these areas are open to him. First, he may (and should) exert leadership in his constituency to narrow the gap between effective desire and constituency interest as he perceives it. The second means, likely to be effective in more cases than the first, is to find some accommodation between the opposing groups, some modification of the original proposal that, at best, might accomplish what each was really after and, at the least, might minimize the frustration of one side without seriously alienating the other. In the case of the anti-closed-shop proposal, a law that permitted the union shop might fill this requirement.

We need not cite further examples, although other combinations of weak and strong, and minority and majority desires and interests are possible and undoubtedly are found in practice. However, a few words about what Wahlke *et al.* refer to as the "consensual role" of legislators are relevant. Members of a legislative body must cooperate with each other in a multitude of ways, of which accepting the leadership of recognized party leaders in the legislative chamber is one, but not the only one. This role may call for behavior in certain cases that is not apparently compatible with what the representative norms would seem to demand. Yet even the requirements imposed by the existence of a group of friends in the legislature

[25] Note that in these examples the Wahlke categories of pressure groups and administration have been included and dealt with as aspects of the context within which the representational norms are applied. Both are suppliers of certain kinds of relevant information.

who frequently support each other's interests in very informal return for like conduct on the part of other members of the group may be indirectly in the interests of the constituents of each of these members. Thus, whether or not the "consensual role" is thought of as distinct from "representation," it in fact may, and, I would argue, should, serve the same ends and be subject ultimately to the same tests of correctness. It is useful to point it out as a separate item; but it would be a mistake not to recognize it as a part of a larger whole whose norms help to define its legitimate claims.

Now a word about electoral considerations, a factor that was deliberately put aside in the preceding discussion. Suppose that our model representative, having made the kind of analysis we have been discussing, decides that he ought to vote for *X*. At this point he considers the probable effect of this course of action on his chances for re-election and decides that they will be decidedly diminished.[26] What effect, if any, should this have on his decision, if he is to stick to the norms of "representing"? In the first place, it might properly serve as a warning to recheck his previous calculations and judgments. Perhaps he had misjudged the intensity of certain desires. Assuming, however, that he found no reason to alter his appraisal, he might have decided to support what he felt to be the true interest of his constituency against its own misguided judgment (for example, in the fluoridation case). Now if indeed he were convinced, after careful study, that this would cost him his seat, should that fact, within the norms of representation, affect his decision? (We must assume that his vote in the legislative body might determine the outcome.) It would appear that the only rational way for him to go about answering this question would be to estimate the alternative to his occupying the seat and the balance of representativeness for the constituency, on all issues, if his opponent held it. By this judgment, barring party and national interest considerations, to be discussed below, he must be bound. In considering the practical operation of this formula, it must be borne in mind that if, for ex-

[26] Of course, this is quite different from saying that he had decided to vote in a way that the majority would oppose. Voters will not necessarily switch their position just because they disagree with the stand of their representative on a particular issue—or, for that matter, on a great many issues! Conversely, even though he had decided to vote in a way that a majority of the voters would approve, his action might still cost him his seat (if most of the majority were made up of members of the opposition party).

ample, voting for fluoridation would cost him his seat, it is highly probable that his opponent would also vote for fluoridation.[27]

But one must consider the question of whether in certain instances a representative may have a higher duty than to represent his constituency (still putting aside considerations of party and national interest). The clearest, if not the only, case would be that of a matter of conscience, a case where justice or moral right might be thought to conflict with constituency desire and possibly even with constituency interest. The case of segregation naturally comes to mind. Of course, if a segregationist constituency has elected an integrationist, knowing him to be such and in the absence of any pledge on his part to support the constituency views in this matter, no problem arises. They have waived any right to object; they have made the judgment that, all things considered, he will represent them better than any alternative that is open to them.[28] But suppose he has kept silent (or equivocated) on the subject and that he is certain that if he cast an integrationist vote it would cost him his seat at the next election. If he acts as a representative, he must go contrary to his conscience (i.e., to another ethical norm).[29] He faces a dilemma in which he must choose between ethical norms, a not unusual circumstance in life, and he must work out his solution by calculating and weighing consequences or by whatever other means his ethical principles may demand.

[27] It is because electoral considerations do play this role, which it is argued here they should, that the matter of apportionment, to which considerable attention is given in this volume, is important. It must be recognized, however, that evidence may be found in support of the proposition that well-apportioned and malapportioned legislatures arrive at very similar policy results. Thomas R. Dye, "Malapportionment and Public Policy in the United States," *Journal of Politics,* 27 (1965), 586–601. Insofar as this finding is generally true, it is at least consistent with the proposition that ethical norms of representation are not without effect.

[28] This reasoning makes the not improbable assumption that on such a salient issue as one involving a sharp conflict between the conscience of the representative and the majority will of the constituency an alternative would have been presented (through the primary election or otherwise) had the majority not been prepared to make the judgment imputed to them in the text.

[29] For the sake of sharpening the issue, it is assumed that constituency desire, and possibly even constituency interest, might reasonably be judged so strong in this case as to override any consideration of an opposing national interest. In fact, it will be only in the rarest of cases that the issue between the dictates of conscience and those of representational norms will be in such direct conflict.

What about the relation of a representative to the minority in his constituency? Do people who did not vote for him and do not expect to vote for him have any claim upon him? Should he take their desires or their interests into account? If we speak now of their desires insofar as they are opposed to those of the majority (and no more intense) and of their interests insofar as they are in irreconcilable conflict with those of the majority—and this is a substantial narrowing of the issue, justified by what has already been taken into account by the preceding analysis—the answer would seem to be that the minority is entitled to consideration within the bounds set by the underlying consensus in the society in question.[30] In addition to recognized rights (see footnote 20), this consensus would normally include commonly accepted notions of justice.

Thus a geographically isolated minority would have a claim on all representatives to supply them with police protection—or bomb shelters—in the same proportion to need as in other parts of the country. At least as far as desire rather than interest is taken into account, this may seldom be a real issue, for one would not normally expect to find situations in which common notions of justice were accepted and yet the majority desired to neglect a minority in this way. Still, consideration of the treatment of Negroes in many places suggests that a wide gap between the implications of generally accepted standards and expressed desires is quite possible.

DISTRICT VERSUS NATION

The second big problem for representational theory, after that of desire versus interest, is that of part versus whole, constituency versus nation.[31] The tension appears only as one moves toward the interest pole of the representational standard; for no one would think that a representative should be influenced, per se, by

[30] It is, of course, the feebleness, if not utter lack, of such a consensus in many new states that makes the operation of representative government in them so precarious at best. It may well be, as Lucian Pye contends, that representation of particularistic groupings is essential for the viability of such polities. The fact is, however, that in many instances leaders' fears that lack of consensus would either lead to civil war or at least prevent all positive accomplishment have led them to seek to impose a national consensus from above at the expense of the effective operation of the elected representatives. Pye, *Aspects of Political Developments, op. cit.*

[31] Curiously, Wahlke does not list the nation among the various "clientele-roles" he enumerates. Wahlke *et al., op. cit.,* p. 14.

the demands (as distinct from the interests) of any constituents but his own, even though they included every citizen of the country save his own constituents. But let us suppose it is a question of a direct conflict between what he is convinced is the national interest on the one hand, and, on the other hand, what both he and his constituents are convinced is their interest. What then?

The situation posed is not likely to occur very often. On most questions the constituency will not be looking.[32] That is to say, very few of its members will have any opinion; nor would an impartial observer believe that the public policy issue involved raised any question of conflict between the constituency and the nation. So we are dealing with the exceptional situation. We are not here considering the question of whether the representative should act solely as a delegate. As at least a partial "trustee," he must inform himself so that he can determine the constituency interest. As a member of a deliberative assembly he should also discuss the matter with his colleagues in further search of sound judgment. But beyond all this, does his membership in an assembly with responsibility for national policy imply pursuit of what Burke called the "general reason of the whole"? Perhaps it would be better to ask, as we did when discussing obligations toward the minority: What is the underlying consensus on the subject in this society? Some obligation on the part of all to support the welfare of the whole is implied by citizenship in any body politic. Without it a body politic would not exist. Surely, then, persons who are selected to represent others in the government of that body politic must, *inter alia,* be expected to represent their interest in and obligation to the whole (even when the constituents themselves might be inclined to overlook it).

This much would appear to be clear. The strength of the obligation of a representative to support the national as opposed to the local interest, where the two clearly conflict, is a function of several factors. First of all, it must be judged in terms of some inevitably crude estimate of the strength in the particular case of each of the interests involved, local and national. Second, the system of government itself is relevant. In Britain, Parliament (including its "Government") is the only vehicle for representation in the legislative

[32] See Donald E. Stokes and Warren E. Miller, "Party Government and the Saliency of Congress," *Public Opinion Quarterly,* 26 (Winter 1962), 531–46.

process. In the United States, on the other hand, the division of labor and responsibility among President, Senate, and House of Representatives somewhat alters the situation, the implication being that the representatives of lesser areas than the whole have some special obligation to espouse local interests. Finally, it is partly a matter of the strength of the particular national consensus. It would appear at least a priori probable that the national consensus in Great Britain is stronger than it is in the United States. (To get a clearer picture of the extent to which this is true would be an interesting aim for an empirical study.) Conceivably, the generally accepted theory in a given country might be that the general interest would be best secured by each locality (through its elected representatives) pursuing its own particular interest exclusively. I personally doubt whether many people in the United States, barring a few sophisticated political scientists, accept this view.[33]

Furthermore, it is perhaps fair to say that where a strong and highly visible local interest seems to be opposed to the national interest, the representative may have to face the possibility of defeat at the next election and thus be forced to make the kind of calculation of alternative that has been described here.[34] Frequently, too, it may be fruitless or detrimental for the representative to vote for the national interest against that of his constituency. Take the case of pork barrel legislation. It may be assumed that the net effect of the legislation will be detrimental to the national welfare but beneficial to the constituency of the representative in question. It is likely that if, during the bill's formulation, he refused to commit himself to support it, he would lose his district's "pork" while not defeating the bill. Under such circumstances, the only effective line for the representative to take is to try to combine with other representatives to create institutionalized procedures to inhibit this sort of legislation. It is a measure of the "national" consensus in Britain that, in

[33] One of the writer's experiences during a British by-election is illustrative of the national differences in question. The constituency was heavily agricultural and highly marginal. On being asked about the attitude of the (traditionally Conservative) farmers toward the election, a Conservative party official showed great moral indignation over the fact that some farmers were actually considering voting for the Labor candidate just because of certain promised agricultural benefits—and contrary, it was implied, to what they must know was the national interest! It seems unlikely that any American politician could make such an argument with a straight face.

[34] See p. 19.

the form of the procedure for private bill legislation, just such action has been taken.[35]

REPRESENTATIVES AND POLITICAL PARTIES

At first glance, at least, the effect of a party system upon the role of representatives appears to create serious difficulties; and it most certainly does add complications. In principle, however, the problem seems fairly simple. Why do parties come into being? If their members were completely like-minded, no problem would arise. But political parties are typically composed of people with some interest in common but also with important differences of interest (or, at the very least, of desire), who find it worthwhile to "trade out" their differences, each giving up something for the sake of gaining support for what he does not give up. What then do the norms of representation say to a representative from a farming constituency whose party leaders tell him he must vote to cut farm subsidies? Let us approach the question obliquely by considering it as if it arose in Britain. In that case there could be little question, assuming that the representative had done his best to press the views and interests of his constituents upon his party leaders, without success. Under the British political system today it is normally part of the understood rules of the game that he should bow to the party (although he might occasionally abstain, if doing so would not endanger the government's majority). His supporters were aware of that possibility when they voted for him. Even if they did not know what stand the party would take on this issue, they desired his party to be in power and were presumably willing to pay the price. Moreover, if the price turned out to be more than they had anticipated and more than they were prepared to tolerate, they could shift their allegiance at the next election.[36]

[35] It may be observed that we in the United States, in limited degree, have such an institution in the form of the President's veto power, and also in certain procedures relating to the authorization and appropriation of funds for public works.

[36] It must be recognized, here and throughout, that we are talking in terms of the informed voter. To bring in the uninformed and apathetic members of the electorate would complicate the discussion but would not, I believe, lead to different conclusions. In fact, it simplifies the representatives' problem, by minimizing the element of desire.

If, on the other hand, we are dealing with the American loose-jointed party system, the same answer does not apply with anything like equal force. But the principles are the same. The conscientious representative must ask himself: To what extent was I elected as a party man? What would my own pre-election statements and actions lead a rational constituent to anticipate what my position on this issue would be? What might my constituency have to gain in other matters from my support for the party on this issue? In other words, with respect to party loyalty, under whatever system, the *ultimate* test remains the desires and interests of the constituency, including the extent to which it shares in a party consensus and a national consensus. But, especially where parties are powerful and can therefore obtain good things for the constituency (which may be things of national as well as of local interest, like effective national defense), this may take the representative a long way from direct response to constituency demand on a particular issue.

Let us press this analysis one step further. Can the tension created for the representative by highly disciplined parties withstand the ever increasing span of governmental functions? As the number and variety of issues increases, any theory of imperative mandate becomes completely unrealistic. Even the kind of theoretical support for a more limited mandate to the party that was outlined above becomes increasingly tenuous. The more functions the government performs, the more difficult it is likely to be for a party to adopt a program on which all or most of its members agree. Consequently, disciplined parties find it increasingly difficult to be programmatic. They may also be forced to accept some relaxation of discipline, as exemplified by the revised code of the British Parliamentary Labour Party, adopted in August, 1966. Perhaps equally as important as either of these developments is the tentative transfer of important representative functions to pressure groups (or "representative organizations") operating directly on government at the administrative level. The great extent of this process in modern Britain, both at the stage of legislative formulation and at the administrative stage, is well known.[37]

[37] See, for instance, S. E. Finer, *Anonymous Empire: A Study of the Lobby in Great Britain,* rev. ed. (London: Pall Mall Press, 1966). Professor Finer also expresses (p. 111) the judgment, relevant to the argument in the text, that the national consensus in Britain "appears to be on the wane."

Research has made it increasingly clear that, in the United States at least, the party government model corresponds only slightly to reality.[38] We also know that electoral accountability (at least as it operates in competitive districts) does not produce that close correlation between voter attitude and roll call votes that common sense might lead us to anticipate.[39] At the same time it appears that in the absence of effective electoral competition representatives seem to represent their constituents to a remarkable degree—or at least that there is a remarkable coincidence of views and votes between representatives and constituency.[40] How does this come about? At least a prima facie case can be made for the proposition that a concept of ethical norms, imposed by the acceptance of the role of representative, vaguely defined though those norms may be, has something to do with this phenomenon. How strong that case may be is a problem for further research.

In conclusion, it will be recalled that this essay began by considering the way in which a regime as a whole is representative. It now appears that the representativeness of a modern democratic government is not achieved through any single channel. In the United States, three sets of constituencies elect representatives at the federal level alone. Moreover, the bureaucracy, and an informal but effective additional form of representation, that of organized groups, provide other avenues of representation.[41] There is good reason for

---

Professor John P. Mackintosh, M.P., makes the point that organized interests, more frequently than not, concede the principle, rather than fight, in Parliament, reserving their efforts to secure a reasonably satisfactory arrangement for the administrative front. See John P. Mackintosh, *The British Cabinet* (London: Stevens, 1962), p. 469.

[38] See, for instance, Stokes and Miller, *loc. cit.*

[39] See Warren E. Miller, "Majority Rule and the Representative System of Government," in E. Allardt and Y. Littunen, eds., *Ideologies and Party Systems* (Helsinki: Transactions of the Westermarck Society, 1964), pp. 343–76.

[40] Miller, *op. cit., pp.* 361–64; and also Charles F. Cnudde and Donald J. McCrone, "The Linkage Between Constituency Attitudes and Congressional Voting Behavior," *American Political Science Review,* 60 (March 1966), 66–72.

[41] To have considered the judiciary, especially in the United States, as itself being, in a measure, a representative organ would not have been inaccurate but would have extended the essay beyond reasonable limits. It should at least be noted, however, that in the very decisions considered in this volume—those dealing with the apportionment of legislative representatives—the court was acting in a way it considered representative of the

this variety. For a person to be represented with respect to all of his interests with which government concerns itself is immensely difficult and inevitably partial and inaccurate, as Rousseau recognized with typical hyperbole. Accountability enforced by elections is one device, a crude one, for making government representative. It has been suggested here that an idea of what representation means, a set of ethical norms, also plays a role. The existence of numerous and varied avenues of representation, each by virtue of its own peculiar nature, seeing, reflecting, attempting to effectuate a slightly different facet of that great conglomerate of desires and interests that make up the electorate, probably produces a more tolerable result than could be accomplished by any one of them alone.

democratic ideals. It attributed these ideals to the Constitution, but perhaps one may be forgiven for suspecting that it found them in the evolving Constitutional morality of the nation rather than in the words of the document or the intention of the framers.

2

PRACTICAL REPRESENTATION

B. J. DIGGS

As a number of writers have recently pointed out, our notion of political representation is clouded by a variety of meanings of the terms "represent," "representative," "representation," and by a variety of interests that persons have in assigning meaning to these terms. For example, one who wants to argue the normative proposition that the best form of political representation is by delegates selected and instructed by a constituency may find himself saying that this is the only "true meaning" of "political representation." And by accepting the true proposition that only someone *typical* of a group is "representative" of the group, one may be led to the false view that only someone typical of a group can be "a representative" of the group—in quite a different sense of "representative."

I shall say just a few words about representation in general and then distinguish a broad type of representation of which political representation, in turn, is only one species. I think there is a strong tendency to overlook characteristics common to different forms of representation and to interpret political representation too narrowly. On the theoretical side, this leads to a puzzle about whether effective representation in a large and complex political system is really possible. On the practical side, it leads to the danger that we shall lose what representation we actually have by not appreciating its forms.

One might well argue that there is a central idea common to the various senses of the term "representation." This is the idea that something, or some group of things, which is said to be "represented," is "made present" or "presented," in some manner or other, by means of an intermediary. Some Latin grammarians refer to the use of the "historical present"—namely, the use of the present tense to recount past events—as a *repraesentatio*. However, the intermediary is usually quite different from a use of tense, and it makes the thing present in a different sense. The intermediary may be a perceptual image, a dream image, a picture, a dramatic portrayal, or a verbal description. It may be natural or artificial, and it may or may not serve a deliberate purpose. Especially if the representation is made for the purpose, we may say *how* the thing is represented (in more than one sense), and in this case we may criticize the maker for representing the thing in the way or *as* he has. There are still other kinds of intermediaries: An individual may represent, not by imaging or interpreting, but by serving as a typical specimen of a class. Or something may serve as a sign or symbol of something else, as a mace represents authority. All these intermediaries contrast with persons who "act for" or "in the place of" other persons whom they are said to represent.

Within these varieties of representation, for purposes of this essay, I want to call attention to a general contrast between pictorial, dramatic, or descriptive representation on the one hand, and what I shall call "practical representation" on the other. In the case of the former, the intermediary is itself often called "a representation"; the representation is a picture, portrayal, description, etc., of something which through or by means of it is known, understood, remembered, and perhaps admired and enjoyed. In the case of practical representation, the intermediary is a "representa*tive*," not a "representa*tion*" (except perhaps incidentally), and this kind of representative, unlike "a representative instance," literally *acts* for or in the place of the represented. The represented in this case is ordinarily a person or persons, not regarded as something to describe or contemplate, but as having practical purposes and problems which the representative serves. Such a representative may describe the persons represented, and thus may "represent them" in the descriptive sense of "represent," for example, as having a certain character or being in a certain state. However, he is not "a representative" simply in virtue of representing them in this sense; artists, actors, reporters, and narrators may represent, but they are not representatives of what they represent, except incidentally. A representative in the practical sense, broadly speaking, is an "agent," in one sense, of persons regarded as active, as "agents," in another sense. He is related to the represented as "another self," as somehow "standing in his place" in the practical arena.

Persons as active beings have needs, desires, goals, likes and dislikes, preferences, and so on. Adult persons, moreover, have "made up their minds" on numerous practical questions; we can say, in this sense, that they have a "will." They also have hopes, opinions, and beliefs, true or false, which greatly affect, in intimate ways, what they want and like, what they will, and how they act. And their desires, hopes, and opinions depend to a great extent on the society in which they live, on socially established techniques, goals which the society makes available, roles which persons can or must occupy within their society. Their interests are thus closely related to the fate of their institutions, whether or not they understand or approve them. In the pursuit of their interests men must thus conform on one side to the way things are in the natural world, and on the other side to that leviathan of their own creation, which makes life possible. In more than one sense and in a variety of ways they can do the wrong thing. We thus have occasion to distinguish what people do from what they ought to do, and what they will from what is really in their interest. There are correspondingly two emphases in practical representation, one on the opinions, desires, and will of persons represented, the other on what a representative takes to be their true interests and well-being.

Because persons pursue their practical interests to a great extent in roles governed by the rules of social institutions, some of these roles voluntarily assumed and others assigned, it might be thought that here is where practical representation comes in. A practical representative stands in place of another, and "a place" in this sense is a "role." Thus one might be led to say that when a person for some reason or other cannot or cannot conveniently do the job that a role requires, or exercise its rights and obligations, then another is found to serve "in his place." A guardian thus represents a child, an attorney a client, a legislator his constituency—each "taking the place" of the represented or principal.

This idea of representation, as we shall see, requires modification. It is, nevertheless, very useful in discerning the extent of practical representation. Persons do have representatives because they cannot "be present" themselves, in a particular role, to do a job, or exercise the rights and obligations of the role. A business needs salesmen to represent it, the local Elks need a representative at a national convention, an academic department needs a representative at a meeting. The need to be represented is similar to the need to be advised. One person cannot be wise in all matters and he cannot be in all places at once. As the pursuit of his goals in a complex society requires him to be in many "places" at once, he has to have help, of which representation provides one form. This function of representation accounts for its ubiquity. The more one undertakes, the more advice and the more representation he is apt to need.

This general view is also useful in understanding the variety of jobs that practical representatives do. A representative may be charged simply with obtaining information being given at a meeting, or he may be asked to present information on the part of his principal; he may be asked to participate in discussion, decide what is best, and vote as he thinks best; he may be directed to argue a case and told how to vote; he may be a buyer or a seller for a business, or a legal representative appointed by a court to defend someone, or a guardian; he may be an officer of a government appointed to perform a diplomatic mission, or a standard assignment; he may be appointed to mediate a dispute, and so forth.

Within this variety of roles and jobs can we find some unity? Is there a generic meaning of "practical representation" common to the various species?

The unifying idea that perhaps first suggests itself is that a practical representative "takes the place of" or "acts for" another simply in the sense that he does a job for another. This sense, however, is too broad to fit practical representation. Where there is division of labor, persons do things for one another without representing one another. Limiting the sense of "doing a job for another" to "doing a job which one gives or assigns to another" does not adequately narrow the conception. My secretary is not my representative, and the mailman is a representative neither of the postmaster nor of the people. Moreover, it is inadequate to interpret doing a job for another to mean acting in the other's interest or in his behalf. Many people may do innumerable things in my behalf without representing me, from closing my windows when it rains to helping me obtain something that I very much want.

It may be thought that doing a job for another is too broad to fit practical representation because representatives do a job which the represented, or principal, himself in some sense is supposed to do; that is, the representative does a job for another as a "substitute" for him. Although there is sense in making such a restriction, the trouble is that the notion of substitute is vague and not immediately helpful. There are many cases of one person's doing a job as substitute for another that are not cases of representation—for example, teaching a class or playing left tackle. And if it be said that the substituting of one person for another in these examples does not constitute the substitute's doing something *for the other* but for the school or the team, the required restriction is still not indicated. For the substitute teacher may see to it that the students reach page 100 in the textbook, at the request of the regular teacher; and the substitute left tackle, on request, may see to it that an opponent gets knocked down, each without representing the other.

Frustrations of this kind may lead one to propose a much more limited conception of "taking the place of" and "acting for" another. A practical representative serves as "agent of" another, and this, it might be thought, should be taken in a rather strict sense, such that, when the representative acts, the agent can be said in some sense to act too. However, it is only in some cases of practical representation that we speak of the principal's performing the act which the representative performs—I may be said to vote by proxy, but I do not usually vote when my representative votes. To avoid this difficulty, one may feel inclined to say that although the principal is not always said to do what his representative (*as* representative) does, nevertheless the principal acts *through* the representative. Thus the people do not literally vote for legislation in Congress, but they do vote for legislation *through* their representative. On this view the representative is conceived as a kind of instrument, but I do not think it is implied that the representative must be thought of as having been instructed how to act by the principal. Something weaker than this is or might be meant. Perhaps we can indicate the possibility of strong and weak interpretations by saying that the principal "acts through the representative" in the sense that he shares responsibility for the act of his representative. If the principal dictates to his representative, the latter is a *mere* instrument and the principal may be wholly responsible. On the other hand, varying conditions would imply varying degrees of responsibility, and the assessment of the responsibility would be an assessment of how the principal acted.

One who adopts this view will need to add qualifications, since a person is responsible for the acts of another who is not his representative—for example, his child or his charge. We do not need to consider the necessary qualifications in order to see that, at best, this view gives a description of only one kind (however extensive) of what I call practical representation. Children and lunatics may be represented; and whether or not they can be said to "act through" their representatives, often they do not share responsibility for their representative's acts. If one is tempted to say that these are secondary or derivative cases of representation, considerable argument would still be required to substantiate the main point. For there are many other cases of practical representation where the principal has little or no choice in the selection or control of his representative. Such an argument would appear to imply prima facie the value judgment that all cases of *genuine* representation *must* be by consent, and so to be question-begging.

It has recently been argued that in cases of representation where there is representation of a principal without consent, the representative acts for the principal in the sense that he performs an act which commits the principal to normative consequences, where normative consequences (and perhaps the act itself) are defined by conventional rules.[1] For example, a trustee's act of selling binds the principal to the conditions of the sale. I cannot here try to supply the kind of elucidation of "normative consequences" that would be needed before this philosophical offering could be really helpful. Even without this, however, it seems clear that restriction is needed. For a military officer by issuing an order can commit a soldier to normative consequences in the required sense; he can make an act

[1] A. Phillips Griffiths, "How Can One Person Represent Another?" Symposium with Richard Wollheim, *Aristotelian Society,* Suppl. Vol. XXXIV (1960), 187–224.

the soldier's duty.[2] Something similar could be said of a tyrant. This, however, is surely not representation. The author of this view in the end modifies his suggestion, saying, as I understand him, that we would not speak of representation in such a case unless the representative exercises a right that the principal has. For example, a trustee of *P* cannot sell the property of *P* unless *P* has the right to this property. As there would be no justification for the right of *P* being exercised by another unless *P*'s interests were considered, when we speak of representation we conceptually imply that the representative ought to consider the interests of his principal.

There are difficulties here. For representatives, as representatives, have many rights (and obligations) that their principals do not have, such as to attend meetings, vote, etc.[3] The line of argument, moreover, although interesting, is curiously indirect. To say that *T* is a trustee of *P* implies, I agree, that *T* should consider *P*'s interests. But this is what trustees are for: they are *charged* with administering property according to the will or for the benefit of another.

After this too brief foray through the thickets, let me summarize results: If one simply does a job for another, whether it be for pay or for the interest of the other, whether it be a job assigned or not, he is not necessarily representing the other. The same can be said if one does a job for another as his substitute. On the other hand, to say that representation occurs only when the principal shares responsibility for the acts by which he is represented is to take too narrow a view, and to say that there is representation whenever one by his acts commits the other to consequences according to rules is to widen it unduly. Representatives, moreover, have rights and obligations that principals do not have, and thus we cannot say that they, when serving as representatives, always exercise rights and obligations of principals, although it may or may not be the case that when they do exercise rights or obligations of principals, they do represent. Should we conclude that in searching for a generic meaning of "practical representation" we are searching for a non-

[2] Hanna Pitkin, "Hobbes' Concept of Representation," *American Political Science Review*, 58: 2, 4 (1964), 328–40, 902–18. Miss Pitkin makes the same point at p. 339. I am indebted to her for her excellent analysis.

[3] In some cases, principals can be said to have a right to be represented—thus to have their representatives vote, etc.

existent genus and that we should proceed to specific forms of representation and content ourselves with "family resemblances"?

Consider the case of the teacher substituting for a regular teacher. So long as the substitute is simply performing the teacher's tasks, whether or not at the teacher's request or in the teacher's interest, there seems to be no representation. But suppose that the substitute is called to a meeting and either states the teacher's views on a school policy, or is informed along with others of a policy that affects the teacher's interests, and agrees to inform the regular teacher. Now there is representation, at least in some contexts. What makes the difference?

I cannot think of a way of stating the difference better than by returning to what at the start seemed to be the central idea in representation; namely, the idea that an intermediary somehow "makes the represented present" or "presents the represented" to another. Unsatisfactory as this concept is, it is helpful in indicating the difference between a substitute and a representative: Most commonly a substitute takes another's place in such a way as to exclude the other, at least temporarily; the job is now the substitute's job, not the regular's job. A representative, if he is not a representative in name only, acts in place of another without excluding him; although he is not the principal, he "stands for" the principal; the principal is "present through him." If this seems mysterious, it may be helpful to compare practical representation with representation of other kinds—for example, with portraiture, or with signification, and to recall that a portrait or sign "portrays," "signifies," or "stands for" something which, as portrait or sign, it is not. *In this respect* practical representation is like other kinds of representation. However, a representative's function, in "standing for" the principal, is not to *portray* or *signify* the principal's needs, opinions, will, rules, or interests, but rather to express them in a different sense, most often to "make them felt" in something of the way the principal could reasonably be expected to do so if he had the knowledge and ability of the representative and could be present himself. In the area of practical representation "stand for" has something of the character of "stand up for." Sometimes a representative is given strict instructions and his job is simply to carry out the will of the principal. More commonly, however, his role as representative requires him to "put himself in the place of the principal" in the way one person advising another is expected to do. He must put himself *in* the place of the principal before *taking* his place. For he goes a step further than one who advises another on how to act: He himself carries out the advice that he would give to the other if he were simply advising him. As representative he is not required to share the principal's interests and concerns, but in part to act as if they were his own. He should gain information that pertains to the interests or will of the principal, or he should otherwise concern himself to promote the principal's interests, or he should present what he thinks *is* (or hopes will *become*) the principal's judgment or will. Just as there may be tensions between the opinions, will, interests, or rules, of the principal, so there may be tensions within the representative's role (and matters may be further complicated by the representative's own opinions, interests, rules, or will). A representative thus does not so much substitute for the principal, in this sense take his *place,* as take his *part*. He conducts business that remains the business of the principal, and he is responsible for conducting it well.

There is another feature or side of practical representation, somewhat analogous to that of other forms of representation, which is equally important. As a portrait is intermediate between the person portrayed, on the one hand, and the person *to whom* it portrays, on the other, so a representative is intermediate between the principal and some party to whom the practical affairs or concerns of the principal pertain. This feature of representation also helps account for the distinction between substituting for, or doing something in behalf of another, and representing the other. Representation is not only *of* someone but *to* someone. The underlying presumption in representation is that there is some need or desirability for the principal to be present before others, or he has some right or obligation to be present—in the sense that some business at hand is his concern, either in fact or according to the rules. The natural locale of practical representation is that in which (1) the principal's interests compete with others' interests, or (2) the principal's opinions, judgment, will have to be presented to others in order to arrive at commonly accepted policy, a working consensus, and cooperative action—and in cases of both (1) and (2), under conditions such that the principal cannot (or cannot conveniently) do this himself. A representative in "taking the part" of the principal "stands for" him before others, thus does not simply "do something for him," act in his interest, or substitute for him.

No time remains to develop this analysis, and yet it obviously needs to be developed much more fully and in more than one direction. The distinction between representation and substitution intuitively appears to be of the greatest importance for a sound theory of democracy: It suggests alternative ways of regarding expertness in government, elections, and the like. Before the force of the distinction can be fully estimated, however, something needs to be said about the relation between representation of interests, and representation of opinion and will. For so long as we conceive the representation of interests as in no way involving representation of opinion and will, it is hard to see how the business of the principal conducted by the representative can in any way remain the principal's business. Moreover, the general analysis of practical representation needs to be supplemented by an analysis of its special forms, including delineation of the conditions in which a special form is particularly appropriate and defensible. I am sure the commentators on this paper are better equipped to do this than I am. Finally, it may be of considerable philosophical and practical interest to develop the comparison between representation and signification. Important mistakes in the latter are likely to have important parallels in the former, and I think that this is in fact the case.

Since these lines cannot be developed in a brief essay, let me conclude with the following remark. A general analysis of practical representation can be expected to reveal only the most general normative guidelines governing its special forms. However, it should be positively helpful not only in clarifying some fundamental issues but also in locating alternative special forms. Negatively, moreover, it may be helpful in revealing special pleading. Even my brief analysis suggests that there is nothing about representation, for example, which requires that the will of the representative conform to the antecedent will of the principal, or that the will of the principal conform to the antecedent will of the representative. These are special theories of representation, and must be either theoretically defended as particularly appropriate to the political domain, or else defended as practical proposals—in neither case as true to the very nature of representation. Generally, we should expect considerable interaction between representative and principal. So long as this interaction consists in a sharing of *reasons,* regardless of who gets the idea first, neither the autonomy of the representative nor the autonomy of the principal is threatened, and fears like Rousseau's can be put to rest.

3

COMMENTARY: THE PARADOX OF REPRESENTATION

HANNA PITKIN

Finding myself in agreement with much of Professor Diggs' paper, I shall indicate only briefly what few bones I think one might pick with him, and then accept his invitation to apply his findings to a further problem about political representation.

Although Professor Diggs' major distinction between "practical" representation and "pictorial, dramatic, descriptive, etc." representation is valid and important, it does not seem to me a sufficiently detailed dissection to take us very far with a concept as complex as representation, even (or perhaps especially) if our real interest is *political* representation. The single, large distinction fails, for example, to tell us the difference between the way representations—pictures, stage productions, and such—represent, and the way symbols represent. Representations may depict or describe or "be a good likeness," but symbols do none of these things. So, while I may be misrepresented, I cannot be missymbolized. Second, we could use a clearer demarcation of the difference (which Professor Diggs touches on) between the way the *maker* of a representation represents, and the way the representation *itself* represents, between making and being a representation (or, for that matter, a symbol).

Of practical representation Professor Diggs says that the represented is "ordinarily" a person or persons. But there is a fairly important difference between representing people and representing—in a practical way—any one of a variety of abstractions. Thus we say that someone "represents the consumer interest," or "represents the cause of the American Negro," or "is acting as the representative of World Peace," or that he "represents law and order around here." (Some of those expressions could be about either practical or symbolic representation, and I think that *that* fact is important.) Then, there is a difference within the category of practical representation between what we might call the form and the substance of representing, between the question of whose official, authorized representative a man is, on the one hand, and the question of whom he really acts for, consults, looks after, is responsive to in practice, on the other. And, finally, there are significant differences between representing a single principal and a multimember constituency.

These distinctions may seem petty, but they are not. For example, Professor Diggs simply asserts that political representation is a subcategory of his "practical" representation. But any number of political theorists have held otherwise, have seen the political representative as portrait or mirror, as sample or symbol or as maker of portraits or symbols. So if we are to see him as a "practical" representative, that view must be *argued,* not merely assumed. And we can't really make or assess such an argument until we are much clearer about what is involved in each of the many different kinds of representing, the presuppositions and implications of each.

But enough toying with the bones that might be picked; let us make some good use of the insights Professor Diggs has given us, on a problem where they do apply. Consider that old and familiar problem of political theorists concerned with representation or democracy, which I call the "mandate-independence" controversy, and to which Professor Diggs alludes when he speaks of the "two emphases in practical representation." The problem is often formulated in some such dichotomy as: Ought a representative to do what his constituents want, or what he thinks best?

What is most striking about this problem is the length of time the controversy has been going on without coming any nearer to a solution, despite the participation of a great many very astute thinkers. Each in turn takes a position—pro "mandate" or pro "independence"—but the dispute is never settled, and the two sides seem to talk past each other. Now, to me at least, this suggests that there might be a conceptual problem, a philosophical paradox involved; and this does indeed turn out to be the case.

The arguments adduced by the two sides of the controversy are legion, and we need not review them here. But what we do need to note is that with fair frequency there appears among them—on *either* side of the controversy—a direct or indirect appeal to the meaning of representation itself. "It just isn't really *representation,*" the mandate theorist will say, "if the man doesn't do what his constituents want." "It just isn't really *representation,*" the independence theorist responds, "if the man isn't free to decide on the basis of his own independent judgment." But rather than putting words into their mouths, let us take a short textual example of each position. For the mandate theorists, let us hear Hilaire Belloc and G. K. Chesterton (speaking jointly in an early book on political parties):

> Either the representative must vote as his constituents would vote if consulted, or he must vote in the opposite sense. In the latter case, he is not a representative at all, but merely an oligarch; for it is surely ridiculous to say that a man represents Bethnal Green if he is in the habit of saying "Aye" when the people of Bethnal Green would say "No."[1]

Speaking for the independence theorists, let us hear from Lord Brougham:

> The essence of Representation is that the power of the people should be parted with, and given over, for a limited period, to the deputy chosen by the people, and that he should perform that part in the government which, but for this transfer, would have been performed by the people themselves. It is not Representation if the constituents so far retain a control as to act for themselves. They may communicate with their delegate . . . but he is to act—not they; he is to act for them—not they for themselves.[2]

[1] Hilaire Belloc and G. K. Chesterton, *The Party System* (London: S. Swift, 1911), p. 17.

[2] Lord Brougham, *Works,* XI, 35–36, cited in Robert Luce, *Legislative Principles* (Boston: Houghton Mifflin, 1930), p. 442.

Confronted by two such arguments, one can see the logic of both positions and wants to say that they are both right. Surely it is true that a man is not a representative—or is at most a "representative in name only"—if he habitually does the opposite of what his constituents would do. But surely it is also true that the man is not a representative—or at most a "representative in name only"—if he himself doesn't do anything. If, for instance, the constituency itself decides all issues by a local vote of the citizenry, and then mails in its decision to a central agency, we would not call the envelope that carries their vote a representative and we would not call the postman or messenger boy who delivers the envelope their representative.

But can both views be right, when they seem to support opposite and incompatible conclusions about the duty of a representative? Perhaps they can, if each has hold of *part* of the truth of what representation is (or means). Professor Diggs suggests as the central idea of representation that something is made present in some manner or other, by means of an intermediary. But of course it must not be made *literally* present; then it would simply be "present" rather than "represented." (For a time, the Latin *repraesentare* does seem to have meant to make literally present, thus, for example, to pay in cash, or to bring a new Pope before a waiting crowd.[3] But *repraesentare* is not exactly "to represent.") For something to be represented it must be made present in *some* sense while nevertheless not really being present literally or fully in fact. As Professor Diggs says, it must be present in or through an intermediary.

I think that this paradoxical requirement, that a thing be both present and not present at the same time, is precisely what appears in the mandate and independence theorists' conflicting views on the meaning of representation. The mandate theorist says: If the situation is such that we can no longer see the constituents as present, there is no representation, and if the man habitually votes the opposite of their wishes they do not seem present in his voting (except, at most, formally, in the sense that he has the authority to commit them). The independence theorist says: If the situation is such that the constituents seem to be acting for themselves directly, if there

[3] Georges de Lagarde, "L'Idée de Représentation dans les Oeuvres de Guillaume d'Ockham," *International Committee of the Historical Sciences Bulletin,* IX (December 1937), 425–51; and Albert Hauck, "Die Rezeption und Umbildung der allgemeinen Synode im Mittelalter," *Historische Vierteljahrschrift,* X (1907), 465–82.

is no intermediary or if the intermediary is a mere puppet in their hands, there is no representation; "*he* is to act, not *they*." Both theorists are right.

Let me close with just two brief comments on the significance of what has been said. In the first place, what conceptual analysis seems to have turned up here is not any kind of a "misuse" of a concept or distortion of its "ordinary meaning." The concept of representation just does seem to be paradoxical in meaning, is intended to express a dichotomous idea. At most one can say that it is a mistake (but not a misuse) to concentrate on only half the paradox rather than the whole.

In the second place, such findings must not, of course, be expected to "settle" the mandate-independence controversy. More is involved in that controversy than the simple philosophical dispute about the meaning of representation. The way the controversy is usually *formulated* itself creates real difficulties which need considerable work. It may be, as the notion of paradox in the meaning of representation suggests, that the issue is usually formulated in such a way that it *cannot* be answered and will not allow a consistent response. There are also, as Professor Diggs has suggested, problems about the nature of "interest," "will," and "opinion" involved. And there are nonphilosophical problems as well—political ones, for example, and questions of policy. While philosophers may argue over whether philosophy would disappear if all conceptual confusions were cleared up, it seems quite evident that political theory would not disappear. The problems of political theory seem to be only partly or sporadically philosophical-conceptual problems; they are only now and then complicated by an admixture of conceptual difficulties. But it is worth investigating just how the political theorist's web of argument changes, if at all, when the thread of conceptual difficulties is separated from the rest of the weave.

4

COMMENTARY: REPRESENTATION AND THE PROBLEM OF IDENTITY

JULIUS COHEN

To a pilot flying without the benefit of instruments, a contour map of a general area drawn from a considerable altitude would, of course, be of value if its avowed purpose were to prevent a landing in enemy territory. However, if the aim is to obtain a report on the pulse of life in the territory below, such a map would scarcely be of much assistance. And so with a contour map of a so-called "practical representative," whose features are drawn from so high a level of abstraction that the more interesting, and perhaps even the more significant, features are left out. Take Professor Diggs' sketch of a "practical representative" as a case in point. At best, it tells us where *not* to land—for instance, *not* to mistake a practical representative for a substitute, *not* to fall into the trap of identifying someone as a practical representative merely because he reflects the principal's interests, or does a job for the principal, or commits him to normative consequences or ascribes responsibility to him, for in all of these instances, these functions could also be performed by someone who is not a representative at all. Thus the danger of mistaken identity.

Such analysis, accurate as it seems to be, assumes that the mistaken identity of the representative has loomed and will loom as a central problem with those grappling with the complex concept of representation—that somehow, for example, there is danger that a substitute might be pawned off as a representative, and that one must be on the alert to ward against it. This assumption, without supporting evidence to buttress it, remains somewhat unconvincing. Judged by the adequacy of the *affirmative* definition that emerges after the effective slaying of the negative straw men, it would seem more worthwhile to concentrate on the problem of the identity of the principal himself than on the analysis of mistaken identities of the representative.

By way of affirmative definition, Professor Diggs suggests that a practical representative is one who somehow stands up for, that is, takes the part of the principal in the conduct of the principal's business with others, as if the principal himself were there, but without necessarily being an exact reflected image of the principal's will or interest. The focus of this definition, as it can be readily seen, is on the identity of the representative and not on the identity of the principal. It is as if in sketching the representative, one's eye were glued to what appeared in the mirror without checking to find out who might be standing in front of it. The mirror image would, of course, be representative of someone. But the question is, of whom? Better yet, *whose* image of that someone?

There are at least two images of a principal—a self-regarding and an other-regarding one—and either of them might in practice be represented by a representative. To assume that the label of "representative" is ascribable only to the self-regarding image of the principal—one in which the principal sizes up himself—does violence to the commonly accepted usage of the term, to which the proffered definition itself is presumably anchored. Take as an example a landmark case in the field of labor law, *Steele* v. *Louisville and Nashville R.R.* (323 U.S. 192 [1944]). In that case the majority of the firemen employed by a railroad were white and members of the Brotherhood of Locomotive Firemen and Enginemen; a substantial minority were

Negroes who, by the constitution of the union, were excluded from its membership. Under the Railway Labor Act, the majority of all of the firemen could elect a bargaining "representative" to negotiate a contract for the entire craft unit; since the majority were union members, the Brotherhood was so designated. Subsequently, the Brotherhood negotiated a contract with the Railroad for all of the employees in the craft unit. The agreement gave the white Brotherhood members considerable economic advantage over the non-union Negro firemen. Among other things, the white employees were given preferential rights to jobs whenever a vacancy would occur, and other restrictions were imposed that made white seniority considerably more valuable than Negro seniority status—all without notice to the Negro employees, or without giving them an opportunity to be heard. The legal issue was whether the Brotherhood acted in conformity with or in transgression of the "representation" function as envisaged by the framers of the Railway Labor Act. The Alabama Supreme Court, in effect, upheld the Brotherhood's version of representation; the Supreme Court reversed, holding that such type of representation was not contemplated under the Railway Labor Act. What is significant for immediate purposes is not as much the outcome of the controversy but rather that such different and competing concepts of "representation" could be so seriously held. Even more significant is the fact that the role and function of the representative varied with the competing views regarding the Negro principals. One view, an other-regarding one, "saw" them through old cultural lenses—as inferiors, not equals; accordingly, the job of the practical representative was fulfilled if the non-union Negro firemen were represented at the bargaining table *as* inferiors. The other view, consonant with the Negroes' self-image, "saw" them as equals; the observing eye was color-blind; the absence of union garb regarded as incidental. With such a principal in front of the mirror, one "sees" the practical representative functioning properly only when he represents all of the members of the craft as equals.

Other examples of the other-regarding image of the principal come to mind: the 20-year-old student who regards himself as mature enough to vote, to marry, to decide about his career, may be represented nevertheless as a minor. A man who views himself simply as a member of the human race may nevertheless be represented as a member of a national, ethnic, or religious group upon whom group sanctions might be imposed or deprivations suffered for the transgressions of its individual members. That the conception of the principal can be other-regarding suggests that before a "practical representative" can be meaningfully characterized as one who acts as if he were conducting the principal's business, it is necessary to ascertain the particular view of the principal that is controlling, for what his business is might well vary with the operative view that governs the determination of his identity.

A glance at a neighboring concept—translation—is perhaps instructive in this respect. Ideally, a literary passage can no more be completely translated than a principal can be completely represented. Something in its identity is usually missing in the shift from one language to another—a shading, a nuance, an inflection, an association that is unique to the original language. Yet efforts are made somehow to approximate the "original" by an act called translation. Both translation and practical representation function to broaden experiences that would otherwise be denied—one the area of communication, the other the area of participation. Both assume that there is an "original" somehow to identify. If the object of the translation is, say, a play or a poem, just what it is that is being translated may well depend on whose view of the text is in command—the author's or the translator's. If the author is not around to complain about the distortions that he sees in the translations, the other-regarding view might well be in control; if he is available for comment, the claim is nevertheless often made that he does not see in his own work of art what others with a different background, range of insight, and experience see in it. How often is it said that he does not quite recognize his own creation and that it has an identity beyond his own comprehension of it? And how often, in such instances, does usage still consider it a "translation"?

One might, of course, object and insist that a translation or a representation ceases to be such when the image of identity is other-regarding rather than self-regarding. If this would be another way of saying that it would not be consistent with usage, even a perfunctory resort to examples in current use would dispel the assertion. If it suggested, nevertheless, that both representation and translation *should* not be considered such unless the self-regarding image is controlling, the problem takes on a normative hue, and could better be attacked by considerations of value than by descriptive analysis alone. Considerations of value also play a role not only in the choice of perspective, but also in determining whether within each perspective identity is to be governed by considerations of what the principal seems to be at the moment, or what he most likely *would* be if a fuller knowledge of his potential development were available. An all too familiar example of this latter consideration is in the functioning of a court in construing a vague or ambiguous legislative enactment. How often one finds a court stating that its interpretation of legislative language is a representation of legislative intent based on considerations of what a reasonable legislative body *would* most likely have intended if it had the experience and hindsight that is now available to the court. A recognition of the role of the normative in this area of analysis should help clarify the meaning of representation by the difficult yet necessary task of distinguishing between representation and *good* representation, as one would hope to distinguish between law and *good* law.

The complexity of the problem of identity as it relates to the concept of representation is compounded by the fact that one is often called a practical representative of a principal even though the individual identity of the principal—especially his will and his interest—is somewhat fragmented, as an ingredient would be when mixed with other ingredients to form a blend that is usually different from the sum of the individual parts. In such an instance, the final product that is represented is a composite of separate ingredients, with a flavor that might vary with their quality, their quantity, their intensity, how they are weighted, and whether the chef regards his role to be recipe-bound, or freedom-bound to exhibit flair and exercise independent judgment. Implicit in this example of representation, common to modern democratic societies, is the assumption that there is somehow a social dimension to the identity of the principal—a view long ago advanced by Aristotle—and that his identity is not exhausted merely by treating him as Mill once did, as an isolated independent entity. Nor is the identity of the principal's social dimension exhausted merely by labeling it social: it is more complex than that. For it includes his identity not only in pluralistic interest groupings, not only as a member of a nation or international community, but possibly as a member of the socially dispossessed, of so-called *antisocial* groupings, organized or loosely knit, which are not accorded legal recognition by the established order. To hold that such a principal is somehow still "represented" in the established order by virtue of residing in a geographic area that has an elected representative gives point to the observation that it is still possible to represent a person without actually representing his interest or his will.

These considerations, brief as they are, should suggest how wanting is a sketch of a representative if the analytic eye that controls the sketching hand fails to focus sharply on the identity of the principal. It is like trying to define one term of a relational concept—employer, parent, obligor, or mortgagor—without exploring the extent to which the meaning of the term might vary with the meaning ascribed to its relational counterpart—employee, child, obligee, or mortgagee.

5

TWO NOTES ON REPRESENTATION

WILLIAM K. FRANKENA

What is representation? When am I represented by *X*? Who are my representatives? One of the things that struck me during the discussions of representation by this Society was the fact that such questions are ambiguous in ways not always noticed. My first note consists of a rough attempt to distinguish some of their main senses or rather families of senses. There seem to be three families of senses of such questions and of the answers to them.

1. There are two *descriptive* senses. In these senses the answer to our questions consists of some kind of an account of American representational institutions. In the first, the answer would consist of a summary analysis of the relevant provisions of our federal, state, and local constitutions and laws. In the second, it would be made up of a more "realistic" study of what happens in practice, for example, of the relevant court decisions, the behavior of political parties, and the like. Taken in either of these two senses, the answers to our ques-

tions would most appropriately come from a lawyer or a political scientist.

2. Our questions may, however, also be interpreted as making a *conceptual* inquiry—as asking for a definition of representation or an analysis of the concept of one person's representing another. Taken in this way, the appropriate source for an answer is a political theorist or an analytical political philosopher. But, even if they are taken in this way, the questions have two kinds of answers. One kind of answer would be an analysis of our actual concept of representation, a definition of what we actually mean when we say that *X* represents *Y*, an elucidation of the rules of our actual use of expressions like "*X* represents *Y*." It might be thought that, if the questions are construed in this way, then sense (2) collapses into sense (1), but this is not the case. It might be that our representational institutions do not in fact embody what we actually have in mind when we speak of representation. Another kind of answer would be to argue that our actual meaning is so ambiguous or so vague as to be of very little help and to propose a definition that would do a better job in one way or another. Such a conceptual analysis would be a recommendation about what we should mean, about how we should use the term "representation."

3. But our queries may also be given a *normative* sense. Suppose I ask, "Does *X really* represent me?" This question can have either the descriptive or the conceptual senses already distinguished. But I may be asking something like, "Is *X rightly* representing me?" Similarly, our original queries may be read as asking, "When is *X* rightly or well represented?" or, "What is a good or the right system of representation?" They are not necessarily normative, but they do sometimes have a normative sense. In fact, there is more than one normative way of putting them. One may ask, "What sort of representation would be just?" Even this is ambiguous: it may mean, "What is just representation?" or it may mean, "What practical set-up would assure just representation?" Or one may ask, "What sort of representation would be most efficient, most useful, conducive to the greatest good of those represented or of society as a whole?" Taken in such normative senses the place to go for an answer to our questions would, of course, be the political philosopher or moralist.

My second note will consist of a few remarks on the question of just representation. Suppose I hold—as I do[1]—an equalitarian view of distributive justice and related matters. That is, I believe that every human being is equally entitled to the best life he is capable of. Am I then committed to the "one-man, one-vote" doctrine? I certainly am committed to saying that each person is to count and be counted as one and only one, since his having the best life he is capable of is part of the Ideal to be promoted. This, however, does not by itself entail everyone's having a *vote*. It does seem to imply that everyone should have a *representative* among those who determine what will be done or not done ("no taxation without representation"), but it does not require that everyone must be free to vote for his representative. To say it does would in effect say that children should elect their parents (since they determine "policy" for their children). Hence, it does not follow, on an equalitarian view, that we have to accord everyone a vote. Who should vote and on what issues depends on what voting regulations are necessary for and conducive to the achievement of the Ideal just indicated.

On the other hand, it would certainly be compatible with an equalitarian view to adopt the procedural principle that everyone is to have a vote on every issue unless there are considerations that justify withholding that right. Presumably, it would be instructive to approach the matter in this way and to see just what considerations are "capable of determining the intellect either to give or withhold its assent" to departures from that procedural principle. Ignorance of certain sorts would be one consideration favoring departures from it, as the cases of children and idiots show, but only if society is trying to remedy the ignorance as far as it possibly can. So, perhaps, would various other kinds of considerations, for example, geographical ones, what these are depending at least in part on the nature of the issue to be voted on.

[1] See *Ethics* (Englewood Cliffs, N.J.: Prentice-Hall, 1963), pp. 38–42; *Some Beliefs About Justice,* a Lindley Lecture published by the University of Kansas, 1966; "The Concept of Social Justice," in R. B. Brandt (ed.), *Social Justice* (Englewood Cliffs, N.J.: Prentice-Hall, 1962).

HISTORICAL DISCUSSION

6

MODERN AND MEDIEVAL REPRESENTATION

HARVEY C. MANSFIELD, JR.

Did we inherit modern representation from medieval representation or do the similarities of practice and opinion mask an essential difference? I cannot decide this historical question and do not propose to consider it chiefly for its historical importance. How to establish representative goverment might seem to be the current version of this historical question, for the principle that government should represent the people is almost universally held today. But the possibility that modern representation is inherited raises a doubt that it is necessary or possible to establish, from reflection and choice, representative government today. It is still disputed whether representative government must become established unconsciously by easy stages through the actions of groups or masses of men or must be legislated all at once (at least in principle) by a few far-seeing men.

Is "social mobilization" for free, representative government a political invention or a social inheritance?[1]

To consider this more general question, one may return to the obvious difference between modern and medieval government: Modern government is secular. I believe that this fact is a necessary truth about modern representation. The medieval sources must be examined in the light of the argument to follow, which shows that modern representation is necessarily secular. Otherwise, current thinking on representation will not be enlightened by historical inquiry because history will be used to support rather than to help us understand the opinions and practices now in favor. Modern representation can be understood only by knowing what was lost or rejected to achieve it.

THE MEANING OF "MEDIEVAL"

Political or philosophical opinion once held that representative government is a modern artifice, and scholarly opinion now holds that it is a medieval inheritance. The former was the opinion of modern representative government in its infancy or, as was then believed, at its founding. *The Federalist,* in claiming a new "wholly popular" representation for the American constitution, acknowledges its debt to "modern Europe, to which we owe the great principle of representation. . . ."[2] Jefferson admits that the idea of representation was "taken, indeed, from a little specimen formerly existing in the English constitution"; and he asserts that "the full experiment of a government democratical, but representative, was and is still reserved for us."[3] The Whigs, to whom these honors were paid, had remained quiet because their revolution in 1688 had not been a partisan venture and they were anxious to maintain the myth of continuity with previous regimes. Of the political philosophers, Locke was reticent as usual, perhaps because Hobbes was not. Hobbes made his claim to originality in the understanding of repre-

[1] Karl Deutsch, "Social Mobilization and Political Development," *American Political Science Review,* 55 (1961), 493–514. Is the "mobilization of society" an objective or a subjective genitive? Cf. *The Federalist,* No. 1.

[2] *The Federalist,* No. 14; cf. No. 63.

[3] *The Writings of Thomas Jefferson,* A. E. Bergh (ed.) (20 vols., Washington, D.C.: 1903), XV, 65–66, 482; see *The Writings of James Madison,* G. Hunt (ed.) (10 vols., New York: 1910), IX, 520; John Adams, *A Defence of the Constitutions of Government of the United States of America,* 3rd ed. (3 vols., Philadelphia: 1797), I, ii-iii.

sentative government quite explicit. He wondered that for six hundred years the king was not considered the representative of his subjects, "the name without contradiction passing for the title of those men, which at his command were sent up by the people to carry their petitions, and give him, if he permitted it, their advice."[4] Rousseau, in opposing the principle of representation, still declared that "the idea of representatives is modern; it comes to us from feudal government. . . ."[5]

After Rousseau, political philosophy became historical and adopted a more favorable view of medieval things. Man was no longer thought to have a fixed nature whose laws could be obeyed by sound policy or historical accident; instead, man was thought to have reached his degree of perfection by his own efforts in reaction against his environment. Since man was certainly not made by God and was now also not a being of nature, the remaining possibility was that he made himself. He could make himself, going beyond merely obeying the laws of his nature, only by cooperating with the accidents of history that challenged him. And so it was that those accidents became necessary to his self-generation or self-creation and that history, having been the lesser arena of politicians as seekers of fame, became the very ground for political philosophy. Since man made himself, he could not be understood otherwise than as free and his history as the history of his freedom in development. With elaboration, this opinion encountered the medieval period, which had been in disgrace under the early modern castigation, and gave it a new dispensation. The universality of Christianity, embodied in a Church that transcended boundaries and was indifferent to regimes, seemed to raise the sight of human freedom heavenward above the horizon of the polis; and Christian symbolism, representing the universal Church in the Pope or the general council, seemed to supply a concrete or political expression of this university, capable of being copied by secular authorities. From being the foremost enemy of freedom, religion thus became a stage of freedom itself. Whereas early modern political philosophers from Machiavelli to Montes-

[4] Thomas Hobbes, *Leviathan,* M. Oakeshott (ed.) (Oxford: 1957), Chap. 16, p. 107; Chap. 19, p. 122; concl., pp. 466–68; see John Locke, *Two Treatises of Government,* II, 13.

[5] *Contrat Social,* III, 15; cf. II, 1. Montesquieu is a seeming exception: he remarked that the idea of the English government "was found in the woods," but not by the French, even though they too had access to those woods. *De l'Esprit des Lois,* XI, 6; cf. XXX.

quieu looked on Christianity as a religion of the East which supports and promotes Oriental despotism, nineteenth-century philosophers began to conceive what is today called "our Judaeo-Christian heritage" as the basis of "Western civilization."[6]

At the same time, Hegel delivered his appreciation of the medieval estates.[7] Reason was not to be found in a fixed human nature, that is, in the behavior of man in the state of nature, but in the behavior of men during the process of civilization. Whereas, according to Hobbes and Locke, individuals were represented in one sovereign artificial collectivity made at one stroke by the laws of reason to be found in human nature, now for Hegel men developed their rationality in several collectivities which could no longer strictly be called "artificial" because of their function in making or developing what had been called "human nature." Further, since the sovereign or the public cannot be made at once, it must be developed in parts: the Estates are one part between the government and particular men. The existence of the Estates guarantees that the government has in fact something to represent: a people formed into a public. The Estates' challenge to the sovereignty of the monarch can be turned to the advantage of freedom, although they may have intended to promote freedom as little as he.

By serving as the medieval contribution to human freedom, representative government was useful to the opinion that man has a history rather than a fixed nature, but it was also *necessary* to that opinion. Man makes himself, but only by stages, for self-creation all at once is a superhuman feat. If man could create himself all at once, it must be true that he could see himself from the beginning. But by postulation there is nothing to see at the beginning. To make himself, man needs the leverage of his environment, something against which he may assert himself: for the making of man by man without the aid of God or nature is not in love but in war. By this "mediation" the stages of human history articulate themselves, each level of creation limited in its assertion by the extent and character of its challenge. Man makes himself necessarily without self-awareness, because there is nothing to survey, no human nature to see,

[6] J. G. Fichte, *Reden an die Deutsche Nation,* VI; *Die Grundzuge der gegenwartigen Zeitalters,* XIII. G. W. F. Hegel, *Vorlesungen uber die Philosophie der Weltgeschichte,* IV, 2. Guizot, *History of the Origins of Representative Government,* A. R. Scobie, trans. (London: 1861), pp. 3, 12. Chateaubriand, *Génie du Christianisme,* IV, VI, 11.

[7] *Grundlinien der Philosophie des Rechts,* 271, 279, 301–02.

until the creation is complete. We can make ourselves on condition that we do not know what we make. "Self-consciousness" is the last stage, and if the last stage has not arrived or cannot exist, self-consciousness is impossible.

Now representative government is necessary to this conception because it is government that represents or reflects something else, culture or society. As the derivative of culture or society, it purports to be government by inattention, unaware of itself, pursuing no end of its own, following the end or ends of its master or author. To be sure, every society needs to be led, but no society can be formed to reach a stage of history that is not implicit in itself. To the opinion that man has a history rather than a fixed nature the idea of a break in history is intolerable.[8] A break would destroy the continuity of human creation whose completion alone makes possible any survey of human history: to see a break in human history would be to admit that man does not make himself. If man can recover himself and rebuild his civilization after a break in history, then he must be able to rely on his nature or on divine aid. He must be by nature, not merely through history, capable of knowing himself; and his government must be capable of giving effect to his self-awareness. The titles of the modern politician seem to understate his importance—leader, premier, president, prime minister, chairman—but they all express the fundamental modesty of representative government. Men who must live in history in order to make themselves cannot rule or form themselves. They must be led to the limit of their stage in history by their representatives.

The question of the derivation of modern representative government has led us to the more general question of whether modern government is an unnoticed transformation of medieval government or a break from it. Those who began modern representative government thought themselves its founders; they thought they had broken with medieval and ancient principles of rule and hence claimed for themselves the fame of the prince who creates "new orders." When political philosophy lost its confidence in the fixed human nature of Hobbes and Locke, their claim to be founders of modern representative government was seemingly exposed as an illusion. They seemed to be hardly more aware of their creation than the philosophers of "Aristotelity" were aware of the cruelty of the priest-ridden regimes they recommended, because both depended on the circumstances of

[8] Guizot, *op. cit.*, pp. 3, 76.

their times. The proof of this conclusion is that Hobbes and Locke contradicted themselves on representative government. They believed the true function of government to be representative and yet themselves claimed to legislate for modern men. Within their doctrines the contradiction is between the limited function of government and the absolute power in the sovereign necessary to establish even this limited government.[9] Against this contradiction the historical school can reasonably protest. The claim of government to represent society can be sustained only if modern representative government asks no exemption for itself and arrives by representing modern society. Representative government is justified only if its founders can be content with the title of leaders.

Recent scholarship on medieval representation has therefore followed the lead of nineteenth-century political philosophy, while disputing its discoveries and refining its conclusions, to show that medieval society made itself representable by modern representative government. Two students of representation, whose names sound an antique ring in the busy chambers of today's political science, Sir Henry Maine and Henry J. Ford, learned from the historical school without succumbing to it. They drew a sharp distinction between medieval and modern representation and defended it with more good sense than philosophy.[10] But others, admitting the differences between medieval and modern representation, accept after much investigation the inner transformation of medieval into modern society. They may be divided into the historical persuasion, deriving from Otto von Gierke and Bishop Stubbs, and the sociological, whose inspiration is the work of Max Weber.

The historians have turned from the study of medieval "ideas" to that of medieval institutions, on the ground that "theory follows the event."[11] An inner transformation of medieval to modern society must be unnoticed and hence not primarily available in the "ideas"

[9] Hobbes, *Leviathan,* Chap. 18; Chap. 30, p. 227. Locke, *Two Treatises of Government,* II, 87, 142. Cf. Guizot, *op. cit.,* pp. 60–62.

[10] Sir Henry Maine, *Popular Government* (London: 1885), pp. 7–8, 59; Henry J. Ford, *Representative Government* (New York: 1924), Chaps. 1, 9. See Francis W. Coker and Carlton C. Rodee, *Encyclopedia of the Social Sciences,* s. v. "Representation."

[11] Helen M. Cam, Introduction to "Medieval Representation in Theory and Practice," *Speculum,* 29 (1954), 348; cf. Gaines Post, "The Two Laws and the Statute of York," *ibid.,* pp. 418, 419; and Cam, "The Theory and Practice of Representation in Medieval England," *History,* N.S., 38 1953), 11.

of either. Accordingly, the historians have examined the charters by which English kings summoned Parliament and the practices of the king's court, Parliament, lords, delegates, attorneys, juries, boroughs, and shires to find the remote causes of England's success in representative government. Comparative analysis reveals the absence of such institutions and practices where representative government did not succeed. These studies and results would seem to oppose the conclusions of the sociological school, which teaches the importance of "ideas." The relevant ideas, according to this school, can be grouped into two world-views, the traditional and the legal-rational (Weber's terms), whose distinction is fundamental.[12] Belief in this distinction is by no means confined to sociologists or those interested in representation. It is current throughout social science today, and appears to be responsible for the similar distinction, found so useful for scholarship and policy alike, between underdeveloped or emergent, and developed or emerged, societies.

On reflection, however, this opposition of ideas and institutions is seen to be incomplete. The ideas are still bound to the historical stages in which they are grouped or which they are said to constitute. They cannot by themselves impel a society from one stage to the next because they are "social ideas" found in society at that stage; they can change only by encounter with new conditions or by abrasion after a period of friction with "the world." One great difficulty in Max Weber's work is how to reconcile his anti-Marxist (but post-Hegelian) emphasis on "ideas" with his view that "the spirit of capitalism" triumphed by the intention of nobody through the good offices of the Puritans. The Puritans authored not the spirit of capitalism but a group of ideas which, contrary to the Puritans' intention, degenerated into the spirit of capitalism.[13] The agency of degeneration was entirely institutional, and the Puritan ideas themselves, being merely social, are afflicted with sociological paralysis.

This difficulty is clear in a passage from Figgis, whose book upholds the long-term influence of ideas:

> Religious forces, and religious forces alone, have had sufficient influence to ensure practical realisation for political ideas. Reluctantly,

[12] Max Weber, *Wirtschaft und Gesellschaft,* 4th ed. (2 vols., Tubingen: 1956), I, 125–39.

[13] Max Weber, *The Protestant Ethic and the Spirit of Capitalism,* T. Parsons, trans. (London: 1950), pp. 98, 154, 174, 184.

> and in spite of themselves, religious societies were led by practical necessities to employ upon their own behalf doctrines which are now the common heritage of the Western world.[14]

"Religious forces" must supply power to political ideas, but "practical necessities" have more power than religious forces. Religious forces are the engine for political ideas on condition that they cannot maintain religious ideas against practical necessities, that is, on condition that they are neither ideas nor specifically religious.

The level of awareness in society is political. A group in society, a "social force," becomes aware of itself when it realizes that it needs and deserves a share in ruling that society. Not only does every "social" opinion have political implications but every "social" group that has its own opinions has political ambitions. This statement is not especially hard on religious ideas, for if they can be considered social, they can be considered political.[15] Those who find a source of modern representative government in the religious ideas of the conciliarist controversy or of Puritan disputation must identify an agency of secularization which makes religious ideas useful for modern secular society. If the agency is new ideas, then these ideas must express the desire of some group to wrest rule from the priests and the priest-ridden; they must be secular political ideas. But if the old ideas wore down or lapsed without dispute from new ideas, the agency must be institutional and the religious ideas merely a reflection of "social forces." Social ideas are transformed passively and cannot impel. Political ideas, on the contrary, can make breaks in history because they express an intention: men cannot make a new society, which they have chosen, without changing their rulers. Political ideas cannot flourish under the modern conception of representative government, for that conception is sociological and non-political; it assumes that the government appropriate to a society is implicit in that society and hence that every social idea contains the political. In this view, the political ideas must reflect and cannot make or form society. Therefore the "ideas" of the sociological persuasion depend on the "institutions" of the historical persuasion, and both presuppose that men make a new stage of society unaware of what they are making.

[14] J. N. Figgis, *Political Thought from Gerson to Grotius, 1414–1625* (New York: Harper, 1960), p. 7. Cf. de Tocqueville, *Democracy in America,* II, I, 5.

[15] Montesquieu, *De l'Esprit des Lois,* XXIV, 1.

This point can be illustrated from the first chapter of J. S. Mill's *Considerations on Representative Government.* There Mill explains that "all speculations concerning forms of government bear the impress . . . of two conflicting theories respecting political institutions. . . ." The first states that government is "wholly an affair of invention and contrivance," while the second regards government "as a sort of spontaneous product," "not constructed by premeditated design" but growing out of the nature and life of a people.[16] Mill argues for a moderated version of the first theory, admitting that the best modern representative government depends on three fundamental conditions—consent of the people, education of the people, and the technology to make possible the public opinion of a large society. But within these limits government is a matter of choice, for, Mill says, opinion is itself a power in society. "To think that because those who wield the power in society wield in the end that of government, therefore it is of no use to attempt to influence the constitution of the government by acting on opinion, is to forget that opinion is itself one of the greatest active social forces."[17]

Mill is attempting to save the importance of politics under representative government, but he cannot succeed. An opinion has power because and to the extent of the power of those who hold that opinion, and persuading powerless men of a new opinion adds nothing to the power of the opinion. When the newly instructed seize power or awe those in power, then the new opinion has power because of the new power of those holding it. If they gained power impelled by their opinion, the opinion is political and the government is more than merely representative of social forces. The "social forces" are in fact political forces. Mill would discover that not every opinion is a social force and that some opinions are much more than a social force if he could try today to convince his followers of his opinion that enlightened despotism is justified in ruling savages.[18] This opinion is not a "social force" if nobody believes it and if it is opposed by the political force of the opinion of those who hold political power. Opinion "itself" has no power; only certain opinions have power. Those opinions acquire power that are accepted by those who hold political power. Revolutionary opinions

[16] J. S. Mill, *Utilitarianism, Liberty and Representative Government* ("Everyman's Library," London: 1936), p. 175.

[17] *Ibid.*, p. 183.

[18] *Ibid.*, pp. 184, 199, 225.

are the opinions of revolutionaries, and the power of the opinions depends on the success of the revolutionaries. Thus the difficulty remains: if opinions or ideas are merely representative or social, they are powerless; if they have effect, they are political rather than social.

The attempt to derive modern society from medieval and modern representation from medieval presupposes that the scholar has dismissed or drastically restricted the importance of "ideas." In recognizing this premise, the historical persuasion is more consistent than the sociological. But the historian may sense the inescapability of ideas in his own need to resort to ideas in speaking against the importance of ideas. The "historian of ideas" would then join the sociologist in seeking the characteristic medieval ideas from which modern ideas and practices may be derived.

What are the characteristic medieval ideas? In philosophy and political philosophy, they are the classical ideas of Plato and Aristotle. Medieval thinkers present their thought as an improvement on ancient thought by virtue of Christian, Muslim, or Jewish revelation, but they never repudiated ancient thought. Their great problem is how to reconcile revelation with Greek philosophy. Their disputes arise between different schools of Aristotelians or between Platonists and Aristotelians. If we consult what medieval thinkers say—and we must, if *their* ideas are to have importance—the fundamental distinction is between philosophy and revelation. We must then take medieval philosophy as derived from ancient, and infer that the fundamental distinction in philosophy is between ancient and modern. No doubt many curious eddies can be found in the backwaters, and unsponsored ideas as well as strange anticipations are entitled to philosophical consideration. In medieval political thought and philosophy, we must also add the influence of Roman law to that of the Greek polis. But in assessing the social or political importance of medieval ideas, one cannot deny that they are on the whole derived from ancient ideas, with the vital exception of revelation. We conclude that if ideas can rule in history and if they ruled at the beginning of modern history, the change from medieval to modern society must be understood (again with the above exception) as a break between ancient and modern ideas. This is how Hobbes and Locke understood their founding of modern representative government.

The very idea of "medieval" is modern. It is possible for a man to say of himself that he lives in a middle age if he refers to a future prospect, perhaps in a providential scheme. The age of the Church militant may look forward to the age of the Church triumphant.[19] It is also possible to conceive of a middle age in the past as a hiatus between ancient and modern; and this was the understanding of those historians and philologists from the Renaissance to the Enlightenment who used the term *medium aevum* or its equivalent. But what distinguishes the modern idea of "medieval" is the opinion that the middle between ancient and modern is a necessary transition from ancient to modern.[20] This precise opinion of Hegel and the historical school—not a vague new love of tradition—is responsible for the revaluation of the Dark Ages in the nineteenth century. History became the royal discipline with the discovery of the necessity of a transition from ancient to modern and therewith of the general necessity of transitions (or stages). Mediation of some kind, whether dialectical or gradual, is the recourse of those who study men without a conception of a fixed human nature. The idea of "medieval" itself contains the assumption of transition between ancient and modern and denies the possibility of a break.

SECULARISM AND DIVINE RIGHT

In regard to revelation, it is generally admitted, however, that the change from medieval to modern society was a break. Those who regard that change as on the whole a transformation should seek above all to explain how a religious society became secularized.[21] Their problem is acute if they have resorted to re-

19 G. L. Burr, "Anent the Middle Ages," *American Historical Review,* 18 (1913), 715, in reference to Otto von Freising.

20 The several studies of the name "middle ages" do not distinguish its prehistory in the first two meanings from its history in the last meaning. See Paul Lehmann, "Vom Mittelalter und von der lateinischen Philologie des Mittelalters," *Quellen und Untersuchungen zur lateinischen Philologie des Mittelalters* (Munich: 1914), pp. 1–25; George Gordon, *Medium Aevum and the Middle Age,* S. P. E. Tract No. 19 (Oxford: 1925); Wallace K. Ferguson, *The Renaissance in Historical Thought* (Boston: Houghton Mifflin, 1948), pp. 73–77, 119–26; Giorgio Falco, *La Polemica sul Medio Evo* (Turin: 1933).

21 Frederick Watkins, *The Political Tradition of the West* (Cambridge, Mass.: Harvard University Press, 1948), Chap. 3; Gerhard Leibholz, *Das Wesen der Reprasentation,* 2d ed. (Berlin: 1960), p. 211; Otto Hintze, "Weltgeschichtliche Bedingungen des Reprasentativverfassung," *Historische Zeitschrift,* 143 (1930), 11; Figgis, *op. cit.,* p. 7; R. W. and A. J. Carlyle,

ligious ideas in order to skirt the influence of Greek philosophy and to emphasize the peculiarly medieval contribution to history. The most peculiarly medieval ideas are to be found where the difference between medieval and modern society is admittedly the greatest, in religion. Where medieval society does not derive its ideas from the ancients, it seems most in opposition to modern society. Yet perhaps the problem of secularization can be solved without relying on the importance of secular ideas. If the secularism of modern representation can be shown to be a mere reflection of the secularism of modern society, then secularism would be accidental to modern representation. The change toward secularism from medieval to modern society would not disturb the important similarity between medieval and modern society, which is representation. One might even hope to find the most important source of this similarity where one seems to see the most obvious difference.

We return to the provisional definition of this essay that representative government represents or reflects culture or society. Such government seems to contrast with government by divine right. When "divine right" is taken in its simplest and widest sense, not merely as the sophisticated doctrine of the divine right of kings nor as the canonists' arguments in favor of the power of the Pope, it gives government the right and obligation to make the people conform to God's commands, whatever they may be. Instead of taking guidance from the consent or the opinions or the feelings of the people, government by "divine right" makes the people conform; instead of reflecting the culture, this government determines the culture. Government by divine right seems to be compatible with any of Aristotle's constitutions of government, including democracy. Certain Puritan sects in the seventeenth century advocated democracy by divine right. It was their view that religion thrives when men are free, that is, when a majority of the community is free to impose severe moral standards, by divine command and with divine sanction, on all the people.

This government is not representative government by our definition. It neither follows nor leads the people as they are in their society or culture; it imposes on the people and rules them. If "representative government" is a term of distinction and implies the

A History of Medieval Political Theory in the West (6 vols., London: 1950), V, 129; Weber, *The Protestant Ethic, op. cit.*, p. 174.

existence of nonrepresentative government, government by divine right would be the prototype of nonrepresentative government.

Indeed, government by divine right seems to have been dominant everywhere before modern representative government arrived and spread. All previous governments seem to have supposed that the relation between man and God affects the relations among men and that God or the gods sanction their rule. Although certain ruling aristocracies, the Roman and perhaps the Confucian, may reasonably be suspected of unbelief, their governments were not secular. They were not publicly based on the sufficiency of this world. Accordingly, these aristocracies used the religion of the people to support their own rule and would have been as shocked at secularism as the most pious believers.

Two of the three religions of medieval times hold closely to the type of divine right government. In Islam and Judaism, a comprehensive revealed Law reigned supreme in the lives of all members of the community. But Christianity is different. Christianity replaces the comprehensive Old Law with the New Law of the New Testament, which does not include penal legislation and does not regulate every detail of public and private life. The New Testament leaves such matters to the law of Caesar, except for certain prescriptions which complement that law.[22] Hence the supreme science of Christianity is theology and its divine law is for the most part otherworldly. Under Christianity this-worldly law developed in two systems deriving from Roman law, canon and civil law, by the efforts of two groups of lawyers, the canonists and the legists.

Then Christianity seems to hold forth the possibility of representative government that is not secular, thus vindicating the derivation of modern from medieval representation. It seems reasonable. Why can a religious people not be represented by a religious government, if their religion distinguishes the sacred realm from the secular and leaves the secular largely in the willing hands of Caesar?

The reason is in the "religious people": one must consider how a religious people becomes religious. According to Christian doctrine, no man is by nature religious; at most man has a natural inclination to God. God created man needing God, hence without a natural awareness of God that would supply his need. On the contrary, man

[22] Ralph Lerner and Muhsin Mahdi (eds.), *Medieval Political Philosophy* (New York: The Free Press, 1963), Introduction, p. 12.

is naturally and was originally recalcitrant; he is a backslider who needs to be reminded of his Creation and its law. The result for a Christian community (as well as communities of other religions) is a religious education resembling Aristotle's moral education. Such education proceeds by habituation in constant practice rather than by demonstration to the intellect, and Christian revelation, however sudden and illuminating, does not obviate the need for repetition and reiteration. Those Christians who served God in these times were not thought to be above the need for routine. Some commentators have found one source of modern representation in the constitution of the Dominican order of 1221 providing for a central representative assembly,[23] but it cannot be supposed that the government of monks reflected the spontaneous habits of the most pious Christians. Nor were the less pious left to their private concerns under the superintendence of secular authorities. Although the education of a Christian community was Christian and concentrated on the most pious, ordinary citizens, however ignorant, were not entitled to develop their own "culture." If they were ignored by their rulers, it surely did not follow that their government represented their ignorance.

The distinction between "sacred" and "secular" does not correspond to the modern distinction between "state" and "society," which confines government to the office of agent for "society." Both sacred and secular authorities could and did interfere in "society"; both regarded themselves as entitled to do so together and disputed how much for each.[24] Paying Caesar's taxes was not meant as a mere gesture of defensive prudence, to placate a subordinate functionary who might otherwise turn vicious. Caesar as well as the Church had a claim for the care of the soul. The "divine right of kings" was maintained, of course, for secular authority.

It was then no accident that those political philosophers who thought they had founded modern representative government argued for freedom of religion. Freedom of religion as they understood it was above all a weapon in their polemic against divine right and the religious education or "cloistered virtue" that supports divine right. By freedom of religion they did not mean the Puritan freedom to

[23] Ernest Barker, *The Dominican Order and Convocation* (Oxford: 1913); Ford, *op. cit.*, pp. 109–10.

[24] Cf. Figgis, *op. cit.*, p. 5; Watkins, *op. cit.*, pp. 58–9; *Lord Acton, Essays on Freedom and Power,* G. Himmelfarb (ed.) (Cleveland: 1955), pp. 86–87.

practice their religion without fear of persecution; that freedom was attainable under the system of divine right. To satisfy the Puritan demand, it was necessary to specify that a sect of the Christian religion was free to capture a country and make it into a theocracy only by majority decision or with majority rule, rather than by the decision of the king. The freedom of religion defended by modern political philosophers was freedom from interference in the lives of citizens by the state or church on behalf of God. Its premise was toleration. Locke, the most celebrated defender of toleration, did not present it merely as the means to a truce between warring religions, on the basis of a formula such as *cuius regio eius religio.*

Toleration is the *principle* that earthly peace comes before any seeming religious duty that may disturb it, the principle to be found in the preamble of the Toleration Act of 1689.[25] This principle does not merely confine each system of divine right to one country and establish the prevailing religion. Rather, it is necessarily intolerant of all divine right, that is to say, of religious intolerance. For divine right is necessarily intolerant. A Christian people, no less than a people of another religion, becomes religious through education in the divinity it holds in reverence, to the exclusion of other gods. While the divinity is by its own word exclusive, the education naturally requires in its routine a shelter from impertinent skepticism. To become "religious" is to learn and practice a religion, which as such and in its practices excludes other religions. Locke was coldly consistent in holding that "those have no right to be tolerated by the magistrate . . . that will not own and teach the duty of tolerating all men in matters of mere religion."

"Matters of mere religion" are distinct from "civil concernments" because God has not given authority to one man over another for the care of his soul. Being his brother's keeper only in "life, liberty, health, and indolency of body; and the possession of outward things. . . ,"[26] the civil magistrate assumes that these cares are sufficient from his standpoint. Because they are sufficient to him, he must ensure that they are sufficient to every authority with power to compel. No one who respects his brother's body and everyone who tries to keep his brother's soul will run afoul of the law. Thus the

[25] H. C. Mansfield, Jr., "Party Government and the Settlement of 1688," *American Political Science Review,* 58 (1964), 940–41.

[26] John Locke, *A Letter Concerning Toleration,* in *John Locke on Politics and Education,* H. R. Penniman (ed.) (New York: 1947), pp. 57, 25.

limitation of secular authority to affairs of the body has the effect of giving a practical or this-worldly sovereignty to those affairs. The churches must not only accept this sovereignty but teach it. It is very striking in Locke's doctrine of toleration that secular authority is limited because secularism is sufficient. But if this were not the case, it would not be possible to limit ecclesiastical authority as well. The principle of toleration that supports modern representative government is the teaching of secularism as opposed to the religious education of divine right.

It may be objected that toleration and representative government are not necessarily secular in Locke's meaning. Kant presented a doctrine of representative government based on the primacy of moral freedom over material interests. His representative government is the embodiment of his "pure" morality, the self-legislation of the moral law through government. Only "pure" morality can be legislated because only morality that bears no relation to material interests can be universalized for every rational being. Hence material or economic interests cannot be represented.[27] Now since morality is "pure" by its lack of reference to the facts of the world, Kantian representation is by intention neither this-worldly nor other-worldly; it is not secular in the sense of being based on the sufficiency of this world. But a pure morality, self-legislated in freedom, must necessarily and by no means incidentally reject every form of divine right: "For in what concerns my freedom, I have no obligation with respect to divine law, which can be acknowledged by my reason alone, except in so far as I could have given my consent to it."[28] Kant replaces the sufficiency of this world with the sufficiency of the reason of the rational beings who happen to live in this world; for God's reason is no higher than the reason of such rational beings. The result is a representative government with the same hostility to divine right as Locke's, if nobler than his.

Deism must not be overlooked in an argument that representative government is necessarily secular, although it is easy to do so. Since

[27] See Carl Schmitt, *Verfassungslehre* (Berlin: 1928), pp. 208–10; Leibholz, *op. cit.*, p. 32; Weber, *Wirtschaft und Gesellschaft*, I, 174–75; cf. Guizot, *op. cit.*, p. 347. Considering the difference between Rousseau's "will" and Kant's "good will," one may suppose the source of this opinion to be Rousseau's remark that will cannot be represented, *Contrat Social*, III, 15.

[28] Kant, "Perpetual Peace," in *Kant on History*, L. W. Beck (ed.) (Indianapolis: 1963), p. 93, n. 2; cf. p. 96, n. 4. See *Metaphysik der Sitten* (Hamburg: 1922), pp. 45–47, 163; *Kleinere Schriften zur Geschichtsphilosophie, Ethik und Politik* (Hamburg: 1964), p. 94.

men cannot be kept from having thoughts on the topics of religion, secularism requires either atheism or deism. Secularism does not quite succeed in establishing the sufficiency of this world. It needs to be protected against those who would arrange this world on the basis of opinions about the other world; hence it needs an opinion about the other world. To be established, secularism must be protected; and to be protected, it must be transcended. Such protection is available from the old philosophic principle that human reason is sufficient, which is different from the new principle that this world (comprising affairs of the body) is sufficient. At the same time it is necessary to confirm the sovereignty of man by the unknowableness of God; if God cannot be known, then man is alone and free. The result is what was called "natural religion" (formerly a contradiction in terms), in which are combined the power of the impotent, rational Aristotelian God and the reason of the mysterious, omnipotent Christian God.

Deism displays the modern mystery of a powerless God, even a mortal God. His sole purpose (to human penetration) is to foreclose the possibility of any relation of governance between God and man, so as to destroy every system of divine right. All varieties of deism, of which many are still alive, have as their consequence and culmination that man is free of divine governance. To arrive at this, it is essential to deny the existence of God's providence; and this may be done directly or by transforming it into a "general providence," through which God, His eye no longer on the sparrow, provides for whole species by the operation of the laws of nature or history. The "elect" or the "chosen people" are now understood to be those who know what they are doing according to these laws. The maxim "God helps those who help themselves" is not deistic, since it acknowledges the necessity and seeks the assistance of God's help. "God allows all to help themselves" is the deistic maxim, for the deistic God is impartial and does not interfere in human affairs. Both government and morality are human, with the guidance of the laws of nature or history found by human reason. In contrast to the religious education of divine right, deism facilitates the education of "religious" men, not in the sense of any religion but in the sense of "religiosity."

Although the morality of toleration attempts to be self-enforcing, still it seems to need the speculative support of deism. It is self-enforcing by its offer of undisturbed private enjoyments in exchange for not disturbing the privacy of others. Such an exchange, it was supposed, does not have to be imposed on any reasonable man. This exchange is the basis for consent to a government that respects and enforces privacy; and government based on this exchange is self-government. The morality of toleration is self-enforcing by virtue of self-government, because the advantages of self-government can be made plain to any reasonable man. But suppose that, by a partial interpretation of the deistic maxim, a man helps himself to what belongs to somebody else; suppose, indeed, that he refuses the exchange, however clearly advantageous, of limitations on himself for freedom for himself. He would refuse it if he thought himself entitled to special consideration as being one of the divinely "elect." Who is to enforce toleration on this unreasonable man? The deistic god can enforce toleration through the laws of nature or history. Those laws, discovered by human reason, may not seem powerful or solid without a divine sanction, for they have been variously understood and hotly disputed. Besides, the unreasonable man who comes to grief by ignoring the laws of nature or history perhaps does not satisfy the spirit of revenge as does the unreasonable man who is punished by god, the author of those laws. In any case, the deistic god is impartial and yet moral, since morality is the morality of toleration; and therefore he is able (if he exists) to enforce a self-enforcing morality. These distasteful paradoxes are essential to the being of a god who does not insist on his divine right. The principle of toleration speaks to its believers—to its decent supporters and its indecent and undeserving beneficiaries—through deism.[29]

Modern representative government, being secular, is emphatically human. As divine right is government from on high, modern representation is government from below. It is government made *out of* the people in its "society" or "culture." It is government determined by its material rather than government impressing a form. It is concerned with the source of its authority, perhaps the original contract by which it was constituted, and surely the implied contract by which it is carried on. What the end of government ought to be is not a theme or problem of modern representation, for that end is

[29] Whether deism is necessary to secularism may be considered the underlying issue in the recent school prayer decisions of the Supreme Court. Does the separation of Church and State have to be maintained by belief in a non-governing (hence nonsectarian) god, or can the belief in separation be indoctrinated without this support?

seen as merely putting into effect whatever the end or ends of society may be. But what ends of a society *can* be represented?

This argument suggests that not every society can be represented by modern representative government, because only certain ends are representable by it. A religious society, or more vaguely, a society of high aspirations, cannot be represented. As men cannot be prevented from holding thoughts on the topics of religion, so also they cannot be prevented from admiring other men and gods or God. Representative government cannot keep people from looking upwards, but it tries to ensure that when they do, they see no government. Representative government is "government from below" not only because it arises out of the people but because it cannot partake of the noble or divine. The cause of this inability, in turn, is not that those qualities cannot be found in the people but that government cannot represent aspirations.

All moral and political aspirations, refusing to accept society as it is, imply the duty to disturb the privacy and impose on the freedom of others. Kant may be said, in his "critical idealism," to have attempted to combine representative government and divine right. He was disgusted at the "empirical" morality of self-interest in the tolerant, representable society of Locke and Hume (as well as in the god of deism), and he tried to make representative government represent the noble in men, including the common man. But Kant did not notice that self-legislation is still legislation and that self-legislated morality is still legislated morality. If it is necessary to compel oneself, it is necessary and no less reasonable to compel others. In the event, Kant's idealism has spent itself in compelling men to be good or in allowing them, with ceremony, to be selfish. For men cannot be represented in that to which they must be compelled or habituated.

Modern representation requires a representable society consecrated by an undemanding god, a society without aspirations. This explains why the Christian division between sacred and secular does not allow modern representation to develop. In the Christian division the realm of the secular has its dignity (insofar as it has dignity) by virtue of the divine right of the sacred, since respect for Caesar was the command of God. To make society representable, it was necessary not to transpose the superior sacred and the inferior secular but to prevent the superior from *ruling* the inferior. In this task, Locke and his friends could seem to obey the division between sacred and secular while attacking it. Having conceived an undemanding god, who binds everyone to help the rest of mankind "when his own preservation comes not in competition,"[30] they could claim divine sanction for secularism from this division. They could claim or imply that the sovereignty of Christian secular authority in its realm authorized the sovereignty of secular authority in a secular society. But was an undemanding god the Christian God?

MEDIEVAL SOURCES OF MODERN REPRESENTATION

From the analysis of secularism and divine right, we return to the explanations of scholars. Without investigating medieval representation, it is possible only to raise difficulties for the arguments by which medieval representation is said to have descended to modern governments. Modern governments embody many medieval ideas and institutions, but if modern representation is secular, it is hard to see how it could have evolved either from ecclesiastical organization or from parliaments by unconscious inheritance. There must have been a break in the history of representation. New "ideas" must have replaced the system of divine right, and those ideas must have been new political ideas, the ideas of new rulers or of old rulers thinking in a new way. A change of regime must have occurred so that these new rulers could build a society representable by a secular representative government. How could this change be unconscious? Unless it is assumed that the natural bent of men is secular or that the "practical necessities" of this world drive them to secularism, the change must have been planned, with an awareness of change, by the new rulers. But when only the modern West has become secular, and at the outset only with the aid of a popular deism, it is difficult to believe that the practical necessities of regimes living under the system of divine right forced them to that change. In fact, the worldly abuses of Catholic Christianity at most inspired a new Protestant system of divine right. Is unconscious Protestantism conceivable? If not, then the much greater change from every form of divine right to secularism would also seem inconceivable. The idea of unconscious inheritance, as we have tried to show, is itself a modern idea not inherited from medieval times—not to mention again the idea of "medieval."

[30] Locke, *Two Treatises of Government,* II, 6.

These thoughts on what is conceivable can neither affect nor discover what happened, but they can direct doubts to some of the explanations of scholars. Since the publication of the third volume of Gierke's vast work in 1881, conciliarism has been held to be a major source of representative government. The conciliarists were clerics (or "publicists") of the late medieval period, writing after the Schism of 1378 to the middle of the fifteenth century to argue that the choice of a Pope should be made by a general council of the Church representing the various orders and divisions of the Church, not including the laity.[31] Gierke said that these writers proposed "a full sovereignty of the council as the representative of the whole community," and that the chief of them, Nicholas of Cusa, "erected a formal system of Representative Parliamentarism" both for the Church and the empire.[32] Figgis gave them credit for treating "the Church definitely as one of a class, political societies." Accordingly they proposed a mixed constitution for Church and empire, the ancestor of modern constitutionalism whose "far-off legacy to our own day was 'the glorious revolution.' "[33] Gierke found this legacy more generally in the philosophic, theological, and legal medieval doctrine, to which conciliarism contributed and which was deposited in the Christian-Germanic idea of freedom. Indeed, according to him, medieval doctrine developed not only this idea but the ancient idea of state sovereignty in opposition to it; and these ideas prepared for combat in subsequent centuries.

Recently these claims for the conciliarists have been reduced.[34] Jacob has written, for example, that Cusa's theory of representation is "as far as possible removed" from the theory of Hobbes. He admits the usefulness of that understanding of conciliarism that regards it as a blow struck for constitutional freedom, but he asserts that the most essential part of conciliarism "has a theological, rather than a political or constitutional, basis."[35] This assertion is inadequate because "the theological" specifies the government of man

[31] Otto Gierke, *Political Theories of the Middle Age,* F. W. Maitland (ed.) (Cambridge: 1951), pp. 57–60; Paul E. Sigmund, *Nicholas of Cusa and Medieval Political Thought* (Cambridge, Mass.: 1963), p. 163.

[32] Gierke, *op. cit.,* pp. 54, 66; see pp. 49–61.

[33] Figgis, *op. cit.,* pp. 56, 63; cf. Hintze, *op. cit.,* pp. 14–21.

[34] Paul E. Sigmund, "Cusanus' *Concordantia:* A Re-Interpretation," *Political Studies,* 10 (1962), 180–97.

[35] E. F. Jacob, *Essays in the Conciliar Epoch* (Manchester: 1953), p. 18.

by God and may include human politics; entirely to separate theological from political is characteristic of secularism.

Figgis stated the point when he conceded against his own argument: "Still we must not forget that it was the politics of a Divine Society that were under discussion."[36] Nicholas of Cusa argued from the existence of an imperial council to the importance of a sovereign council in the Church; he moved back and forth in the analogy of ecclesiastical and secular authority because he regarded all authority as divinely endowed.[37] It is also easy to argue the analogy of ecclesiastical organization and the state in a secular society. For example, Hobbes and Locke declared that the sovereignty of the Pope in the Catholic Church was incompatible with the secular sovereignty of a free government.[38] In reverse direction, from church to state, churchmen may argue today from the liberty of interpreting sacred texts to freedom of speech, or from equality of men under God to racial integration. But how is it possible to argue from a system of divine right in whose premise, the government of God, both church and secular authority agree, to secular society whose rejection of divine government is shared by church and state? The ecclesiastical organization of a "Divine Society" may draw upon the practices of secular authority in that society, but how could it be the model for representation in a secular society? Conciliarism might make a convenient authority in a political argument of a secular society, but only out of its context. In fact, its greatest influence was on Protestantism.

These remarks need not be varied (though they would have to be elaborated) when applied to Luther, Calvin, or the Puritans.[39] Whatever they changed of medieval Christianity, they changed to preserve Christianity and divine right. From this generally accepted truth it follows that their influence on secular society was not *their* influence but the convenience of secularized men and secular disputants. Anticongregationalism, antipresbyterianism, antiepiscopalism, antipapalism, and anticlericalism do not singly or in sum make secularism; nor do the worldly abuses of the papacy and other ecclesiastics which these movements opposed. Infallibility in the

[36] Figgis, *op. cit.*, p. 64.

[37] *De Concordantia Catholica,* II, 13, 14, 18, 23, 32; III, 4, 12.

[38] Hobbes, *Leviathan,* Chap. 42, pp. 357, 366, 373, 378; Chap. 44, p. 399; Chap. 47, pp. 452–53. Locke, *A Letter Concerning Toleration,* p. 58.

[39] Figgis, *op. cit.,* Chap. 3; L. F. Brown, "Ideas of Representation from Elizabeth to Charles II," *Journal of Modern History,* 2 (1943), 23–40.

Church cannot supply the model for absolute sovereignty, since the absolute sovereignty of modern representative government requires and was intended to sustain human independence of God's governance. The absolute sovereignty of modern representation represents the absolute sovereignty of man in the state of nature, who has, contrary to the Bible, the right to all things which he may suppose necessary to his preservation.[40]

Conciliarism proposed a mixed government for the Church and empire and the whole government divided between them, but neither mixed nor divided government within the system of divine right is the same as, or analogous to, the limited government of modern representation. Modern representative government must be limited, we have suggested, so that government can reflect the society or culture without forming it; and absolute sovereignty may be needed to transform those elements in society, such as the clergy and the aristocracy, that have been nourished by divine right. The secularism of modern representation explains its strange attachment to both limited government and absolute sovereignty.[41] Mixed government, on the other hand, aims to secure the consent of all elements to an interfering government that may be divided, in varying and disputed proportion, between sacred and secular authorities. The mixture and the division seek to prevent tyranny by one authority but they do not serve to limit all authority to the protection of private liberty. The natural law characteristic of divine right stands above government in an uneasy relation with divine law; but it also stands above the people as the ends to which their government must bring them. The natural law of modern representation in the political philosophy of Hobbes and Locke stands above government, requiring the consent of the governed, but it also protects the people not merely from misrule but from every unnecessary interference with private liberty.

The other source of modern representation is the medieval parliaments. Speaking of England in his lectures on representative government (delivered in 1820–22), Guizot said that "the creation of a Parliament" was "the birth of a representative system."[42] In studying

[40] Georges de Lagarde, "L'idée de représentation dans les oeuvres de Guillaume d'Ockham," *Bulletin of the International Committee of the Social Sciences,* 9 (1937), 441; Hobbes, *Leviathan,* Chaps. 13, 14; Locke, *Two Treatises of Government,* I, 86; II, 4, 8, 11, 13.

[41] Cf. C. H. McIlwain, *The High Court of Parliament and Its Supremacy* (New Haven: 1910), pp. 352, 373.

[42] Guizot, *op. cit.,* p. 334.

medieval parliaments, scholars have attempted to compare parliaments in different countries for the ultimate purpose of explaining the varying destiny of modern representation in those countries;[43] and the success of representation in modern England has made the medieval English Parliament and the English shires and boroughs glow with significance. In the different histories of parliaments, the change from medieval to modern representation appears almost unnoticed as a transition, for modern representation is thought to have been the gradual consequence of developing modern societies.

Thus the problem is, according to H. M. Cam, "What is the community being represented?" Representation itself is so little a problem that it began when someone exclaimed in the primitive din: "Don't all talk at once—who will speak for you?"[44] With this origin, representation loses its special character entirely; one could find it not only in medieval times but in antiquity, and not only in the ancient confederations but in the cities themselves. Even the difference between representation and "direct government" would disappear, since the assembly of a "direct government" could not proceed unless it prevented all from talking at once and required one to speak for many.[45]

Every government has the problem of consent, and many governments seek consent by offering offices to members of the groups whose opinion they find valuable or indispensable. Medieval representation used such "representative machinery" to secure consent. But "representative government"[46] is government that uses representative machinery because it is authorized solely and entirely by consent. Strictly speaking, only modern representation amounts to "representative government." The medieval phrase from Roman law, *Quod omnes tangit ab omnibus approbetur,* illustrates the difference. "What touches all should be approved by all" is merely permissive and implies that some matters do not touch all and need not be approved. In any case, the initiative is with the Crown.

In modern representation, the initiative is with the people who

[43] Otto Hintze, "Typologie der Standischen Verfassungen des Abendlands," *Historische Zeitschrift,* 141 (1929), 229–48; Robert von Mohl, *Staatsrecht, Volkerrecht und Politik* (Tubingen: 1860), pp. 33–64; H. M. Cam, "The Theory and Practice of Representation," *op. cit.,* pp. 11–14.

[44] Cam, "The Theory and Practice of Representation," *op. cit.,* p. 18.

[45] J. A. O. Larsen, *Representative Government in Greek and Roman History* (Berkeley: University of California Press, 1966), p. 2.

[46] This distinction is implied in Larsen, *ibid.,* p. 5.

consent to government and who may thereby consent to the use of prerogative by a king or president. Because modern representative government is limited, its every act must be authorized; everything is assumed to touch all so that no unnecessary interference will be allowed. In order to argue that the medieval English Parliament was becoming more and more representative of the public, scholars must examine the growth of public legislation and the use of the *commune petition* there. But since the Settlement of 1688,[47] Parliament has assured the omnicompetence of the public's representatives by its own sovereignty. Increasing public legislation and changing conceptions of the public interest since that time have not added to the extent of possible public intervention.

How much discretion for representatives is a question for both medieval and modern representation, but the question is posed differently. When Edward I summoned a Parliament in 1294, he made sure that it could commit the taxpayers to the taxes it voted by demanding that the representatives appear with *plena potestas*.[48] The French Constitution of 1791 included a provision that its members must represent the nation rather than any particular department.[49] Against the Radical doctrine of "authoritative instructions," Burke maintained in his Bristol speech of 1774 that members of Parliament must represent the people by using their own judgment instead of reflecting the popular will. The difference is not that modern representation is discretionary and medieval mandated;[50] it is in the understanding of the people being represented. The modern debate assumes that the people are a whole to be represented *by* their government, while the medieval debate assumes that the people are a part to be represented *to* their government.

Therefore medieval representation was "dualistic" or "*en face*."[51] The English king faced the people's representatives because he was

47 Mansfield, *op. cit.,* p. 938.

48 Gaines Post, "Plena Potestas and Consent in Medieval Assemblies," *Traditio,* 1 (1943), 368, 374, 402.

49 Georg Jellinek, *Allgemeine Staatslehre* (Berlin: 1905), pp. 561–62.

50 Weber, *Wirtschaft und Gesellschaft,* I, 172; II, 674, 792. Because of his distinction (traceable to Kant) between ideal and material interests, Weber supposed that the "free representation" of the former was the essential specific of modern representation, as distinct from the tethered "technical representation" of material interests by the agent. See also Leibholz, *op. cit.,* Chap. 3.

51 Hintze, "Weltgeschichtliche Bedingungen," *op. cit.,* p. 1; Lagarde, *op. cit.,* p. 428.

not a member of the people himself. He was a member of the realm. In his private capacity he was a member of the realm whose head he was in his public capacity; and in this public capacity he represented a community that included a king. His "representation" of the people in this capacity was his responsibility, divinely or naturally given, for their good. The people did not make him king by making him their representative. In the analogy between the human body and the realm, the king was head or heart. But the analogy of Hobbes is quite different: the sovereign is an entire human body, which is therefore entirely artificial. Hobbes' sovereign, even if he is a monarch, was no better than any other man before he was chosen as representative;[52] and modern representation follows Hobbes' analogy. Modern representative *government* is not part of that community which it represents, and modern *representatives* in their private capacity are mere members of the people that first consent to government. The medieval representative constitutes part of the community he represents, whereas the modern representative is made entirely by his "constituents." Some recent studies have suggested that the medieval community represented in Parliament was formed in great part by royal policy and by the administration of the king's court.[53]

The vital difference is that, according to the modern conception, the people are a whole having no ruling part. Everyone belongs to the people. The people themselves are not potentially a ruling part, and they cannot be divided into ruling and ruled parts. It is less important whether the people are a whole of many individuals, as for Hobbes, or an ordered "culture" or "society," as for modern sociology (so long as the orderedness is not political). The people to which Marsilius ascribes sovereignty contain the celebrated *valentior pars,* a stronger or superior part; and the people to which

[52] *Leviathan,* Chap. 18, p. 113; for Locke also, when such a man is not the representative, he is "a single private person without power." *Two Treatises of Government,* II, 151.

[53] Was Parliament originally a limitation on the king or a device of the king? The current is now running against Stubbs, who held the former opinion. D. Pasquet said: "The nation did not demand representation in the king's parliament. It was the king who imposed on his subjects the duty of sending him their representatives." *An Essay on the Origins of the House of Commons,* R. G. D. Laffan, trans. (Cambridge: 1925), p. 225; see also Albert B. White, *Self Government at the King's Command* (Minneapolis: 1933); J. R. Major, *The Estates General of 1560* (Princeton: 1951), pp. 73–75; Charles R. Young, *The English Borough and Royal Administration, 1130–1307* (Durham: Duke University Press, 1961).

Nicholas of Cusa gives the power of consent to government contain the "wiser and more outstanding" (*sapientiores et praestantiores*), who have a natural right to rule.[54] But the Hobbesian people are equal in strength and wisdom in the state of nature and hence have no natural ruling part. Modern representation requires that all government be artificial so that it may be impartial, reflecting the interests of all groups and ruling according to the desires of none. That such a government be made by contract is not decisive, for the social contract appears in premodern thought. What does distinguish modern representation from medieval is the equal bargaining power of all parties to the contract. As a result of this contract, a part of the people may be awarded a leading role and the majority may be expected to defer to them. But such leaders are not rulers and deference to them is a kind of consent. Modern representative government, Jefferson recognized, is not incompatible with an elite of "natural aristoi." It is incompatible with the idea, as he put it, that some men are born with saddles on their backs and others with spurs.

Because the "people" of modern representation have no ruling part it does not follow that modern representation is democratic. The people can consent to a government that holds no elections, never mind universal suffrage. But it does follow that modern representation is secular. A people having no ruling part has no ruled part; if the people cannot be understood as the numerical majority seeking to rule, then also it cannot be considered receptive to rule. Divine right holds that the decisive relation of governance is between man and God, not among men; and the equality of men under God is from this standpoint an equality of subjection. If all men were created equal by the God of divine right as opposed to nature's god, then they owe obedience to Him above all and consequently to the government He appoints. Their recalcitrance would not affect their duty. The manner by which God appointed the government—immediately or by translation from the people—would affect the character of the government, but again would not affect the duty of obedience. But the people of modern representation have no such duty.

To distinguish modern from medieval representation one must define modern representation and know its medieval sources. For

[54] Marsilius of Padua, *Defensor Pacis,* I, 12, 3–4; Nicholas of Cusa, *De Concordantia Catholica,* II, 14; cf. III, pref.

most scholars the implicit basis of this definition is the English Parliament since 1688; the sources of its qualities are in question. We have argued here that modern and medieval representation are different ways of life, not merely different kinds of representative machinery, and that the difference is most visible in the secularism of modern representation. The break between medieval and modern representation, if it occurred in 1688, would then be found in the policies rather than in the institutions of the English Parliament. The problem of self-examination for modern representation is that its way of life denies the possibility of legislating a way of life and yet must be legislated.

7

AN AUGUSTAN DEBATE: NOTES ON THE HISTORY OF THE IDEA OF REPRESENTATION

ISAAC KRAMNICK

Edmund Burke was an unabashed admirer of Sir Robert Walpole. The zealous missionary of party had only praise for the party man Walpole.

> Sir Robert was an honorable man and a sound Whig. He was not as the Jacobites and discontented Whigs of his time have represented him, and as ill-informed people still represent him, a prodigal and corrupt minister. They charged him in their libels and seditious conversations as having first reduced corruption into a system. Such was their cant. But he was far from governing by corruption. He governed by party attachments. The charge of systematic corruption is less applicable to him, perhaps than to any minister who ever served the Crown for so great a length of time.[1]

[1] Edmund Burke, *Appeal from New to Old Whigs* in *Works* (Boston:

There was, moreover, another feature of Augustan political life to account for Walpole's appeal to Burke; in those early years of Whig ascendancy Walpole had emerged as spokesman and champion of the theory of representation that would receive its classic statement in Burke's famous letter to his Bristol constituents.[2] The occasion for Walpole's statements on the nature of the representative function was the full-blown debate between his press and Bolingbroke's Opposition in 1732 over the Government's excise bill.

Fanned by Bolingbroke's weekly *Craftsman* and William Pulteney's agitation in the City, the opposition to the rather mild tax measure was powerful enough to bring about one of the most dramatic Parliamentary setbacks dealt to Walpole in his long administration. Walpole withdrew his proposal in response to the public outcry as manifested in the widespread petitioning, instructing, and even threatening of members of Parliament by interested constituents. Lest anyone misconstrue the precedent of his having had to bow to public pressure, Walpole turned angrily to a theoretical attack on any such radical principles. His writers lashed out at the dangers implicit in petitioning and instructing members of Parliament. The legislature of England, replied the *London Journal,* is the sole authority in England; the people have no voice over this supreme authority. To claim that they do is to speak of rebellion and of their taking the government into their own hands.[3] The power of the people extends only to the constituent act of establishing the

---

1881), vol. IV, p. 107. Not only was Walpole a "party man," but, moreover, his journals were one of the few voices heard with anything favorable to say about the principles of party in general. His *London Journal* suggested that all free countries would have parties. To those who claimed that no country in the world was ever as infested with parties as England, the *Journal* replied, " 'Tis so far from being a reproach, that 'tis an honor to us; and shews, that we have a sense of liberty and public virtue." No. 777, May 18, 1734.

[2] The views herein attributed to Walpole are found mainly in the party press which his administration subsidized and distributed "speedily" and "without charge" through His Majesty's Post. (These are charges found in the Opposition weekly, *The Craftsman,* No. 265, July 31, 1731.) For details on Walpole and the distribution, subsidization and authorship of his press which included the *London Journal, The Daily Courant, The Free Briton,* and *The Daily Gazetteer,* see J. H. Plumb, *Walpole* (Boston: Houghton Mifflin, 1956), vol. II, pp. 314–15; Lawrence Hanson, *Government and the Press 1605–1763* (Oxford: Oxford University Press, 1936), Chap. IV, "The Government Press"; and *A Further Report From the Committee of Secrecy appointed to enquire into the Conduct of Robert, Earl of Orford, During the Last Ten Years* (London: 1742).

[3] *London Journal,* No. 758, January 5, 1734.

government. When the government is settled and the power of legislation given to a body chosen to represent the community, "then the original power of the people in their collective body ceases, for the sole power and the sole authority is invested in the persons chosen, who are to judge and act for us in all matters relating to legislation."[4]

Walpole's *Journal* was careful to anticipate the radical retort implicit in Locke's discussion of the "Dissolution of Government" in the *Second Treatise*.[5] The *Journal* insisted that when Locke talked of a supreme power of the community to save itself from the legislature's invasion of property and liberty, he meant a residual power to be called upon for something much more fundamental than a tax on tobacco. Only when the constitution itself was threatened by the legislature could the government be dissolved, it suggested, and only then, when dissolved, did the people regain their power and authority. While the constitution was preserved, the *Journal* reasoned, the people had no right to instruct their members on what laws they should make and how taxes should be raised.[6] The members of the legislature might ask advice and the subjects might even petition them, but that was all.

> We have no authority over them, we cannot command them; we gave them power to make laws for us, and chose them, because we judged they had abilities and integrity enough to do their duty. But they must judge what laws are best for us; what taxes are most proper. If we don't like what they have done, we are at liberty, when the time is expired, to chuse [sic] others; this, and this only is our power. But we have no right to send threatening letters, and insolent instructions, authorisation orders and commands to those persons in whom we have lodged the supreme power of legislation.[7]

In their objection to the instructions and "commands" ordering members of Parliament to oppose the Excise Bill, Walpole's writers opposed the implied theory of representation as radical, democratic, and a threat to the mixed constitution by increasing the power of the people. Walpole's theorists rejected the Opposition's juxtaposition of the people and Parliament and the radical inference that the people had the supreme authority. Were the people allowed this

[4] *Ibid.*, No. 726, May 26, 1733.

[5] John Locke, *Second Treatise on Civil Government,* Peter Laslett (ed.) (New York: Cambridge University Press, 1965), paragraphs 222, 430.

[6] *London Journal,* No. 758, January 5, 1734.

[7] *Ibid.*, No. 726, May 26, 1733.

power the mixed constitution would fall before an omnipotent popular branch, dependent on the fancies of the mob. In 1734, the *London Journal* wrote, "What enormous nonsense is this: The King is to know no voice of the people, but by their representatives. The Parliament is the only voice of the Nation he is to hearken to."[8] To refute this nonsense, the *London Journal* called upon the authority of the great Whig and Republican hero, Algernon Sydney, whose *Discourse concerning Government* contained views similar to those being stressed by Walpole. The *Journal* quoted his comments:

> Every county does not make a distinct body, having in itself a sovereign power, but is a member of that Great Body which comprehends the whole NATION. 'Tis not therefore for Kent or Suffix, Lews or Maidstone, but for the whole nation, that the members chosen for those places, are sent to serve in Parliament . . . they are not strictly and properly obliged to give an account of their actions to any, unless the whole Body of the Nation for which they serve could be assembled.[9]

Burke's views on the relationship of the representative and his constituents had roots deep in the Whig past. One could, for example, go back even to Coke's *Institutes of the Laws of England* where it is written that "though one be chosen for one particular county or borough, yet when he is returned, and sits in Parliament, he serveth for the whole realm."[10] In the eighteenth century the little-noted statement of the principle by Walpole provides yet another source for Burke's views. Here was one more reason for Burke to be impressed by this "honorable man and sound Whig."[11]

The radical theory of the representative as delegate of his constituents is deeply rooted in the medieval constitution. As far back as the fourteenth century the notion of the representative as attorney for his constituents' interests can be found.[12] This view of the mem-

[8] *Ibid.*, No. 755, December 15, 1733.

[9] Quoted in No. 755.

[10] Quoted in C. S. Emden, *The People and the Constitution* (Oxford: Clarendon Press, 1962), p. 23. Emden is in error when he attributes these Burkean attitudes to the *Craftsman*, p. 24.

[11] There is an additional source for Burke's views among eighteenth-century writers on representation. See "Of the First Principles of Government" in *Hume's Theory of Politics*, F. Watkins (ed.) (Edinburgh: T. Nelson, 1951), pp. 151–52, for views virtually identical with the Walpole-Burke view.

[12] See May McKisack, *The Fourteenth Century* (Oxford History of England) (Oxford: Oxford University Press, 1959), pp. 194–99; and Samuel

ber of Parliament as a local representative was revived in the constitutional crisis of the seventeenth century, which saw many instructions from freeholders to their delegates in Commons. In 1681, Shaftesbury actually circulated a form of instructions suitable for use by county constituencies in instructing their representatives on exclusion.[13] Another significant example of this practice is found in Andrew Marvell's correspondence with his constituents in the corporation of Hull. Marvell wrote the corporation in 1670: "What is your opinion at Hull of the Bill from the Lords for general naturalization of all foreigners that shall take the oaths of allegiance and supremacy?"[14] This conception of the representative's role would be central to later eighteenth-century radical thought. In the Augustan years its spokesman was Lord Bolingbroke, the erstwhile Tory leader, and head of the Opposition to Walpole—to his excise and his regime.

Bolingbroke, whose partisan interests were well served by the people's claim to instruct their representatives against the Excise, adhered to the delegate theory. His weekly journal, the *Craftsman,* objecting to the *London Journal*'s attacks on the application of the constituencies to their representatives answered: "There may be cases put, where the very best things be turned to an ill use, but instructions from corporations have been, and may be, of singular use to the cause of liberty, on some important occasions."[15] Bolingbroke's newspaper asked the *Journal* "whether the members of the House of Commons are the people's representatives or not; and whether, unlike all other deputies and trustees, they are absolutely independent of their principals and constituents?"[16] The *Craftsman*'s position was, to be sure, founded more firmly on medieval precedent than on any fundamental democratic instincts which would prompt the Wilkes-Jebb-Cartwright radicals; but even the medieval argument would be part of this latter position. Parliaments, the *Craftsman* wrote, were formerly called on particular emergencies of state, at which time the people were informed of the problem for which the Parliament was called, "and therefore were enabled to acquaint

---

Beer, *British Politics in the Collectivist Age* (New York: Knopf, 1965), pp. 6–7.

[13] Gilbert Barnett, *History of My Own Times* (Oxford: 1823), vol. II, p. 281.

[14] Cited in Emden, *op. cit.,* p. 19.

[15] *Craftsman,* No. 389, December 22, 1733.

[16] *Ibid.*

the elected with their sense of the matter, before they came to town." Should anything unexpected occur during the sitting, the Commoners usually "desired leave to consult their constituents, before they came to any resolutions."[17] The *Craftsman* was not above drawing upon the radical strain in Locke to prove its point. Like the later radicals, it did not hesitate to confront the Parliament with the extraparliamentary political community.

> The community says he [Locke] perpetually retains a supreme power of saving themselves from the attempts and designs of any body, even of their legislators, whenever they shall be so foolish, or so wicked as to lay and carry on designs against the liberties and properties of the subject.[18]

Bolingbroke's newspaper proclaimed itself the champion of such a community, whose members had sense and virtue; whereas Walpole, the *Craftsman* wrote, considered the common people "stupid, dregs and vulgar."[19]

The debate on the nature of representation was revived in an even more bitter exchange during the last years of Walpole and immediately after his fall. The positions were the same; Bolingbroke's Opposition upheld the right of constituents to instruct their delegates, while Walpole and the government Whigs denounced this as a radical innovation destructive of the balance of government. The historical props for this second stage of the debate were the many petitions and instructions sent to members of Parliament demanding a declaration of war against Spain, or, this having been done, the continuation of war grants. There were also instructions to representatives calling for place bills, triennial Parliaments, and investigation of Walpole's financial manipulations. As would be the case in the Wilkes affair, so too in these years from 1739 to 1743 the center of popular agitation was in the corporations of Westminster and London, although instructions on the war often came from the merchants in interested cities such as Bristol. Lord Egmont's government tract, *Faction Detected by the Evidence of the Facts,* criticized the Opposition's radical tactics. A small misguided group in Westminster, he wrote, had drawn up instructions to their members in Parliament. "This notion of it being the duty of every M.P. to vote in every instance as his constituents should direct him is a thing in

[17] *Ibid.*
[18] *Ibid.*
[19] *Ibid.,* No. 372, August 18, 1733.

the highest degree absurd." It is a fundamental change in the constitution which presumes "that no man, after he is chosen, is to consider himself as a member for any particular place, but as a representative for the whole nation."[20] The Opposition's principle would alter the constitution, making it into a democracy. The people, wrote Egmont, were erroneously setting themselves up as superior to the whole legislature and thus resuming that vague and loose authority that all peoples who enter into political society "divest themselves of and delegate for ever from themselves."[21] Such an attitude made the representative a mere creature of the people, as among the Dutch. At last the government was able to turn a favored Opposition charge against its authors; the Opposition, it seemed, was guilty of importing evil Dutch practices! The government newspaper, *The Daily Gazetteer,* added in 1742 that instructions to members left representative government totally uncertain and chaotic. Its views were thoroughly compatible with those of Burke's later reaction to similar radical demands.

> But surely a representative is one who stands in the place of another, with power to act for that other as if he, or if he represents more, as if they were present, and acting for themselves. Yet instructions quite alter the case, and from a representative make such a member a mere deputy, governed by other folks' sentiments which nothing in our constitution warrants, and which the whole frame of it tacitly condemns.[22]

In the renewed debate of 1739 to 1743, the Opposition once again sponsored the delegate theory of representation. In the *Craftsman* and in the same set of pamphlets that answered Egmont's attack on the continuation of the Opposition, the people's case was defended from the criticism of the Establishment Whig government. One Opposition pamphlet answered Egmont by denying that the people, in originally divesting themselves of power to their representatives, ever intended "to delegate it forever from themselves."[23] It proceeded to attack the government's view that the people had obtained too much power by quoting Bolingbroke's *Remarks on English*

[20] Egmont (Lord Percival), *Faction Detected by the Evidence of the Facts* (London: 1743), p. 100; see also *Seasonable Expostulations with the Worthy Citizens of London, Upon Their late Instructions to their Representatives* (London: 1742).

[21] Egmont, *op. cit.,* p. 134.

[22] *Daily Gazetteer,* No. 2309, November 23, 1742.

[23] Egmont, *Opposition, Not Facism* (London, 1743), p. 33.

History to the effect that the people had had more freedom in Saxon England than in Walpole's England.[24] The *Craftsman,* still the leading spokesman for the Opposition, commented in 1739 that "the collective body of the people have a right to petition or instruct their representatives in answer to the ministerial writers who have laboured the contrary."[25] Has not any man, it asked, "a just right to instruct his attorney, trustee, delegate, representative, or by what ever other name he may be called, in all points relating to his interests"? Surely, no man in his right senses "would continue such a person in his trust, if he refused to follow his directions, or acted contrary to them."[26] The *Craftsman* was adamant in its insistence that such practices had a hallowed place in the medieval constitution; three years later it wrote: "The claim of the people to instruct their representatives is no novelty, and their right to do it was never called in question before."[27]

Several decades before the Burke-radical debate on the people's role in instructing their representatives, the same battle was waged between Walpole's Whigs and Bolingbroke's Opposition, first over the excise and then over war with Spain. It is clear from Burke's later comments on these events at the end of Walpole's reign how disturbed he was by the precedent they seemed to establish for popular control of political decisions. He was convinced that Opposition politicians, Opposition poets, and the mob forced Walpole and his party government into a war they did not desire.[28] One more item had been added to the list of objections that Burke had against Bolingbroke, for not only was the latter the great enemy of organized religion and parties, but even worse, in terms of his views on representation he was a radical. It may have been wishful thinking then when he asked "who now reads Bolingbroke?"[29] All the more reason, too, for Burke to praise the memory of Sir Robert, who in those Augustan years waged battle, albeit not that successfully, against the radical theory of representative government.

[24] *Ibid.,* pp. 42–43.

[25] *Craftsman,* No. 702, December 22, 1739.

[26] *Ibid.*

[27] *Ibid.,* No. 857, December 25, 1742.

[28] Edmund Burke, *On a Regicide Peace* in *Works* (Boston: 1881), vol. V, pp. 288–89.

[29] Edmund Burke, *Reflections on the Revolution in France* (New York: Library of Liberal Arts, 1955), p. 101.

> Sir Robert was forced into the war by the people, who were enflamed to this measure by the most leading politicians, by their own orators, and the greatest poets of that time. . . . When I was very young, a general fashion told me I was to admire some of the writings against that minister [Walpole]; a little more maturity taught me as much to despise them.[30]

[30] Burke, *On a Regicide Peace, loc. cit.*

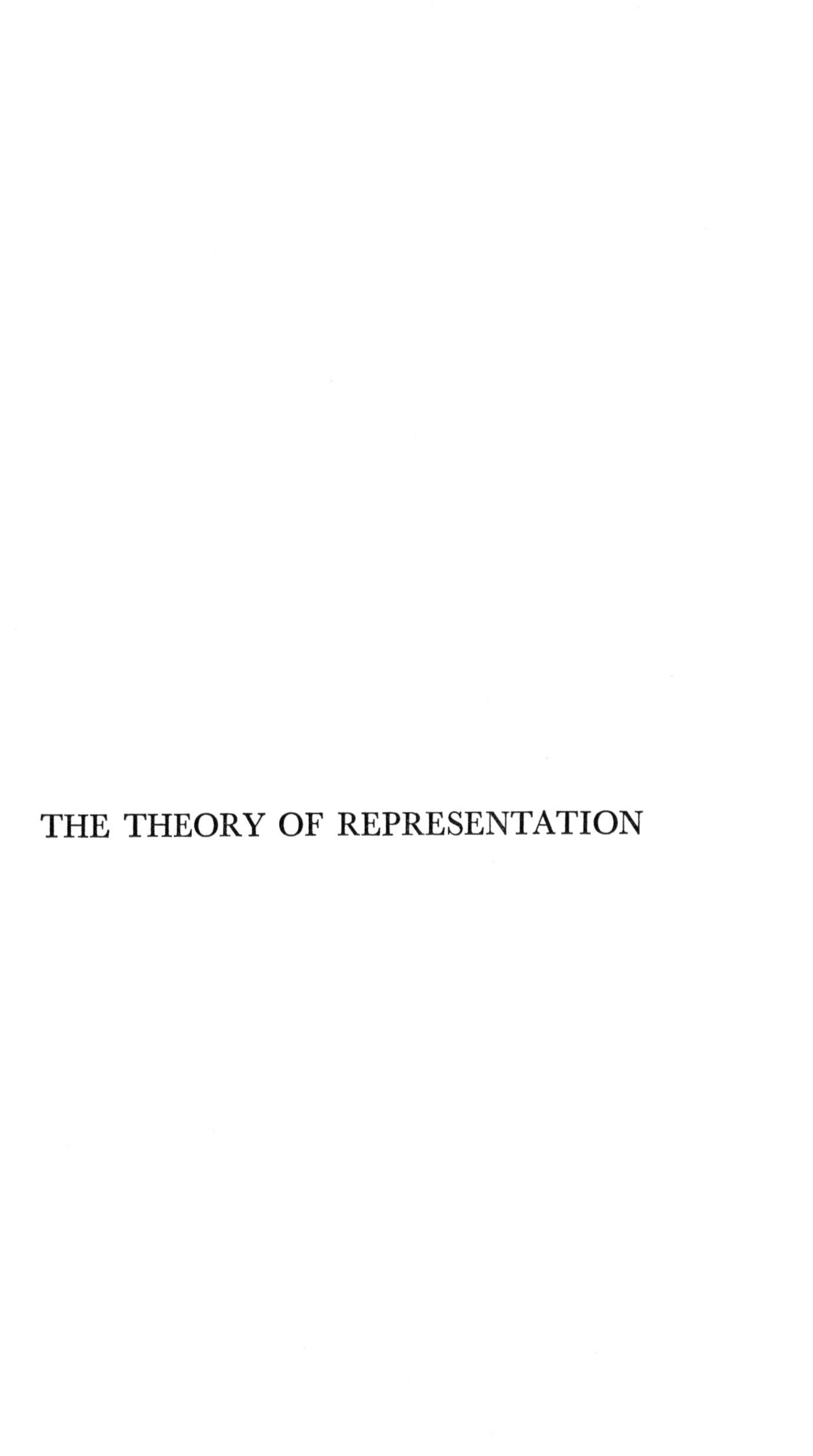

THE THEORY OF REPRESENTATION

8

ELECTORS AND REPRESENTATIVES: A CONTRIBUTION TO THE THEORY OF REPRESENTATION

MAREK SOBOLEWSKI

In the theory of representation, the relation between electors and their representatives is the most fundamental problem. The way in which it is resolved determines the content of the general theory of representation. That is obvious: Representation means the relation between the subject represented and the representative acting on his behalf.

It is in this perspective that I shall discuss the problem in my essay; not as a marginal, detailed study on political behavior in the frame of a single constituency, but as an introduction to the general theory of representation.

CLASSICAL CONCEPTS OF REPRESENTATION

There are two classical concepts regarding the relation between the electors and their representatives: the concept of a "free mandate" and the opposite one of an "imperative mandate." In spite of much criticism of these rigid and formalistic notions, they dominate, in fact, both in the modern constitutions and in political science and political philosophy.

In most constitutions in the Western world, the member of parliament is defined as the representative of the whole nation, and cannot be legitimately bound by any mandate or pressure coming from his electorate. This is not a purely formal statement, a form of juridical traditionalism; it still has important practical consequences. In the Federal Republic of Germany in 1958, the Constitutional Court declared unconstitutional an attempt to organize a consultative referendum on atomic armament, because it would constitute illegal pressure on parliament, entitled to decide freely and independently the policy of the country.[1] In France in 1960, President de Gaulle refused to call an extraordinary session of parliament, arguing that the deputies were acting under the unconstitutional pressure of some professional organizations (the farmers' unions) while they were obliged by the constitution to act independently.[2]

The Marxist theory of government evidently takes the opposite view of the issue. It was Marx himself who made the famous statement that in a capitalist state the electors are only entitled to decide every three or six years by whom they will be *"ver-und-zertreten im Parlament."*[3] Since the time of the Paris Commune the principle of responsibility of representatives to their electors and the right to recall the representatives have constituted the firm bases of the socialist theory of representation, stated in every constitution of socialist countries today.

[1] Though in the formal sense the judgment of the Court was based on considerations derived from the principle of federalism, the arguments concerning the theory of representation were largely discussed. See *Die Entscheidungen des Bundesverfassungsgerichts,* Bd. pp. 116–18. See also my paper (in Polish, with an English summary) "The Parliament and the People in Federal Germany," in *Zeszyty Naukowe UJ-zeszyty prawnicze* No. 6 (Cracow, 1959).

[2] See President de Gaulle's letter to the President of the National Assembly, *Le Monde,* March 19, 1960.

[3] K. Marx, *The Civil War in France* (Pol. ed. Dziela Wybrane, I, 489).

In spite of the essential rigidity of the respective constitutional principles and doctrines all over the world, the reality of political life takes on quite different features. In fact, even the detailed provisions of a constitution and the established constitutional practice often contradict the admitted principle of mandate.

In all capitalist states, notwithstanding the accepted principle of the free mandate, there are political parties, which steer and control the parliamentary behavior of deputies. Rigid party discipline in parliament is no longer held to be contrary to the constitution. The principle of the free mandate protects the member of parliament only against the loss of his seat before the next election. It by no means gives him freedom of action and independence vis-à-vis the party leadership.

In many countries (e.g., in Federal Germany for the Landeslisten [states-elections]) only the political parties are legally entitled to present candidates for an election. In the parliamentary regulations only political parties (or large groups of deputies, which means the same) are entitled to participate in the organs of assemblies, to propose motions, and so on. In Federal Germany, the Constitutional Court has declared invalid and null the mandates of the deputies from parties declared illegal, in spite of the fact that formally they were the duly elected representatives of the whole nation.[4] The idea of an independent representative of the whole nation seems to be totally obsolete. I must agree with Professor Leibholz' statement that the modern Western states are no longer representative in the classical sense,[5] but that they are party states, which makes the concept of the free mandate an anachronism.

The situation is not different with the concept of imperative mandate in the socialist countries. In Poland the constitution affirms the right to recall the deputies to the Diet. But in the fourteen years of our constitution, the parliament has failed to enact the detailed provisions concerning the procedure of recall, and the deputies could not be recalled. The law governing elections to the local councils provides for the procedure of recalling the councillors; but the procedure is so complicated that it has never been applied, and in practice the councillors have been revoked in other ways (by de-

[4] *Die Entscheidungen des Bundesverfassungsgerichts,* Bd. 2, pp. 72 ff., and Bd. 5, p. 392.

[5] G. Leibholz, *Der Strukturwandel der modernen Demokratie* (Karlsruhe C. F. Müller Verlag), particularly p. 13.

cisions of the council itself). Moreover, the formal rights to propose recall belong to the political parties or to the National Front, i.e., some sort of union of political parties and other organizations. Not the electors directly, but the parties, judge on the opportunity of recall of the representatives. It would seem that the situation in other socialist countries is different in detail but similar in general trends.

We may also conclude that the classical concepts of free or imperative mandate, notwithstanding that they are accepted in constitutions and sometimes by political practice, are generally out of date. They do not give us any relevant information as to the real relation between the electors and their representatives; they are even misleading. Since we do not find such information in the legal provisions or legal doctrine, we have to find it by sociological analysis.

But we must bear in mind that while such analysis may elucidate the real relations between the electors and the representatives, it cannot change the constitutional, legal provisions concerning the status, the rights, and duties of deputies. It cannot be substituted for the legal definition of representation. It may, at best, serve us as a basis for interpreting legal principles in a more reasonable fashion.[6]

In this essay I am concerned only with the elaboration of the theoretical basis for the sociological theory of representation. I am not concerned with the effects of this concept on the legal principle of representative government; that I have done elsewhere.[7]

RELATION BETWEEN ELECTORS AND REPRESENTATIVES

In the political process of the modern state, the relation between electors and their individual representative—the deputy—is of minor importance. There are, of course, exceptions to the rule. In some particular situations this relation may be more significant;[8] that is generally supposed to be the case with elections of members

[6] See my paper (in Polish, with English summary) "On the Interpretation of Constitutional Principles and of Corresponding Legal Concepts," in *Zeszyty Naukowe UJ-zeszyty prawnicze* No. 10 (Cracow, 1963).

[7] In my book (in Polish, with an English summary) *Representation in the Modern States of Capitalist Democracy* (Cracow, 1962).

[8] See, e.g., S. Rokkan, "The Comparative Study of Political Participation," in A. Ranney (ed.) *Essays on the Behavioral Study of Politics* (Urbana, Ill.: University of Illinois Press, 1962), p. 51.

of the Congress in the United States; that was supposed to be the case with the Radical Party in the French Third Republic. In such situations the personal characteristics of the candidate outweigh the party label, his responsibility to his constituency outweighs party discipline. We may assume that in such circumstances local interests and local opinions on political issues may influence to a greater degree the course of national policy. But even that assumption is not always true. We know that often just the popular local notables enjoy a great margin of freedom and tolerance vis-à-vis their locality.

In most countries the individual representative plays a different political role. He is a symbol of his party. As we know from many electoral studies, the electors often do not know the name of their representative, not to speak of his personal opinions or characteristics. He is expected to represent the party program. He is often an important source of information on the mood of public opinion to his party leaders. But his personal role in politics depends on his status in the party ranks, not on his relations with the constituency.

For the electors, the representative may play also an important function as an intermediary to the governmental offices. He has to intervene in these offices to promote personal or local interests. In addition to public meetings, at which the deputy explains the policy of his party, such intervention forms the greatest part of his job. The situation in Poland also seems to fit this pattern.

Only the relation between the electors and their party has real political importance in the elections. When we speak about the mandate of the electors, we refer to the party, not to the individual representative to whom this mandate is addressed. I say "party" and I mean that body in the political party which determines the political behavior of party members in parliament and government; for the purpose of this study it is not important to indicate what kind of body that is.

RELATION BETWEEN ELECTORS AND THE PARTY

Apart from the discussion on the electorate mandate, we may take it for granted that every party seeks the approval of its program, and that every party is compelled to respond in a certain way to public opinion. On the other hand, every party does possess a certain freedom of action and is never totally dependent on the opinion of its electorate. I do not try to measure the relative strength of these opposite trends. I do not know if that is at all possible. I should rather enumerate groups of factors that stimulate each of these two opposite trends.

The freedom of action of the party, the possibility of tactical maneuver in face of the electors' opinions and demands, is based on several groups of factors. I am going to outline them only briefly, because their operation is commonly admitted and undisputed.

The first group is related to *the nature of opinions on political issues held by the electorate.*

A number of factors current in modern communities contribute to the fact that knowledge about public affairs as well as interest taken in them are, for the vast majority of the public, rather slight. In any case the rise, if there is any, in these indices does not keep pace with the growing activity of the state, which results in an immense extension of the scope of public affairs. This makes impossible a sufficient spread of opinions on public issues as well as the formation of opinions that would be both sufficiently concrete and detailed. The same observation can be made on voters' familiarity with the party programs and electoral platforms. In contemporary political science one speaks rather about the voters' image of the parties than about their detailed orientation to party programs and attitudes on particular issues.[9]

The operation of these factors enables the parties to build up their programs in a very general and stereotyped manner. Thus, it is always possible to interpret the program in many different ways, according to the demands of the moment. In such circumstances the party program can hardly be viewed as a detailed and rigid mandate, if as a mandate at all.

The second group of factors promoting the party's independence in politics is connected with *the nature of party identification.*

Several voting studies have emphasized that the party identification precedes the voters' electoral decisions, and determines that decision.[10] The party preference, it is affirmed, is largely independent of the concrete electoral program and even of the actual policy of the party. To use the formula of W. E. Miller, the party serves

[9] For the attempt to define the notion of the party image, see J. Blondel, *La société politique britannique* (Paris: A. Colin, 1964), pp. 79–80.

[10] A. Campbell *et al., The American Voter, an Abridgment* (New York: John Wiley, 1964), p. 73.

rather as a point of reference for its followers.[11] In establishing the sources of party identification one puts a great stress on irrational motivation.

This crucial problem certainly deserves further study as it has not been clarified sufficiently. What is certain, in my opinion, is that party identification is closely connected with the party image in the voters' eyes. That image is general enough to grant the party great freedom of action. Once shaped, it shows itself to be of lasting value, and to a high degree independent of changes in the party's current policy. In this sense we may speak about traditional party affiliation, the party being a reference point to its supporters. But this tradition-rooted support has—as I see the problem—certain definite limits, which limit also the party's independence in face of the political opinions of its electorate. I shall discuss the problem later in more detail.

The third group of factors determining the party independence from the opinions and demands of its electorate is connected with the *characteristics of governmental decision-making and popular perception of governmental policy.*

The government has to decide on many questions that are never mentioned in electoral platforms or statements; on questions which were not foreseen, which have arisen suddenly in an unexpected way; on questions of a technical and specialized nature, on which the public has no ideas and no opinions. Consequently, the government (or better—the party in government) has a great freedom of decision on all these issues.

The government, too, notwithstanding that there may exist a clear public opinion on some issue, could be forced by external pressures and circumstances to behave in a different way. No government, even one of superior powers, is immune to such pressures, which constitute the external limits for a virtually representative government.

Further, the government knows that even a very unpopular decision could after some time be forgotten or accepted as a *fait accompli*. Human memory is rather short, and a conservative attitude inherent in most social groups helps to validate *ex post facto* many decisions previously resented. It is only before elections that a government must, and does, pay greater attention to public opinion.

[11] W. E. Miller, "Party Preference and Attitudes on Political Issues," *American Political Science Review* (March 1953), p. 50.

Last but not least, the government often has to decide against the mood of popular opinion in the interests of the nation. There are many examples of popular opinion being false on a vital issue. Some necessary measure could be very unpopular, as for instance, the policy of raising taxes. But representative government does not mean only responsiveness to the demands of the people. It means also leadership; that is, the obligation not to respond to popular but irrational demands. There is a chance that after a period of time and experience, the rightness of such a decision will be totally accepted by the people.

More generally, the operation of all these groups of factors constitutes a setting in which the principle of representation and representative government must be seen and interpreted. This setting excludes the interpretation of representation in terms of a detailed and ever-binding mandate for government. The notion of imperative mandate is totally inadequate to the modern political situation.

PARTY DEPENDENCE ON PUBLIC OPINION

I have previously stated as obvious the fact that the party is to a certain degree dependent on its electorate, on public opinion. Let us now examine the factors that cause that dependence.

I have accepted the view that the voters' party preference is determined by the party image. That image, as we know, is general enough to grant the party a great freedom of action. But it cannot be concluded from this statement that the party image and thus the party preference are totally independent of the voters' own political opinions. The greatest shifts in party preferences occur mainly in periods of strong political tensions and revaluation of accepted values and opinions. This is clearly shown by American studies, the Civil War and the Great Depression of the 1930's being chosen as examples.[12] In Europe it was the period following the Second World War; in France, in addition, the Algerian crisis (1958). This coincidence seems to indicate some deep connection between the voters' political opinions on crucial social and political issues and their party choice.

The same conclusion could be drawn from the analysis of the

[12] Campbell, *op. cit.*, p. 278.

party changers and the floating vote. It is generally admitted that such voting behavior is characteristic of people with the worst information, at the lowest level of education and interest in political life.[13] With no opinion of one's own on political issues, however general and vague, there does not exist a party image.

The most characteristic indices are brought by the large-scale analysis of voting behavior. I fully agree with Professor S. M. Lipset that however irrational and accidental may be the individual voting behavior, group analysis indicates the existence of rationality in the voters' choice.[14] The workers tend to vote for the Communist and Socialist Parties. They are greatly overrepresented in the electorate of these parties. The middle class in Great Britain, as shown by J. Blondel, votes in a proportion of over 80 per cent for the Conservative Party.[15] The correlation between the economic interests of the social groups and the party preference is obvious.

In spite of his unfamiliarity with the party programs and the current political issues, the voter forms his party image not as irrationally as is often suggested. Behind his choice there is a lifelong observation of parties and governments.[16] Maybe that cannot be tested by polls, but for this only our present research technique is to blame.[17]

This rational correlation between the voters' political predisposition, party image, and electoral choice is clearly perceived by the party leaders. I do not mean the elaboration of the party slogans and programs, which is also correlated with the supposed political preference of the electorate. I mean that the policy options of the parties generally reflect the main preferences of their electorate, particularly in the field of economic policy. In the long-run perspective we have seen how changes in the social structure and social status of the large groups of workers in the Western countries have influenced in the past three decades the programs and policy of Socialist Parties. To a considerable degree, as far as the attitude to the welfare state was concerned, it has influenced also the options

[13] Blondel, *op. cit.,* p. 69.

[14] S. M. Lipset, *Soziologie der Demokratie,* Luchterchand Verlag (German ed. of *Political Man*), p. 307.

[15] Blondel, *op. cit.,* pp. 54–56.

[16] In this sense, see also A. H. Birch, *Representative and Responsible Government* (London: Allen and Unwin, 1964), p. 186.

[17] I agree with the criticism of current research techniques by D. E. Butler, *The Study of Political Behavior* (London, 1958), pp. 63–65.

of conservative and liberal parties. That is also true in respect to particular issues, of special importance to the given social group. Let me pick just two examples. The French Radical Party, before the Second World War, was inclined to pass in government coalitions from the socialists to the moderate right. But as was shown brilliantly by F. Goguel, before each general election the Radicals withdrew from such coalitions and came back to their traditional socialist alliance.[18] In contemporary Italy the Communist Party attitude toward religion and the Roman Catholic Church is dictated mainly not by doctrinal premises, but by the attitudes held by the Communist electorate in that country.

I should conclude this point by two statements. First, the policy of the parties is generally based on corresponding group interests and must be kept consistent with these interests and their perception by the electorate. In this respect the class interpretation of politics is still of the first importance, though it is not sufficient to explain all details of the politics of representation. Second, the dependence of the policy of the parties on the attitudes of their electorate is especially marked in issues of particular importance to the given group.

The next factor that contributes to the dependence of the party on the political attitudes of the electorate is the existence of pressure groups. The influence of pressure groups is very often opposed—as illegitimate, as particularistic by definition—to the legitimate influence of the electorate. It has been treated as a challenge to the influence of "public opinion." I am not convinced that this is the right approach. The members of pressure groups are part of the electorate. They express their special interests for which there was no place, or not enough place, in the party program. They try to ensure the realization of these interests. The action of pressure groups could be seen as supplementary to the representation by elections. To be sure, these are particular interests. But taken as a whole, they all represent strong and persistent interests of the electorate, which have to be legitimately taken into account by the representative government. As they are mutually inconsistent, or even antagonistic, the government is in a good position to bargain and look for a compromise. But it is through the pressure groups that the electors have the best chance to influence the policy of govern-

[18] F. Goguel, *La politique des partis sous la IIIe République* (Paris, 1946).

ment on the issues most vital to them. That is an unequal influence, to be sure. That is why the Western countries are still capitalist democracies, the influence of capitalist pressure groups being greater than the influence of the others. In individual cases this may undermine the principle of representative government, giving predominance to obviously minority opinions and demands. But in general the operation of the multitude of pressure groups serves to correlate better the action of government with the demands of the people interested in such action.

The last factor I should like to mention here is the willingness of the democratic government to respond to the demands of the public. We cannot deny that such an attitude does exist in democratic countries. It grows from the deep-rooted ideas on society and government, and is the result of long-established traditions of democracy. It is also determined by the very fact that modern government cannot be run without loyal and willing cooperation by the people concerned. This means also bargaining rather than enforcement as the method of government.

REPRESENTATION AS A PROCESS

This short description of background for the concept of representative mandate makes criticism of this concept legitimate. It seems obvious that the juridical theory of the imperative mandate, however desirable we may hold it, is unrealistic and utopian. The concept of the free mandate, however, is no more realistic. The whole theory of representation built upon either of these principles is not adequate to the political process of modern democracies.

The most important reason for the failure of this theory can be seen in its rather static formulation. The idea of representation is based on the concept of status: of the concordance between two separate and definite qualities—the will of the represented and the policy of the representatives. In the classical concept there should be a rather metaphysical identity between the will of the nation (*volonté générale*) and the action of representatives. In the modern concept there should be a real political identity between the will or opinions of the voters and the action of representatives; to use the famous words of M. Duverger, we have to deal with a model and his portrait or his photograph.[19]

[19] M. Duverger, *Les partis politiques,* 3ᵉ éd. (Paris, 1958), p. 409.

The trouble is that in reality there exists neither the *volonté générale* nor the model to be photographed. The policy of a government must be, and usually is, coherent and uniform. But on most issues there is no uniform will or opinion of the people or the majority of the people. There are several mutually inconsistent opinions of different groups of people, and a mass of largely uninterested persons. There is a changing diversity of interests, demands, and opinions. If we ask with which opinion the policy of representatives has to be coordinated, the proper answer would be very difficult to find.

The governmental process in a democracy can be conceived rather as an exchange of views, opinions, and pressures between the government and different social groups. Every side tries to influence the other, to win it for his opinion. When we take a single issue, there is usually a group of people interested in it, more active than others and trying to influence the governmental decision. The government must take these demands into account. But it must also realize that the satisfaction of these demands could bring up other, concurring demands of another group, though these demands do not even exist at the time.

The character of the political process leads me to the conclusion that representation has to be interpreted in terms of a process rather than in terms of a status. I would agree with the definition given by Lipset that representation is a system of actions which have "to facilitate interchange between authority and the spontaneous groupings of society"; a system which includes "most major attempts to influence authoritative decisions."[20] In terms of a process, it is a process of interaction between various social groups and the government. The forms of interactions are highly differentiated. For the most part they are carefully organized and planned, but there is also a large margin for rather spontaneous interaction. The main established, institutionalized forms are the elections, the press campaign, the action of pressure groups and political parties, demonstrations, strikes, petitions. Every form is equally legitimate from the standpoint of representation, and no single one is by itself sufficient to achieve the aims of the process of representation.

The political aim of this process is to build up a popular consensus on governmental policy taken as a whole. That is the central

[20] S. M. Lipset, "Party Systems and the Representation of Social Groups," *European Journal of Sociology,* No. 1 (1960), 51.

idea of democracy, and practically the indispensable condition of every democratic government. The interaction leads to consensus through the creation of a certain similarity between the course of government policy and the attitudes of the people interested in it. There cannot be consensus without this similarity of views and attitudes as to the items of state policy. For people not very much interested in the issue, and for the judgment on the whole policy of the government, no more is needed than the similarity of basic attitudes and shared values. For those more interested in the issue a closer similarity of opinions is required.

Thus, political representation could be interpreted as a process of mutual interaction which creates the similarity of the policy of the government and the attitudes of the people, those more interested in the given action in the first place. The similarity does not mean identity or concordance. It has no relation to the "general will." The degree of similarity will vary in time, on different issues, and in the relation to different social groups. What is required from the representative government is the continuation of the process of interaction, the opening of all possible channels of interaction, and the resulting minimum degree of consensus on the actual policy of the government.

9

REPRESENTATION, GOVERNMENTAL STABILITY, AND DECISIONAL EFFECTIVENESS

ERIC A. NORDLINGER

"Representation" is thought to be a political "good" for a variety of reasons. It has been said that a representative system best ensures that governments act in the interests of the governed, that the governors are held accountable for their actions, that a representative system is usually found in conjunction with an "open" or "free" society, that it ensures the dignity of the individual, and, assuming that all forms of government involve some corruption and maladministration, that a representative system decreases the magnitudes involved. The attribution of these and other desired values to representative systems has been often suggested, and even more frequently, they have been implicitly assumed. What has not been widely argued is that over and above these advantages, the representative subsystem of a democratic political system[1] may contribute markedly to the system's stability and decisional effectiveness.

This is the theme that will be explored here, although much of the result is closer to educated speculations than to highly plausible hypotheses supported by substantial evidence. An attempt will be made to delineate the ways in which differing conceptions of political representation, the actual operation of the representative subsystem, and the nonelite's beliefs about the degree to which their democratic system is genuinely representative, tend to impinge upon the total system's stability and decisional effectiveness.

Stability refers to viability—to the persistence of constitutions and governments over time. Is a democratic system able to operate according to the procedural rules set out in the constitution, or does it become necessary to substitute another constitution in times of crisis? Is the life of governments calculated in terms of months or years? An effective government is able to govern, taking decisive decisions when these are thought to be called for by pressing conditions; an ineffective one is hampered by structural, constitutional, or cultural impediments. Representativeness refers both to the translation of electoral outcomes into the party make-up and policies of governments, public opinion being reflected in the government's political complexion, and to the exercise of decision-making responsibilities by those institutions that are constitutionally accountable—decisions being made by the executive and the legislature rather than by the civil service, the army, or particularly powerful interest groups.[2]

As the term "representation" is commonly used, it tends to refer exclusively to the idea that the representative is somehow charged with acting on behalf of a group of individuals. What is often overlooked is that the representative's actions are also accepted by these

1 By a democratic system is meant a political system in which there is a genuine competition for governmental office, with the majority of the population choosing from among the competitors. Such a democratic system will then have an analytically and partly empirically differentiated representative subsystem, by which is meant the representatives' nomination and election, and their interaction in the legislature and the executive.

2 These characteristics of stable democracy are spelled out in greater detail and given operational meaning in Harry Eckstein, " 'Measuring' the Effectiveness of Democracies," 1962, mimeo., and Harry Eckstein, *Division and Cohesion in Democracy: A Study of Norway* (Princeton: Princeton University Press, 1966), Appendix A.

individuals as authoritative. In fact, Weber goes so far as to write that "the *primary* fact underlying representation is that the action of certain members of a group, the 'representatives,' is binding on the others or is looked upon as legitimate so that its result must be accepted by them."[3] This dual conception is aptly summarized in the term "representative authority,"[4] including in the representative's role the right to issue directives or requests that are carried out without the use or threat of force, his authority resting on respect, deference, loyalty, and, at times, persuasion.

To make the point in a parallel fashion, a democratic government is charged with the two often conflicting responsibilities of representing the citizens and exercising authority over them. As a government, it must be able to lead, concomitantly binding the electorate to its actions; as a democratic government, it must respond to the wishes of the electorate.[5] To fulfill the first requirement, a democratic government must be accorded a sufficiently wide scope of independent authority by the electorate so that when conditions and events demand it, decisions can be taken without first having to consider public opinion, and perhaps even taking actions that are distinctly unpopular among the voters. Without this leeway there is a high probability that the government's decisional effectiveness will be impaired, in turn leading to governmental instability and perhaps even to major constitutional crises.

THREE CONCEPTIONS OF REPRESENTATION

If this reasoning, following from the twofold conception of representation, is accepted, it suggests that not every type of repre-

[3] Max Weber, *The Theory of Social and Economic Organization* (New York: The Free Press, 1947), p. 416; italics added.

[4] *Ibid.* Similarly, Talcott Parsons views elections and voting as the mobilization of "generalized support for leaders so that they may assume and discharge responsibility." William C. Mitchell, *Sociological Analysis and Politics* (Englewood Cliffs, N.J.: Prentice-Hall, 1967), p. 140.

[5] Harry Eckstein has placed the appropriate label of "balanced disparities" upon these two necessary activities of democratic governments; *Division and Cohesion . . . , op. cit.,* Appendix A. The point that contradictory demands are placed upon democratic governments—the balance between "power and responsiveness" as Almond and Verba call it—serves as the starting point of these two writers' theory of stable democracy. See Gabriel Almond and Sidney Verba, *The Civic Culture* (Princeton: Princeton University Press, 1963), pp. 476–479. Also see the related theory in Eric A. Nordlinger, *The Working-Class Tories: Authority, Deference and Stable Democracy* (Berkeley: University of California Press, 1967), pp. 210–52.

sentation is suitable for stable and effective democracy. Representation may be based upon at least three different criteria. First, a person can represent others by virtue of a contract between them, as in the case of an agent or *delegate* who is charged with looking after the specified interests of those they represent. In this case representation refers to the particular role of the representative after he has been chosen.[6] Second, a person may also be a representative because of his personal attributes, being *typical* of the electors through a sharing in such characteristics as religion, social status, education, or communal membership. Here representation refers to the resemblance of the representatives and their constituents in terms of existential attributes. Third, representation may take on a *procedural* definition, referring simply to the means by which representatives are chosen, that is, their nomination and election. Procedurally, representation refers only to the fact of election, without including any assumptions regarding the representative's role or his personal attributes, although it is assumed (as in the case of the other two conceptions of representation) that periodic elections have the effect of making the representative responsive to the electors.[7] Only this third conception of representation, with the implicit degree of independence it allows the representative, is thought to be eminently suitable for democratically stable and effective systems, given the postulated necessity of balancing governmental authority and responsiveness.

The French case is a poignant illustration of the debilitating effects of a political culture in which a delegated conception of representation is strongly emphasized. The diffuse and intense French fear of entering into authority relations with others—what Crozier has termed *l'horreur du face à face*[8]—is intimately bound up with the adherence to a form of representation that places severe

[6] For a discussion of American state legislators' conceptions of their roles as "delegates," "trustees," or "politicos," see John C. Wahlke, et al., *The Legislative System* (New York: The Free Press, 1962), pp. 267–86.

[7] Although there are other types of representation besides the three mentioned here, they appear to be the most important types in terms of both their frequent appearance in democratic systems and in writings on representation. See, for example, A. H. Birch, *Representative and Responsible Government* (London: Faber, 1964), pp. 14–16; and Giovanni Sartori, "Representational Systems," in *The International Encyclopedia of the Social Sciences,* forthcoming.

[8] Michel Crozier, *The Bureaucratic Phenomenon* (Chicago: University of Chicago Press, 1964), pp. 213–36.

limitations upon the representatives' independence. Authority becomes absolutist, something that the individual citizen alone possesses and that cannot be shared with others. In the popular and culturally attractive Radical doctrine of Alain, democracy becomes nothing more than the control of the governors by the governed—a system of surveillance rather than one of leadership and responsiveness. The placing of these excessive restrictions of delegated representation upon the "representative authorities" is largely responsible for the system's inability to offer continuous noncrisis leadership.[9]

Moreover, the necessarily complex and hierarchical structure of national political systems means that individuals adhering to the idea of delegated representation will soon become disenchanted (if not alienated) from the democratic system, making them available for mobilization in antisystem mass movements. According to this hypothesis, a mass-movement politics should be prevalent when there is a conjunction of an extremely centralized political system and widespread notions of delegated representation—as is the case in France, which has experienced the democratically disabling effects produced by the semi-Fascist movements in the 1930's, and Communism, Gaullism, and Poujadism in the short life of the Fourth Republic.

Given the importance of intermediary associations and the participation of their members, it is worthwhile noting that a delegated conception of representation provides a discouraging context for the growth and effective operation of associations. As Kornhauser has persuasively pointed out, the existence of intermediary associations, serving as buffers between the individual and the political elites, is an effective safeguard against the development of those mass movements that are so destructive of democratic stability and effectiveness.[10] A proliferation of associations prevents nonelites from being

[9] It is not only the French nonelite that adheres to this conception of representation. The most characteristic and significant feature of French parliamentary behavior is a rebelliousness against authority, an inability to allow "representative authority" to parliamentary leaders, or to engage in organized action entailing superordinate-subordinate relations. The deputies' tenacious adherence to the delegated conception of representation is evidenced in the widely accepted generalization that the premier is "tolerated only when he is at everyone's disposal: resistance (or an error) on his part provokes demands for his resignation." See Constantin Melnik and Nathan Leites, *The House Without Windows* (New York: Harper & Row, 1958), p. 108.

[10] William Kornhauser, *The Politics of Mass Society* (New York: The Free Press, 1959).

easily "mobilized" by the elites; and at the same time, associations protect the elites from an overbearing influence on the part of non-elites.

Yet, when representatives are thought to be closely and solely responsible to their electors, little room is left for the political role of voluntary associations mediating between the two. France again provides a useful case in point. The country's weak associational life and its attitudes toward representation are closely interdependent. Politics is about the isolated individual on the one hand, and his closely instructed delegates on the other, out of which emerges the mystique of the general will. Going back to Voltaire, Rousseau, the revolutionary tradition embodied in the Loi Le Chapelier outlawing labor organizations in the name of liberty, and coming down to the contemporary political culture, the notion of the general will (or its modern Gaullist variant) at best provides only a restricted political role for intermediary associations.[11]

Another set of debilitating consequences for stable and effective democracy could follow if representation were widely taken to mean being typical of the class of people who elected the representative. Having people with the same socioeconomic backgrounds as representatives may be desired because it is thought that such men would best understand and be most attuned to the particular needs and desires of the electors. This is certainly not an uncommon belief.[12]

[11] Although the impact of representation as delegation has been far less widespread in America and Britain than in France, even in these two countries it has weakened both intermediary associations and the cohesion of political parties. See Samuel H. Beer's discussion of "radical democracy" in *British Politics in the Collectivist Age* (New York: Random House, 1965), pp. 39–43, 52–61. While realizing that the connections have not been established empirically, it is still worthwhile raising the issue of France's impact in this respect upon her former African colonies. In attempting to account for the greater affinity of French- rather than English-speaking Africans for the idea of a one-party state, Aristide Zolberg focuses upon French conceptions and experiences of representation. "It could indeed be suggested in 1959 that the one-party ideology was peculiarly 'French,' perhaps because party pluralism, associated with the ineffective Fourth Republic system, could be dismissed without difficulty; because the one-party ideology had some affinity with De Gaulle's plebiscitary democracy; and because France had shown less concern with the institutionalization of pluralism during the process of decolonization than Great Britain." *Creating Political Order: The Party-States of West Africa* (Chicago: Rand McNally, 1966), p. 50.

[12] However, "There is no guarantee that people with typical interests will, when they are put into positions of authority, pursue those interests, thereby doing what the people 'want' them to do. . . . A new environment and new responsibilities often give rise to new interests, and even though the governor

But given the association of socioeconomic status with educational levels and achievement, the obvious difficulty then arises of having as representatives men with typical minimal educational training and average intellectual abilities. Notwithstanding the implicit disapproval of some political scientists who, having discovered that legislators have far better educational backgrounds than their constituents, interpret this as a manifestation of social and economic inequality, surely it must be admitted that the contemporary complex conduct of government would suffer—and thus its effectiveness and stability—if representatives had only minimal educations and average intellects.[13] The argument that appointed "experts" and "intellectuals" in the higher civil service could make the intricate decisions, as in the area of fiscal policy, is a poor answer to the problem.[14] For if there were a wide intellectual gap between elected and appointed officials, only two outcomes are possible: The civil servants may intellectually dominate the representatives with arguments that the latter are unable to evaluate independently, thereby reducing the authenticity of democratic government; or the representatives may disregard the advice of the civil servants, bringing us back to the original problem of the representatives' abilities for the conduct of twentieth-century government.

Moreover, to the extent that a minimal social distance separates the electors from their representatives, the possibility that particularly heavy substantive and representational demands will be placed upon the representatives is enhanced. In an important sense, a status gap separating electors and representatives performs one of the functions carried out by intermediary associations—the function of mediating between the nonelite and the political elites so that the former does not make excessive demands upon the latter. Without a distinct status gap separating the two groups, the electors might assume that being "one of them," their representatives owe them special considerations, concomitantly feeling familiar enough with them to press their demands in an uncompromising fashion. And, when the representatives are dependent on constituents that appear as special

---

was typical in his origin, that he remains typical cannot be presumed." See C. W. Cassinelli, *The Politics of Freedom* (Seattle: University of Washington Press, 1961), p. 42.

[13] Francis X. Sutton, "Representation and the Nature of Political Systems," *Comparative Studies in Society and History*, October 1959, pp. 9–10.

[14] Cf. Carl J. Friedrich, *Man and His Government* (New York: McGraw-Hill, 1966), pp. 306–307, 311.

interest groups, the regime's legitimacy may well suffer in the eyes of competing groups.

Furthermore, in those societies in which men with a high status in a nonpolitical hierarchy also enjoy the respect of others as political leaders, this transfer of respect from a nonpolitical to the political status hierarchy helps support stable and effective democracy in both Western and non-Western countries. In the new and unstable systems of the underdeveloped areas, the primary prerequisite for a stable democratic future is the institutionalization of governmental roles and procedures.[15] These roles and procedures must become regularized and legitimized, and one of the few ways that this can be done within a short time span is to have the respect paid to traditional institutions and roles transferred to the political system by having high-status individuals move into the representative subsystem, as in India and Northern Nigeria. And in those industrialized societies featuring politically transferable status hierarchies, such as England, the high social status of representatives strengthens the trust and the respect paid to the political elite, thereby allowing the government a broad sphere of independent authority.[16]

From the perspective of the representative's own attitude toward his role as a political leader, it is advantageous to have men of relatively high social rank as representatives, especially in those societies in which high social status is accorded particular respect in the political sphere. For the man who believes that he has a "right" to his position—in this instance, because of the legitimacy of the electoral process in combination with his high social status—will tend to be a more confident and effective "representative authority" than a man who is somewhat hesitant or uncertain about the propriety (if not the legitimacy) of his position. A comparison of English and American political elites led Shils to conclude that the confidence and assurance provided the elite members by their high social status and the deference accorded them by the nonelite may underpin the

[15] See Samuel P. Huntington, "Political Development and Political Decay," *World Politics,* 17 (April 1965), 386–430.

[16] The English manual workers' attitudes toward the high social status and the authority of their "governors" are analyzed in Nordlinger, *op. cit.,* chapters I, III, and IV. In attempting to account for the correlation between the level of formal authority and high social prestige of incumbents, Frederick W. Frey develops the general hypothesis that "the recognition of the fact that another individual holds power over oneself tends to be psychologically repugnant"; yet when the incumbent enjoys high social prestige it becomes easier to admit and accept his power. *The Turkish Political Elite* (Cambridge, Mass.: M.I.T. Press, 1965), pp. 400–406.

protection of political liberties, thereby contributing to the system's democratic authenticity.[17] In contrast, a representative who believes that he owes his position, at least in part, to his being "typical" of the people who elected him might find it difficult to diverge from his constituents' expectations without sacrificing the confidence that he has in his "right" to hold office.

These last few points referred to only one type of existential attribute shared by the electors and the elected, that of social class and status. In a different manner, the operation of democratic systems is also associated with these and other types of existential attributes held in common by the representatives and their electors—especially those of a religious, linguistic, regional, and tribal nature in sharply polarized societies. The term "associated with" has been used advisedly; for when representatives are typical of the particular group or strata that elected them, it is not nearly so much this overlap that may produce democratic instability as it is the conditions that promoted this overlap in the first place, that is, the deep cleavages themselves. But although it is of secondary importance, this congruity does not provide the means (or more accurately, the mechanical arrangements) for mitigating the underlying political cleavages. And this congruity may have the additional effect of making compromise and coalition-building more difficult as political positions are hardened in the process of self-insulation, with interaction being limited to other individuals who share the same political and existential attributes. Such an overlap between representatives and their constituents may then exacerbate already existing cleavages and democratic weaknesses by further polarizing the differences between the conflict groups, adding one more layer to a congruity of geographical, tribal, and economic attributes, as in most of West Africa and Uganda.[18]

[17] Edward A. Shils, *The Torment of Secrecy* (New York: The Free Press, 1956). The broad question of the leader's attitude toward his own position is discussed by Roger Holmes, "Freud, Piaget and Democratic Leadership," *British Journal of Sociology* (June 1965), esp. pp. 125, 137. It might also be that in the non-Western areas high status individuals have a more highly developed sense of loyalty to the nation relative to lower status groups. Evidence for this highly tentative generalization comes from a survey study carried out in India. See Joseph W. Elder, "National Loyalties in a Newly Independent Nation," in David E. Apter, ed., *Ideology and Discontent* (New York: The Free Press, 1964), pp. 81–83.

[18] In effect, this argument transplants Truman's thesis, that crosscutting memberships in intermediary associations provide for moderation and co-

These, then, are the difficulties involved in the notions that the representatives are the delegates of the electors or typical of them if the representatives' authority is to be respected, or in broader terms, if the democratic system is to be stable and decisionally effective. In contrast, the procedural conception of representation guarantees neither directly, but at the same time it does not have any built-in disadvantages for stable and effective democracy, consequently providing a not unattractive context for its development.

The argument that the procedural conception of representation is the most viable one for achieving democratic stability can also be supported by asking the basic question: What is the function of elections? Sartori's answer is that we vote, "not to make a democracy more democratic, but to make democracy possible: that is, to make it function. In the very moment that we admit the need of having recourse to elections, we minimize democracy for we realize that the sytsem cannot be operated by the *demos* itself. Clearly, then, the purpose of elections is to select leadership, not to maximize democracy."[19] Even if this argument is not accepted as a statement of the sufficient functions of the electoral system, it remains eminently valid as a statement of one of its singularly important functions. Recalling some of the appropriate points that were already alluded to, it then turns out that a procedural orientation toward representation is the "proper" one for the efficient implementation of the electoral system's function of selecting leadership. Whereas the two alternative conceptions of representation, even when they are not mutually exclusive with the procedural concept, tend to restrict the electoral system in the performance of what is perhaps its most important function.[20]

---

hesion in the democratic system, to the representative subsystem. David B. Truman, *The Governmental Process* (New York: Knopf, 1951), esp. pp. 167–68. However, neither Truman's argument nor the point made here need necessarily hold true, as in the case of the Netherlands, where a bargaining and compromising political style prevents the sharp polarization of parochial and partisan loyalties from disabling the system. See Hans Daalder, "The Netherlands: Opposition in a Segmented Society," in Robert A. Dahl, ed., *Political Oppositions in Western Democracies* (New Haven: Yale University Press, 1966).

[19] Giovanni Sartori, *Democratic Theory* (New York: Frederick Praeger, 1965), p. 108.

[20] If the argument is accepted, the next problem for analysis might be an inquiry into the historical conditions that engender attitudes toward "representative authority," emphasizing the representative or the authority dimension. Such an inquiry might very well *begin* with a comparison of the

THE OPERATION OF THE REPRESENTATIVE SUBSYSTEM

Having explored some influences that the widespread attachment to three different conceptions of representation have upon the operation of democratic systems, the second part of this essay is devoted to a discussion of the ways in which the success or failure of the representational subsystem's performance affect stability and effectiveness by first influencing the beliefs and behavior of the nonelite.

The poor performances of the representative subsystems of the Weimar Republic and the French Fourth Republic played a singularly important part in the demise of these two systems. These representative subsystems were characterized by a lack of responsiveness to the electorate, with changes in cabinet personnel taking place quite irrespective of the nonelite's opinions and values, while the situation of *immobilisme* meant that governments were largely unresponsive to the electorate's needs in terms of their policy-making activities.

The representational subsystems' poor performance then further decreased the genuineness or authenticity of German and French democracy by allowing nonrepresentative institutions to fill the void. The inactivity and low prestige of these legislatures allowed for an increase in the civil service's and the army's power—two institutions that were beyond the control of the electorate. The civil service's independence was also enhanced by the constant reshuffling of ministerial positions; ministers could hardly manage effectively to control their civil servants when they themselves had neither the time nor

---

historical development of England and France, since these two countries apparently emphasize the opposite dimensions of the "representative authority" formula. England's gradual historical development allowed democratic notions of controlling the representatives to merge with traditional notions of independent authority, forming a political culture in which representatives are expected to govern, not just represent, the citizens. In the France of the *ancien régime* the centralization and arbitrariness of monarchical authority produced an intense suspiciousness of all types of authority. And when the "democratic revolution" arrived, it not only introduced notions of equality into the political culture that were antithetical to the independent prerogatives of elected representatives; the antics of a Louis Bonaparte, a Boulanger, or a MacMahon could only reinforce these sensitized fears and suspicions of authority, except when no other alternatives remained open, and a crisis leader was temporarily installed.

perhaps the inclination to master the bundles of materials, data, and techniques of departmental business.

Under such conditions it was no wonder that vast segments of the German and French populations became disenchanted with their democratic systems. Since there was only the most tenuous of connections between a party's electoral program and the implementation of that program (even if the party managed to form part of a coalition government), and since the legislature was unable to act in any important sphere of policy, the voters could only become exasperated by, if not alienated from, the democratic system. In both the Weimar and the Fourth Republic practically all the opponents of the two regimes had one thing in common: they wanted the government to govern. Their final objectives and their means for attaining them were of course radically different, but nearly all the opponents of the two republics were critical of the representative subsystems' inactivity and cabinet instability.[21] In the case of Weimar, ineffective parliamentary government produced an extensive desire for a powerful authority to replace the seeming anarchy of party government, President Hindenburg receiving national support as an Ersatzkaiser in order to restore political order and governmental effectiveness. Moreover, when a legislature is in a state of paralyzed inactivity it often becomes essential to challenge the entire system rather than to work within its confines, if the protest is to have any effect. And in the case of the Fourth Republic, the goal of the two most important "surge" movements—Gaullism and Mendèsism—of making structural alterations in the representative subsystem only made for a greater stubbornness and hostility on the part of the threatened parliamentary leaders. The poor performance of the two representative subsystems thereby provided the heady political environment that was eminently conducive to the rise of mass movements, which then further discouraged and obstructed the governments' effectiveness and eventually led to the collapse of the two constitutional frameworks.

[21] The national surveys carried out by the Institut Français d'Opinion Publique indicate the widespread dissatisfaction with the operation of the Fourth Republic's representative subsystem. In July 1956, 78 per cent of a national sample replied that the seven-month average life span of cabinets was too short, with only 3 per cent saying that it was just right. And in August 1958, when asked to reflect on the reasons for the poor functioning of the Fourth Republic, 95 per cent agreed with the statement that the governments changed too often.

Curiously enough, the power that was thrust upon the German and French bureaucracies, owing to the representational subsystems' incapacities, helped to alienate the civil service from the democratic system. The German bureaucracy never provided the Weimar Republic with any outright support. It was still staffed by the traditional administrative elite of the Wilhelmine monarchy, and prided itself on its purity as an apolitical institution. Yet when the pressure groups focused their efforts on the civil service, inexorably drawing it into the political fray, it underwent strains and tensions that further alienated it from the Republic.[22] Although it occurred in a more diluted fashion, a good part of the French bureaucracy experienced similar pressures. The ministries of Education, Agriculture, and Colonies were most heavily "colonized" by pressure groups and were given the least amount of guidance by the cabinet, resulting in their heightened demoralization and disenchantment with the institutions of the Fourth Republic. Thus, contrary to the assumption that the civil service can enhance a democratic system's stability when the representative subsystem is malfunctioning, the flow of power to the civil service without a concomitant level of guidance from the representative institutions may actually help to undermine rather than support a democratic system's longevity.

If poorly functioning representative subsystems detract from the system's over-all performance, the reverse is also true. When the nonelite believes that the outcome of elections directly influences the personnel and decisions of government, not only do such beliefs go a long way in broadly legitimizing the political system, they also secure the important requirement of independent governmental authority by encouraging the "representative authorities" to do what *they* think best for the interests of the country.

This point is brought out in a survey study of the English working class. The respondents were presented with a situation in which a Government staffed by members of the party that they *oppose* (i.e., the Labour voters were faced with a Conservative Government, and vice versa) was said to favor a particular policy with which a majority of the electorate disagreed. The manual workers were then asked whether or not such an "opposition" Government should carry out its policy, and their reasons for saying so. Approximately half the workers replied that this "opposition" Government ought to go

[22] Charles E. Frye, "Parties and Pressure Groups in Weimar and Bonn," *World Politics,* 17 (July 1965), pp. 645–46.

ahead with its policy in the face of the majority's disagreement.[23] It is most unlikely that such a high proportion of workers would have assented to such independent exercise of governmental authority if they did not believe that the electoral process had legitimized the Government. In fact, in explaining why they would permit such independent Government action, many of the workers mentioned the theme of governmental leadership in conjunction with the Government's election to office. ("We [the voters] put them in power to get on with the job." "The Government is there to lead, we elected them, didn't we?")

There is yet another way in which the authenticity of the representative subsystem indirectly affects democratic stability and effectiveness. In his discussion of the different social and psychological factors that shape the individual's feelings of political effectiveness—the belief that one could do something to influence governmental decisions—Lane suggests that perhaps "the sense of political efficacy relates less to deeper personality qualities than to the actual responsiveness of the governmental authorities."[24] By "responsiveness" Lane means very nearly the same thing as the authenticity of the representative subsystem—the extent to which the personnel and policies of government are attuned to electoral outcomes.

In turn, feelings of political efficacy are related to the system's stability and decisional effectiveness. Almond and Verba's five-nation study indicates that people who believe themselves to be politically effective tend to be more satisfied with their government's substantive outputs, in the sense that these outputs are thought to have contributed to an improvement in their own lives.[25] Their support of the democratic system is thereby enhanced, although such attachments may not be sufficiently durable to survive periods of crisis. However, and more important, Almond and Verba's analysis also led them to the conclusion that individuals who see themselves as politically effective have a greater sense of attachment or diffuse loyalty to the system.[26] These individuals can therefore be counted on to support

[23] Nordlinger, *op. cit.*, pp. 82–84.

[24] Robert E. Lane, *Political Life* (New York: The Free Press, 1959), p. 151.

[25] Almond and Verba, *op. cit.*, p. 244.

[26] *Ibid.*, pp. 246–47. However, Germany constitutes an exception to this generalization. See Sidney Verba, "Germany: The Remaking of Political Culture," in Lucian W. Pye and Sidney Verba, eds., *Political Culture and Political Development* (Princeton: Princeton University Press, 1965), esp. pp. 144–46.

the government not only when it is satisfying their demands, but also in times of adversity and crisis when popular support becomes crucial for the system's stability. If major crises are to be successfully resolved, the "representative authorities" must be able to exercise the authority dimension of their roles, and it is the nonelite's diffuse support that allows, and even encourages them, to do so.

One of the "immediate" causes for the decisional ineffectiveness and breakdown of democratic systems is the legislature's refusal to accord the executive a sphere of authority commensurate with its responsibilities. The importance of the executive's leadership and energizing role is evidenced in the fact that it has now become almost a truism to say that when the executive is overly circumscribed in its activities the democratic system's stability and decisional effectiveness are sharply impaired; a "strong" executive is a pre-eminently necessary condition for democratic stability. On the other hand, to make a similar statement about the legislature would be far more problematic.

This leads us to ask if there are any paths by which attitudes toward representation serve to strengthen the executive's position, even at the expense of the legislature—traditionally the representative institution par excellence. Such interconnections are found in the beliefs that the executive is a more dignified, efficient, and authentic representative institution than the legislature.

The clash of interests, the recourse to undignified, crude compromises, and the making of decisions that are mutually incompatible take place in both the legislature and the executive. But there is an important difference. They are more visible in the legislature. The electorate can more easily see "politics" taking place in the legislature; and even when it is hidden from view, the electorate continues to assume that it is there. This is, of course, partly a function of the structural fact that legislatures are made up of numerous individuals and groups who, if they are to produce any decisions, usually do so through the medium of "politics." In contrast, the executive power is almost always embodied in a single individual. From the vantage point of the electorate, it can therefore be assumed both that decision-making in the executive is more orderly and that the decisions themselves are meaningfully coherent in the context of the full panoply of public policy. The President has a "program." The executive is thus seen to be carrying out its representative activities in both a desirable and efficient manner in contrast to the legislature whose representative activities often take the form of unedifying squabbles and self-contradictory measures. The executive consequently "deserves" the special support of the electorate, even at the expense of the legislature.

This last point has special relevance in the "new states." Whatever else may have been said of the former colonial governments, in their outward appearance they embodied Weber's legal-rational authority. The actual decision-making process was covered by a patina of unity, effectiveness, forcefulness, and dignity—outward manifestations that can only help to undermine the respect accorded to post-colonial legislatures embracing widespread patronage and corruption. In this we see a further contrast with the leaders of non-Western states in their multi-hued, deference-inspiring mantles of authority—mantles that often combine charismatic qualities, traditional symbols, and modernizing appeals.

The executive may also be viewed as a better representative to the extent that he is seen to act for the *general* welfare. He becomes the organizer of the public good, as opposed to being the promoter of group interests—something with which the legislature is frequently identified. Whether he actually conceives of his role as such or not, the executive can pose as the representative of the general interest, rising above the supposedly particularistic, selfish, and petty interests of the legislators. Moreover, because the executive represents the entire electorate, whenever a group exists whose demands are being ignored by the legislature—a group that is in some way "underrepresented"—it is the executive who can be called to redress the balance. Since the executive is a national representative, in contrast to legislators who only represent sections of the electorate, the former may be accorded the special respect due to a representative of all the people. When this "extra" measure of respect is accorded the executive, it may contribute to the system's decisional effectiveness, especially when the executive faces an obstructionist legislature.

THE "DECLINE" OF ELECTIONS

The increasing importance of the executive relative to the legislature in the post-1945 period is related to another long-range development—the decreasing significance of elections as they influence public policy. The increasing complexities of governmental affairs, which have made voting for one party or one candidate over another inappropriate as a guide for arriving at governmental decisions; the enlarged areas of foreign and defense policy with their necessary secrecy and dependence on international developments removing the decision-making sphere even further from the electorate; and the increasing importance of electorally unaccountable civil servants and pressure groups in a continually expanding welfare state, have all made signal contributions to the shrinking role of the electoral process as it patterns many types of governmental decisions.[27] It is therefore not inconceivable to compare the electoral system today with the English monarchy at the beginning of the nineteenth century. Both are declining in the performance of their manifest functions in the decision-making process; both serve as a common political reference point for their societies; both serve as a set of rituals, ceremonies, and symbols that tend to integrate the society in the form of a unified political system; both legitimize governmental authority through their continuation, even while the importance of their manifest roles is shrinking. To some extent, then, the point made by Bagehot regarding the desirability of conserving the "ceremonial" elements of government in order to attract loyalty and respect—or more broadly, to integrate the society—is beginning to become applicable to the electoral system. As elections begin to lose their "efficient" content in certain industrialized countries, their symbolic content—their capability for generating emotional attachments—may become increasingly important in integrating societies into stable democratic systems.

If this trend has been reliably stated, and assuming that it continues into the future, how might the operation of democratic systems be affected if elections turn out to have a minimal influence upon governmental policy outcomes? If elections succeed only in placing individuals or parties in office, without, however, exercising a significant influence over policy outcomes? It is certainly not difficult to conceive of such a democratic system, one in which there is genuine competition for office, but in which elections, and even the elected representatives themselves, have little influence upon particular policy outcomes. Nor is it necessary to assume that such a

[27] A similar conclusion is reached by a different path in Stein Rokkan, "Mass Suffrage, Secret Voting and Political Participation," *European Journal of Sociology,* II: 1 (1961), 152. Also see C. B. MacPherson, "Technical Change and Political Decision," in Roy C. Macridis and Bernard Brown, *Comparative Politics* (Homewood, Illinois: Dorsey Press, 1964), esp. pp. 442–43.

democratic system would be unstable, ineffective, *or* unresponsive. To a large extent Norway already fits this description; it is a system in which corporate interests are largely the prime movers in the decision-making process, with the representative subsystem providing only a legitimizing and balancing backdrop.

According to Stein Rokkan, in Norway,

> Votes count in the choice of governing personnel but other resources decide the actual policies pursued by the authorities. . . . The crucial decisions on economic policy are rarely taken in the parties or in Parliament: the central area is the bargaining table where the government authorities meet directly with the trade union leaders, the representatives of the farmers, the smallholders, and the fishermen, and the delegates of the Employers' Association. These yearly rounds of negotiations have in fact come to mean more in the lives of rank-and-file citizens than the formal elections. In these processes of intensive inter-action, the parliamentary notions of one member, one vote and majority rule make little sense. Decisions are not made through the counting of heads but through complex considerations of short-term or long-term advantages in alternative lines of compromise. . . . [The cabinet] stands at the top of the electoral hierarchy, but it is only one of four corporate units at the bargaining table.[28]

Given the additional fact that the Norwegian Labor Party has continually governed the country for the past three decades, it is especially significant that neither the voters nor the opposition parties are negatively oriented toward the system. A 1957 survey study indicates that only a minority of the supporters of the opposition parties prefer even a change of government. And only one of the three opposition parties is seriously interested in establishing a basis for an alternative government, and even in this case the primary motivation is not the winning of government office.[29]

Norway thus provides an example of a system in which the influence of elections upon policy outcomes is secondary at best, yet it remains an eminently stable, effective, and responsive democratic system. In a way, this is not overly surprising. For although the very real possibility remains that large segments of an electorate will be-

[28] "Norway: Numerical Democracy and Corporate Pluralism," in Dahl, *op. cit.*, pp. 106–107.

[29] *Ibid.*, p. 105. For a penetrating and broad-ranging analysis of Norwegian political culture patterns that could be used to account for these attitudes, see Eckstein, *Division and Cohesion . . .* , *op. cit.*, esp. pp. 121–54.

come politically alienated from the system when elections cease to perform their manifest function, there are three alternative responses which do not entail an unstable, ineffective, or unresponsive system.

The first possibility is that the electorate may remain unaware of the diminishing influence of its votes, and the representatives themselves might operate under an invalid definition of the situation. Although it is unlikely that the electorate would operate under such a delusion for more than a generation (if nothing else, the accumulation of pertinent questions asked by pollsters will begin to have an effect), the result might very well be only a half-conscious or hazy awareness of political reality. Given their normative attachments to elections as the efficient and symbolic elements of democracy, the voters' perceptions of this reality might be partially blocked by their democratic preconceptions, forming a set of attitudes toward elections not unlike British attitudes toward their monarchy: a high value is placed upon its continuance, all manner of legitimacy and stabilizing political benefits are thought to derive from it, yet it is recognized that the monarch herself does not play a significant part in the decision-making process.

A second related possibility arises when we ask why citizens vote. It is only a minority of voters who go to the polling booths in the expectation or hope that their votes will influence governmental policy. Rather, voting turnout is primarily a product of a sense of duty and an expression of long-standing loyalty to a political party, and, as such, the decline of elections is tangential to the operating characteristics of democratic governments. Another possibility is one that has already been mentioned in the Norwegian case. To a lesser extent, the same may be said of the United States and many other European countries: pressure groups that speak for sections of the electorate give detailed and primary shape to governmental policy, but they exercise this vast influence because there is always an election around one corner or another. It may be possible for other institutions to perform those manifest functions usually accomplished by elections and representatives. Nor is it unthinkable, once its performance becomes unsatisfactory to large numbers of voters and politicians, to envision the procedural reformation of the representative subsystem, gradually adapting what is largely a nineteenth-century institution to twentieth-century demands. At a minimum, there could be an alteration in the widespread beliefs regarding the most important functions that elections are thought to perform.

To make the point in a sentence, given the existence of at least four possible responses to the diminishing role of elections, only one of which would necessarily detract from a democratic system's stability, effectiveness, and responsiveness, there is perhaps less reason to be unduly pessimistic about the present and future decline of elections (and legislatures) than is commonly supposed; it would by no means be the worst of all possible worlds so long as power is balanced by responsibility—even though the chain of responsibility does not lead directly to the electorate.

CONSTITUTIONAL DECISIONS AND THE THEORY OF REPRESENTATION

10

REPRESENTATION IN LAW AND EQUITY

CHARLES L. BLACK, JR.

Like most men who make their living by trying to think, I have sometimes attempted to be a philosopher, but, as happened with the man of whom Boswell tells, cheerfulness keeps breaking in. I am a member of a political science department, but no elephantiasis of vanity brings me to view the official act that made me so as anything but a deed of kindness, the opening of a charitable umbrella, and the most I can hope is that my political science colleagues may find profit in using me as what the anthropologists call a native informant, when their own concerns impel them to seek insight into the ways of the tribe to which I do in truth belong. I am a lawyer; I know you will expect me to talk like a lawyer, and I will start with the apportionment cases, which have given our subject most of the high current interest it possesses.

In the fall of 1961, when I started off my constitutional law seminar, the prevalent rule on judicial intervention in election districting was thought to be represented by the case of *Colegrove* v. *Green*,[1] then fifteen years old—a case in which four of the seven Justices sitting (though not all for the same reason) refused altogether to act on the inequalities of Illinois districting for Congress. By the fall of 1964, some 1,100 days later, one looked about and saw that, in a very large number of states, the federal courts were deeply concerned, as an accepted part of judicial business, in redistricting plans for both houses of state legislatures and for Congress.

Why did the dam break?

Shortly, there existed a widespread practice—the practice of drawing district lines for representation so as to enclose widely varying populations—morally offensive to many, and in their view (not an implausible one), damaging to their material interests. The note of complaint—improper representation—was one that set strings vibrating a long way back in time. No broad theory was or perhaps could be tendered to justify the practice on the merits. It was, inevitably in our culture, claimed to be unconstitutional, and the claim was not clearly wrong. Yet this claim was repelled from the courts, without examination, on the basis of a doctrine—the "political question" doctrine—without content or structure. The water was strong; the dam was weak, and poorly located.

Three cases mark the main points of fracture: *Baker* v. *Carr*,[2] decided in 1962, *Reynolds* v. *Sims*[3] and its companion cases, in 1964, and *Wesberry* v. *Sanders*,[4] in the same year. *Baker* v. *Carr*, exhibiting a pattern of unequal apportionment in districting for both houses of the Tennessee legislature, held the Fourteenth Amendment "equal protection" question to be justiciable and remanded the case for hearing. *Reynolds* v. *Sims* and its companion cases held that the "equal protection" clause required an approximate equality of population in districts for *both* houses of each state legislature. And *Wesberry* v. *Sanders*, relying on Article I, §2 of the Constitution, rather than on the Fourteenth Amendment, held that the same requirement applied to districting for Congress.

The Congressional case, *Wesberry* v. *Sanders*, and the state legislature cases, *Reynolds v. Sims* and the rest, look very much alike at first glance. One principal thing I want to discuss is the vastness of

[1] 328 U.S. 549 (1946).
[2] 369 U.S. 186 (1962).
[3] 377 U.S. 533 (1964).
[4] 376 U.S. 1 (1964).

the difference between them, in the frame of reference of federalism.

Wesberry, on the one hand, was an intervention by one branch of the federal government in a matter concerning the structure of that same government, a matter over which, by common concession, some part of the federal government possesses paramount authority. No objection to the decision could be made on purely federalist grounds—no objection, that is to say, on the ground that the national government was interfering in a matter which belongs, under the federal plan, to the states. The "federalist" objection, if it could be called such at all, would have to be that the state decision on districting was immune from any but Congressional interference, a contention hard to distinguish from those commonly proffered in a purely interdepartmental contest, such as the one the Court thought to be involved when President Truman tried to seize the steel mills.[5] In the state legislative districting cases, in sharpest contrast, the federal power, through one of its organs, is intervening in a matter which is not only a state concern but *the* state concern—the very structure of the state government, the constitution of the state in the central sense of that word.

Closely connected with this difference are others. In *Wesberry,* the general desirability or constitutionality of a pattern of balances within government was not at stake. The focus was exclusively on one component in the machine. With the Senate at the other end of the Capitol, with the Supreme Court itself developed and accepted as a center of power, with the constituency of the Presidency organized on its own lines, the Court had to make the relatively narrow decision whether it was the fair implication of the constitutional text that the election of members of one House in one branch was to be protected against systematic regional discrimination—whether, in that sense, the lower House was to be held to embody the popular principle. By contrast, the requirement of *Sims* and other cases is an equality in district populations in a class of state elections not yet defined. We know that elections to both Houses of the state legislature must meet the test. *Gray* v. *Sanders,*[6] a case I have not yet mentioned, held, further, that a county-unit system for electing and even for nominating statewide officers, such as the governor, is unconstitutional, where the units ultimately counted represent varying numbers of voters. At a minimum, then, every component of the legislative and executive branches of a state has to be elected on the

[5] *Youngstown Sheet and Tube Co.* v. *Sawyer,* 343 U.S. 579 (1952).
[6] 372 U.S. 368 (1963).

"one-vote, one-value" principle. But the rule of these cases may go further than that, and reach into aldermanic elections, for example, or elections to the school board; if there is a stopping-place, it is now hard to project.[7]

What we have, then, is, on the one hand, a rather specific and narrow intervention by one organ of federal power into the manner of constituting a part of the federal government, and, on the other, a sweeping intervention by the federal power into all the important elections, and perhaps all the elections, of the states. I have said that the sweepingness of the intervention is not unconnected with the federal-upon-federal as opposed to the federal-upon-state incidence of the intervention. This is so because, in general, and saving a few specific provisions not important here, the federal Constitution inhibits the states only in the broadest terms—"equal protection," "due process," "republican form of government." In our constitutional plan, it is usually hard to find a textual or technical ground for finely gradated federal interventions into state affairs. The paradigmatic federal requirement is state abstention from racial discrimination, which applies across the board, to every possible form of state activity; the traditional office of legal acumen in these matters is not to make distinctions, but to drag these to the light and to exhibit their insufficiency.

So much, for the moment, for the political differences between the state-legislative and the Congressional cases; let me briefly summarize the respective constitutional grounds offered by the Court; I think the connection with what I have already said will be clear.

In *Wesbury* v. *Sanders,* decision was based on the first article of the Constitution. That article commands:

> Section 2. The House of Representatives shall be composed of Members chosen every second Year by the People of the several States, and the Electors in each State shall have the Qualifications requisite for Electors for the most numerous Branch of the State Legislature.

The article then proceeds to apportion the membership of the House, as among the States, on a population basis.

On this text, the Court proffers an argument which I may restate, somewhat fleshing out its bare bones, as follows:

[7] See Jack B. Weinstein, "The Effect of the Federal Reapportionment Decisions on Counties and other Forms of Municipal Government," *Columbia Law Review,* 65 (1965), 21.

First, the requirement that the representatives be "chosen" by the "people" fairly implies that, in a single-constituency election, such as an election of a state's Congressional delegation "at large," or without districting, each vote shall have a unit value.[8] It may be well to note here that the Constitution says nothing about districting, that even its permissibility has to be inferred, and that Congressional elections have sometimes been held statewide under Article I, §2; moreover, the "electors" of Article I are set up in that article as a single class, with no suggestion that any "elector" is to have a status, as such, higher than that of any other elector; as new states are, by implication and not by textual command, to be on an "equal footing" when admitted to the Union, so it might be inferred that these electors are to be on an "equal footing" with respect to the power of the vote of each, in a single-constituency election. This first step in the argument apparently commands the assent of every member of the Court except Mr. Justice Harlan, for in *Gray* v. *Sanders,* the county-unit case, Justices Stewart and Clark, the only Justices other than Harlan who failed to join the *Wesberry* opinion, joined in a concurrence which said, "Within a given constituency, there can be room for but a single constitutional rule—one voter, one vote."[9] If this is right, then one thing clearly forbidden would be weighting of votes as a function of the place of residence, in a statewide election of one or more Congressmen.

Second, to continue with a paraphrase of the Court's opinion, the division of a state into unequal districts is functionally similar to and effects much the same unequal distribution of political power as would the unequal weighting of votes by districts in a statewide election—the thing forbidden if one accepts the first step in the argument.[10] Now constitutional law is literally suffused with this idea of functional similarity as a ground for similar treatment. *Brown* v. *Maryland*[11] treated an occupation tax on an importer as a tax on imports was to be treated. *Guinn* v. *U.S.*[12] knocked out the "grandfather clause" as a voting requirement, because it would function in practice much like a racial test. *Boyd* v. *U.S.*[13] voided an order to produce one's papers oneself, on the ground that this

8 376 U.S. at 8.
9 372 U.S. at 382.
10 376 U.S. at 8.
11 12 Wheaton 419 (1827).
12 238 U.S. 347 (1915).
13 116 U.S. 616 (1886).

was functionally tantamount to an unreasonable search and seizure. It is to be noted, moreover, that it is a perceived functional *similarity*, not an exact equivalence, that underlay the holding in each of these cases, and in many more. Similarly, the *Wesberry* court found, in the unequal districting plan, something much like the inequality in the weighting of votes by districts in the statewide poll.

I may say that this argument looks pretty good to me. As a mathematical demonstration, of course, it fails, as all important constitutional arguments fail. But it seems to me to pass the test, and the only test, that constitutional arguments have ever had to pass; it is more sensible than any argument that has been produced to the contrary. But I am not concerned now with your acceptance or rejection—I merely draw attention to the modest scope of this argument. It has no tendency to reach one inch further than the Congressional districting problem. When a case reaches the Court on asserted inequalities in Presidential elections, for example, the argument of *Wesberry* should have no application. It rests on no broad premise, but on the interpretation of the very provision dealing with the matter at hand, and with that matter alone.

The contrast with the doctrine underlying the state legislative districting cases is nearly absolute. "No state shall . . . deny to any person within its jurisdiction the equal protection of the laws."[14] The juristic method that brings these words down to the requirement of equal districts in elections for both houses of a state legislature is essentially different from the method of *Wesberry* v. *Sanders*. I will talk about some of my problems with it, and describe the position I now uneasily occupy.

This clause, in the cases interpreting it, really has two separate aspects. It outlaws racial discrimination, absolutely and without reference to the arguable reasonableness or unreasonableness of the particular act; that is the upshot of all the racial cases. Then, in its more general aspect, it forbids action which is "unequal," in the sense that differences in treatment have no tenable rational ground; in this aspect, the clause has been sparingly applied, for it is not easy to satisfy the stated condition.

Now the possibilities of the application of this clause to the districting problem are several.

As it stands, without the addition of any major heads of inter-

[14] U.S. Const., Amend. 14.

pretation, it could be held to forbid districting patterns wholly without rational basis, patterns that cause counsel's mouth to gape when a Justice leans across the bench and asks "Why?" There would have been room for some judicial action even here.

By a simple expansion, easily suggested by its text, the clause might be held to require that the state follow its *own* laws on redistricting, thus extending their "protection" equally to those disadvantaged. When *Baker* v. *Carr* came down, the defendant state in that case, and a good many others, in the face of *state* constitutional provisions, had not redrawn district lines in more than half a century; others had drawn the lines with no regard to the state constitution's requirement of equality. In this, there was room for more judicial action.

Beyond this, a radical operation had to be performed, for under the new decisions substantial population differences in legislative districts are apparently outlawed, whether or not reasons of some weight could be proffered for their existence, and whether or not state law commands equality. The exact form of the surgery is not quite clear, but the result is plain enough—the right to vote in a district approximately equal in population to every other district has been given, within the equal protection clause's coverage, a status resembling that of the right to be immune from racial discrimination. That is to say, the right is something like an absolute, or, to put the matter another way, no reason for infringing it is good enough.

We have to ask, then, whether this radical operation is justified. I will state and try to uphold the view that it is in part justified—but not, I must confess, with the feeling of confidence which I have in the result in *Wesberry*. My reasons can be rather briefly stated. It would not be hard to show, I think, that it has been the *vote,* and the influence of the vote, that our political society has regarded as the chief of all *protections* against wrongful or undesired exercise of governmental power. This protective function of the vote might be an adequate ground for elevating the immunity from systematic inequalities in voting power to a special position under a clause which, after all, speaks primarily of "protection." I think it could even be shown that protection, rather than participation in the making of policy, was the primal function of representation, for that is the idea that must underlie the medieval conception of representation as a mode of giving or withholding assent to governmental actions originated by others than the representatives.

But if it is the protective or defensive function of the vote that centrally justifies the elevation of voting equality into something like an absolute, the standards that emerge ought to respond to that rationale. A thoroughgoing equality of voting weight, as to every election for every office, is not self-evidently required—one might be tempted to say it is self-evidently *not* required. For my part, I would have wished to see the Court, first, in the cases presenting themselves, explore the possibilities in well-settled doctrine and in doctrine not very far from the well-settled—the pruning away of the rather purely arbitrary inequalities, and the insistence that state laws on redistricting be applied—surely a condition to their being equally applied. Further assessment of the aptness of the districting system to furnish "equal protection" seems to me a much more intricate task than the Court has so far made of it. The question, I should think, would have to be, not whether a particular electoral device is in itself altogether egalitarian, but whether the political system within which the device operates can be said, as a whole, to be affording "equal protection," by distributing voting power in such a way as to give adequate protection to all sections. Plainly, the state with both legislative houses grossly malapportioned in favor of the rural and small-town interest is not doing that. But, with the utmost respect, I have to confess that I cannot confidently make the same assertion of a state whose governor and lower legislative house must depend for election predominantly on the larger urban centers, but whose upper house is skewed in the rural and small-town interest. Indeed, if Congressional districts are to go by population, if the state's Presidential electoral vote goes by population, if the United States Senators are elected by population, if the governorship goes by population, if the lower house of the state legislature is districted purely by population, then it might seem that the skewing of a single state chamber is no more than a needful redress of the balance, to prevent utter defenselessness, entire lack of "protection," for the inhabitants of sparsely populated districts. This is a judgment, of course, relative to time, tradition, and history. It is a judgment that rural and small-town America, though it must consent to a very large diminution of influence as its people flow away, still has enough importance to be left with some minimal means of defense. While these are, as stated, purely political considerations, I believe they could be adequately restated as grounds for differentiation under the "equal protection" clause. And I have to say that it seems to me the Court did not, in deciding for a rigid egalitarianism even with respect to the second state chamber, adequately confront the analogy of the United States Senate. It is not that it is hard to see the differences, or to see that for some purposes they are important differences. The problem really is, "What question is being asked?" The questions that I would ask are, "Is the allocation of representation, in one House of a state legislature, on the basis of unequal populations, badly out of line with our warranted national concepts of equality? Does it violate our notions of what it takes for a government to be looked on as one which gives its people 'equal protection'? Is this true no matter what the rest of the structure of the government is like, no matter what kind of power it elsewhere gives the densely peopled sections?" If these are the questions, then I fail to see how the federal analogy can be altogether irrelevant. Far from its being irrelevant, it would have seemed to me that the federal analogy might have given the Court just that parallel needful to justify the drawing of a maintainable line between the doubly and grossly malapportioned state legislatures which have existed, and the legislature which, in one of its chambers, would give some protection to sectional interests now threatened with political obliteration.

I must content myself with this brief treatment of the cases as cases, leaving much unsaid. It must interest us here to go on and try to place this whole controversy, this whole drama, in the wider setting of Western man's thoughts about representation. I have tried to do this in my own mind, but the result has been largely negative.

One need not wonder at this; I have already given the explanation in my opening remarks. I would regret the insufficiency of what remains more than I do, were it not that what I am doing here is to open what I do not doubt will be a full and illuminating discussion of those philosophic issues to which the reapportionment decisions direct the mind; this being the case, it may not have been wrong to start by focusing mainly on the decisions themselves. Nevertheless, until cheerfulness breaks in, I shall give you my few impressions of the wider setting.

First, it has to be said that there is not and never has been, at least in recent times, any general theory of representation that could with any warrant be seen as dominant. This is not surprising. What we call representation in the narrow sense, that is to say, the assembling of elected representatives for the purpose of their formulating policy and devising new laws, is a thing that may be seen as having started, in recognizable form, perhaps four hundred years ago—five human lives the length of my father's. Figuring a career at about fifty years, eight careers have seen the development of this system, which is said to be, truly I think, the chief political creation of modern man. When historians see us in the kind of perspective which makes us think of William the Conqueror and Henry II as rather close in time, they will probably see the English Reform Bill of 1832, and the decision of our Court in *Baker* v. *Carr,* as nearly connected steps in the formation of a set of practices which were later to receive the theory adequate to explain them.

The theoretical problem is made the more complex by the fact that there are modes of representation other than the one arising from election. Surely our ambassadors represent us; it is a shallow doctrine of representation which cannot find it in the person and office of the policeman on his beat. The Supreme Court itself, I think, must be looked on as representative, having been put and kept in its position of power by acts of the more immediately chosen popular representatives, who might in any ten days since 1789 have weakened it or destroyed it. A satisfactory concept that stretches over all these kinds of representation must include components of social psychology as well as of games theory, and that concept has not yet won its way to the point of being visible to at least one lawyer.

There have, however, been several continuing debates about special issues, and it may be interesting to turn to some of these.

The most teasing of them concerns the problem of "virtual" rep-sentation. Can a representative ever be said to represent anyone other than those who have chosen him? You may think this problem archaic, but something rather like it, a species, perhaps, of the same genus, remains with us, at the very center of the process of election, and indeed of the theory of majority rule. Let us look again at the requirement of Article I that the Congressman be "chosen by the people." Now no Congressman is ever, in the full literal sense, "chosen by the people." He is chosen by some of the people, while others of the people either choose one of his opponents, or do not choose anybody. In a two-party state, it is probably in only a minor fraction of the cases that a Congressman is chosen even by a majority of the "electors" in his district, for enough "electors" stay home to convert all but the landslide victory into a "choosing" of the victor by a minority of the "electors" Where there are three candidates the victor may be "chosen" by as few as one-third plus one of those voting, which in an off-Presidential year, when voting is relatively light, may be a small fraction indeed of the "electors" as defined in Article I, §2, and a smaller fraction by far of the "people." Yet few would assert that the people of the district are not all represented, and this shows, I think, how much of a necessary or at least a seemingly inescapable mysticism—"virtualness," if you like—remains in our common concepts about representation.

I doubt that any constitutional decision can say anything very clear about the set of puzzles nestled in the concept of "virtual" representation. The decisions we are examining evidently do not do so, unless it be in a very partial and doubtful way. I believe some of the apologetic for malapportionment has suggested the representative from the sparsely populated district really represents the interests of all in the state, so that the inhabitant of the more populous district is as fully represented as if apportionment were equal. This kind of fractional virtualness is something I find hard to take very seriously; if you take it seriously, you will see in the decisions we are examining a rejection of this much of the theory of virtual representation. But the really radical problem—how can the whole people of any constituency be said to be represented by a man only some of them chose—is not touched in the least by the apportionment decisions.

Another much discussed question has been: Is "representation" to be of people or of communities? Here, again, I think that the new decisions touch very little if at all on an ancient question. It is true that some special pleaders for malapportionment have tried to invoke the community-representation principle. But in probably the large majority of the cases, the inequality of districting complained of did not rest on the community principle. The Congressional district, for example, has no communal existence—it is a geographical division set up for the single purpose of electing a congressman. On the other hand, where true communities are represented, no insuperable problem is posed by the equality requirement, for the communities can be represented *pro rata,* and if that results in too large a group of representatives, votes in the chamber can themselves be weighted.

One of the most interesting questions, through centuries, has been—is a representative a "trustee" or a "delegate"? Is it his function to do what he thinks right, or to do what his constituents think right? If the former, is the right to be defined in terms of his constituents' interest or of some wider public interest, with all the difficulties inherent in defining either? Insofar as either the interests or the views of his constituents are relevant, is he to regard only those who voted for him, or all those in the district, or those among whom he thinks he can form a successful re-election coalition? So one might begin a set of questions which could be followed into shadings and combinations of greater and greater subtlety. As to all of them, it seems plain that much is to be said on both sides, and that any conscientious representative has to steer and does steer a tortuous course, the vector of which at any time is a function of more numerous and complex factors than can be put into a structured relation. What can interest us here is that the reapportionment decisions do not bear at all on this set of questions, that the representatives of equally apportioned districts must face them in just the same form as before.

Perhaps only one ancient line of thought about representation is really connected with these decisions. Is the representative body to be a "replica of the realm," a reduced-scale map of the people? In one sense of this question—that which goes to the quality of the representative, to his typicalness as against his superiority—the decisions have nothing to say. In the other sense, the sense of John Adams' call for proportional equality of interests within doors and out of doors, these decisions, it seems hardly needful to note, have a limited but definite relevance. They do not, emphatically, ensure the attainment of that proportion; where election is by plurality, no districting system can ensure the presence indoors of the interests of the near-plurality. But, insofar as the old districting systematically favored the rural districts and the small towns, and insofar as those areas have special interests, there has been a certain systematic departure from the Adams principle, beyond what is necessitated by what seems almost the inherent nature of our politics. The decisions, obviously, go no further than the wiping out of this particular systematic skewing disfavoring the large urban centers. The skewing itself has been denied or minimized, but if those who so argue are right, then it seems strange that the decisions should create any furor or be much objected to, since nothing material is at stake, and the actions of the Court, though perhaps futile, were harmless.

Before I close, let me mention one more problem. It may be that the most important thing of all is that people feel adequately represented. Though our ideas about representation have changed, now as in the Middle Ages the assent given through representatives is the active ingredient in legitimacy. It seems likely that more and more politically conscious people had come to feel, particularly since the War, that the representation given them, particularly in the state governments, was a sham. These decisions, when implemented, ought to dispel that feeling. But it seems to me that the Court ought to take thought whether a similar feeling, perhaps justified, may not come into being among the inhabitants of districts of relatively light populations, when absolute egalitarianism is taken to the extreme of rejecting the retention of some protective balance for them anywhere in the state government.

11

BLACK ON REPRESENTATION: A QUESTION

STUART M. BROWN, JR.

My discussion here is concerned with a single question which Professor Black raises and tentatively answers at the very end of his interesting and illuminating paper. I do not, that is, challenge or discuss his analysis of *Baker* v. *Carr, Reynolds* v. *Sims,* and *Wesberry* v. *Sanders*. But I should here confess that I am at least as uneasy as Black is about the first two of the cases, those concerned with representation in state legislatures, and that I may be even more disquieted than he about the principles used to justify these two decisions. But I have nothing to add to his analysis of the cases themselves, though the reasons for my disquiet about the principles will, I think, become clear in the course of my remarks on the one question I shall treat.

The question is: What bearing, if any, do these two court decisions concerning apportionment for state legislatures have upon the traditional problems and theories of representation? Black thinks that the court decisions have little or no bearing upon the traditional problems and theories. I, on the contrary, think that the decisions have a very strong bearing upon some of the traditional problems, and I am disquieted precisely because I think they do. With regard to this question, therefore, there is, at least prima facie, a strong disagreement between us, but it may turn out that our disagreement is apparent and verbal rather than real. The problem is that Black does not use the term "bearing" in any precise logical sense. Nor does he use the term "implication." Instead, he undertakes to place the controversy about these cases in the setting of "Western man's thoughts about representation" and finds that there are few, if any, important relationships between them; that is, between the issues raised by the court cases and the thoughts of Western man about representation. Thus, he does not clearly specify the kinds of important relationships he is seeking to discover, and he may find none because there are none of the sorts he seeks. I, on the other hand, looking for the logical relationships which are of special interest to philosophers, may find a number of important ones. If this is the source of our disagreement, as I believe it to be, our disagreement is verbal but not at all trivial.

Now in one clear and important sense these court decisions have no bearing upon the traditional problems and theories of representation: they offer no solutions to any of the traditional problems and require no modifications in any of the traditional theories. But the reason why this is so is that a court decision to reapportion, no matter how sound or unsound the supporting arguments may be, expresses a court's judgment of a course of action to be taken. It does not express the court's view of the proper solution to the traditional problems about representation or the court's view of the correct theory of it. Even if it did, even if in the course of its argument the court expressed its view of the traditional problems and theories, the fact that it did would not constitute solutions to these problems or establish the correct theory. What solves problems in political philosophy and makes one theory of representation better than another is quite independent, logically, of any court decision on apportionment. Court decisions are concerned with specific legal and constitutional questions arising under a given legal system and not with the very general, philosophical questions of political theory. Court decisions, therefore, cannot conceivably solve the problems or logically require changes in the theories. This is true of all the problems considered by Black: whether representation can and ought to be virtual; whether people or communities ought to be represented; whether representation ought to provide a replica of the realm; and whether representatives are to be properly conceived as delegates or trustees.

In much of his discussion, Black is inquiring about this kind of relationship and answering correctly that none exists. In his remarks about theories of representation, he notes that there has been no really dominant one in recent times and suggests what some of the requirements of an adequate general theory would be. The main implication of this section is that the court decisions make no contribution to the problem, and this is surely correct. Again, Black's discussion of virtual representation poses an abstract, theoretical question: How can all the people of a constituency be represented by one man whom only some of them elect? Having elaborated this question, he concludes correctly that the court decisions do not touch upon it. In all these cases, however, the court decisions make no contribution, because they cannot. The problems are understood in such a way that no court decision can solve them.

Although the court decisions cannot solve the traditional problems or require modifications of the traditional theories of representation and in this sense have no bearing upon the traditional problems and theories, the principles used by the court in making these decisions do have a momentous bearing upon them. And because the court decisions are not independent of the principles on which they are based, the decisions as based on principles have a momentous bearing upon the traditional problems and theories.

The argument is in two steps: First, these court decisions are not independent of the principles on which they are based. This is to say that these court decisions are not bare judgments ordering reapportionment. They are judgments which are allegedly based upon certain principles. Any existing malapportionment is to be understood and made out in terms of these principles, and any acceptable system of reapportionment must conform to them. The principles, therefore, function both as the premises of the legal arguments supporting the decisions and as the criteria of adequate representation to be achieved by reapportionment.

Second, these principles of representation, functioning in these two ways in the court decisions, bear upon the traditional problems and theories in the sense that they are logically compatible with some and incompatible with others. The principle "one-voter, one-vote" or "the equal protection of the laws" interpreted as implying "one-voter, one-vote" is, as stated in the decisions, a principle of unrestricted egalitarianism. It is consistent with some conceptions of democracy and the theories of representation appropriate to them; it is inconsistent with others. The decisions, therefore, beg questions about which traditional conceptions of democracy and representation are correct. The Court, begging these questions, acts to change the character and balance of power in our political life. Whether or not the question is begged in accordance with our own prejudices and our view of the Constitution, the bearing of the decisions is direct and momentous.

The concept of democracy is notoriously vague, and in particular with respect to two features which appear antithetical. One is that in any democracy the interest and will of the majority of citizens must prevail without restriction. The other is that though in general the interest and will of the majority must prevail, certain restrictions must be placed upon majority rule because the interests of a majority can be adverse to the equally valid interests of minorities and of the whole community. Democracy is and over very long periods has been commonly conceived in terms of one of these alternatives to the exclusion of the other, both conceptions prevailing side by side within the Western democratic tradition, and one of them, that protecting minority interests, being more conservative than the other.

Not surprisingly, the traditional problems reviewed by Black polarize on these two alternative concepts. For example, the theory that representatives are primarily trustees rather than delegates implies a view of democracy in which the interests of the whole community, including the interests of minorities, are to be protected. Representatives would be chosen as trustees, and presumably the method of election would be biased in favor of men qualified by education, position, and character to act as trustees. This requirement could and has been used to justify systems of unequal representation. By contrast, the theory that representatives are primarily delegates implies a view of democracy in which the interest and will of the majority are to prevail without restriction. Representatives would be chosen as expressing directly the interests of the electors and the system of representation would so far as possible provide equal representation, give every elector an equal opportunity to be represented by his own delegate. Obviously, the principle "one-voter, one-vote" implies this latter view of democracy, in which representatives are to be conceived as delegates rather than trustees. The court decisions as based on this principle do not address themselves to the question whether representatives ought to be trustees or delegates. They beg the question in favor of the delegate theory and the concept of democracy associated with it.

Similarly, the principle "one-voter, one-vote" implies that it is people as individuals rather than communities which are to be represented. It fails to answer the traditional question as to which should be represented. It begs that question in favor of people as individuals.

Perhaps the most interesting point of disagreement between Black and me is concerned with the replica of the realm theory of representation. Here he thinks the apportionment cases do have a bearing: because they correct an existing bias favoring rural areas, they will provide a closer approximation to a replica of the realm. I cannot, of course, dispute the obvious fact that whatever corrects a bias in a system of representation provides in fact a closer approximation to a replica of the realm. But the principle "one-voter, one-vote," or "the equal protection of the laws" interpreted to imply "one-voter, one-vote," is not itself a principle for protecting the interests of each distinct component of the community against exploitation by the others. It is not a principle for creating and preserving a pattern of representation that will be a replica of the realm. On the contrary, this principle, applied without restriction, would not in the long run and in general preserve minority interests. In the long run and in general it would sacrifice them to the interests and will of the majority. It is therefore logically incompatible with a replica of the realm theory and with the theory of democracy underlying it. Again, the court decisions are not addressed to and do not answer questions about the merits of the replica of the realm theory of representation. On the contrary, they beg the questions, in this case against the theory, not in favor of it as Black thinks.

These questions about the replica of the realm theory and the protection of minority interests raise what seems to me to be the fundamental question about representation posed by these decisions. The question is whether these decisions, as based on the "one-voter, one-vote" principle, imply the acceptance by the Court of an unrestricted egalitarianism which is inconsistent with the concept of democracy expressed in the Constitution of the United States. The answer is that the decisions do imply this. They imply a view of democracy in which the protection of minority and regional interest is not a central and definitive feature. Yet this is the view of democracy in the Constitution. Unless this were the view, many of the most distinctive features of the Constitution, like the bicameral legislature and the acknowledged sovereignty of the states, would make no sense. I do not wish to put myself in the false position of arguing for any traditional version of states' rights theory or against reapportionment. I am not in favor of any traditional version of the former nor against the latter. Reapportionment indeed is long overdue in most states. What I am protesting is the principle on which the reapportionment decisions were made and what seems to me to be the incompatibility between the concept of democracy implied by the principle and the concept of democracy expressed in the Constitution of the United States.

I do not for a moment believe that the use of the "one-voter, one-vote" principle will lead to the exploitation of minorities or the abandonment of the institutions which protect regional and minority interest. Unlike Hobbes, I have no fear that everything bad and possible under some set of principles will in fact obtain. What I find most distressing about these court decisions is the carelessness with which the Court acts upon and invokes principles which are at least prima facie incompatible with the concept of democracy underlying the Constitution. I am distressed precisely because these principles do have implications for problems about representation and democratic theory and because the Court of all our institutions ought to be most fully aware of and sensitive to them.

12

POLITICAL PARTIES IN THE NORMATIVE THEORY OF REPRESENTATION

DONALD E. STOKES

Law and power are seldom strangers, but their relationship is peculiarly close in the reform of representation now being forced on the legislatures of our states. As in most great constitutional changes, the Court is proceeding in this one with scant help from the Constitution itself. What the Fourteenth Amendment gives is no more than a diffuse prescriptive premise—that all citizens must receive equal protection of the laws. To move from this premise to detailed prescriptive conclusions the Court has had to consider the effects of apportionment schemes on political power.

What Professor Black (see Chapter 10) finds wrong is not that the Court has performed such an analysis but that it has failed to perform it well. What seems to him questionable in *Reynolds* v.

Sims and its companion cases is not that the Court has invoked the equal protection clause in this area but that applying the clause here is "a much more intricate task than the Court has so far made of it." We might indeed say that the real divergence between the Court and its critic is over an appropriate political theory—a body of descriptive or predictive generalizations about representation and political power which can connect normative premise and prescriptive conclusions in this debate.

This is a situation well calculated to make the student of politics believe that he has something relevant to say. Certainly the political scientist ought to be especially sensitive to phenomena of power within the legal forms of representation. My own view is that political representation must be comprehended a good deal in terms of two complementary problems of power or influence: on the one hand, the power of a citizenry over its political leaders, the great problem of democratic theory; on the other, the authority of leaders over the led in the sense of the acceptance by a mass citizenry of decisions made by representatives in its behalf. Since the legitimacy of the regime is so settled a matter in the American context, it is the problem of democratic control which has received the wider attention. But these dual aspects of power in representation are related through the fact that the public's perception of its influence on political leaders is part of what confers legitimacy on the decisions of leaders, a fact recognized by Professor Black in speaking of "the active ingredient in legitimacy."

Any student of politics who looks at the classical theory of representation in terms of power is unlikely to feel very satisfied. The writings which still come first to mind when the topic of representation is broached, especially the enormously influential works of Edmund Burke, do not carry us very far toward the kind of theory which would help the Court, or anyone else, to reach sound prescriptive conclusions in this case. Professor Black's brief call of the roll is revealing. In none of the classical issues of "virtual" representation, of individual or communal representation, of "trustee" or "delegate" representation, or of representation of a "replica of the realm" does he find any real help in thinking about the problems which now occupy the Court.

Part of the difficulty is no more than a matter of what ideas we have conventionally associated with "representation." Political theorists have by no means been blind to the empirical relationship of representation to power since the time of Burke, but their work is usually phrased in other language. I would offer as a main example analyses of the role of political parties. In this century—earlier indeed in America—parties and party systems have played an immensely important role in developing the public's control of leaders and conferring legitimacy on the regime. This contribution has not gone unnoticed, but it is rarely connected to the concept of representation.

It is therefore remarkable, but not in the least unusual, that a critic such as Professor Black should have been able to work his way through an extended consideration of the political theory of representation without once mentioning political parties. I would feel that parties deserve to be at the center of our thought about representation and that once they are, the problems reviewed by Professor Black have a very different look. It is clear, for example, that many of the mechanisms protecting the interests of particular groups are to be found within the party system rather than within the formal structure of government. Professor Black is faithful to an important element of American experience in speaking of the "defensive nature of representation"; John C. Calhoun may indeed be our most authentically American political theorist. But the means of defense have to a notable degree been provided by the political party rather than by elaborately contrived blocking mechanisms of formal government itself, as Calhoun would have wished. Indeed, the embracing, nonsectarian character of our parties has to an extraordinary extent made the aggregation and adjustment of competing interests a function of the party system.

It would be still more remarkable to overlook political parties when we turn to the positive functions of government. The success that parties have had in marrying government action to popular consent has converted the modern doctrine of party government into what is really the most widely accepted normative political theory of representation. Of course, the American experience lies a good ways off from any pure model of government by tightly disciplined and popularly responsive parties. And yet there can be no doubt that our party system has channeled the expansion of governmental power in ways that are broadly acceptable to a public whose support is sought in free elections. Despite the strong tendency toward fragmented authority in a system of separated powers, the parties have increased the chances of coherent action by placing government in the hands of partisan leaders who have common policy beliefs and tactical goals.

I think that much of the dissatisfaction with the old basis of apportionment in the states arose precisely from the fact that the unequal weight given rural areas so often blocked affirmative action by party leaders whose programs carried majority support in the state electorate. To be sure, the gains of reapportionment are not limited to strongly competitive states. The Court's first intervention came in a state that is only marginally competitive, and many states —for example, Georgia—where the gains are most dramatic are less competitive even than Tennessee. All the same, the recurrent image of a party winning a statewide mandate only to be blocked by one or more malapportioned chambers of the legislature did much to create the political support for judicial action, a support that has indeed been essential in keeping the Court's power over state apportionment from being impaired.

The rightness of the Court's present doctrine must therefore be judged partly in terms of political representation through the party system. From such a perspective, I am impressed by one great advantage of electing both houses (as well as the executive) on a strict population basis: it will tend to deliver control of the several organs of government to the same party. This is not John Adams' principle that the proportion of interests indoors and out-of-doors should be the same; it is easy enough to show that under a single-member system limited swings in popular support will produce much wider swings in legislative seats, at least in a state where both parties have strong support. The principle is rather that the party which has won an electoral majority should gain the control it needs to give its policies effect.

Both predictive and normative objections can of course be raised against this principle. Predictively, it may be argued that the relationship of votes to seats introduces some random variation into the connection of popular support to actual power and that it is by no means certain that a party with a statewide majority will gain control of a legislative chamber apportioned strictly by population. The argument is valid but of limited importance. If the popular majority is at all large, the probability that it will fail to yield legislative control vanishes under any but the most pathological districting system.

If the heirs of Elbridge Gerry were clever enough to produce pathologies of this sort, they could expect their work to receive the judicial attention it deserved.

Normatively, this principle can be opposed by the tradition of defensive constitutional arrangements so richly evident in American thought, a tradition to which Professor Black's paper belongs. I am prepared to believe that there are political communities whose survival depends on blocking arrangements of this kind. I do not believe that ours is one of them, not at least in this century. Nor do I feel that the social element which is the object of Professor Black's solicitude is particularly well chosen. If we were to start afresh to identify a portion of American society which most requires special political advantages to achieve equality of power, I think we could make a better choice than the small-town and country dwellers who happened to be advantaged under the antique apportionment plans. A much more persuasive case could, for example, be made in behalf of the economically depressed racial and ethnic groups of our great urban areas, groups which could easily be separated out in geographic terms. My own feeling, however, is that any such award of special constitutional points creates more problems than it solves.

Therefore, I find myself much more in sympathy with the prescriptive conclusions drawn by the Court. An analysis of the role of parties in political representation has of course not been a main element in the reasoning by which the Court moved from premise to conclusion. But reasoning in terms of such an analysis would lead to conclusions similar to those the Court has drawn, particularly on the question of whether both houses of the state legislature should be apportioned by population. The success of representative institutions—even, as Professor Black suggests, the legitimacy of these institutions—will in the long run depend on how well they respond to needs felt widely in the community. This sort of response needs to be encouraged by constitutional arrangements which deliver effective power to partisan leaders who have the widest electoral support.

13

STANDARDS FOR REPRESENTATIVE SELECTION AND APPORTIONMENT

LEWIS A. DEXTER

I

Courts, and writers on political questions, have in recent years tremendously *over*emphasized the weight to be attached to the principle of "one-man, one-vote." From a practical standpoint, no great harm, as yet, appears to have been created by this overemphasis. Potentially, however, it is dangerous to the American public welfare. And bearing in mind that there is a tendency in some countries to adopt or to be greatly influenced by American Supreme Court dicta, it is worth pointing out that the adoption of the "one-man, one-vote" principle would be very dangerous in some other societies. Finally, the *over*emphasis on this principle is not intellectually very rigorous, from the standpoint of either jurisprudence or political philosophy.

For, in general, American judges are supposed carefully to circumscribe the application of any principle to immediate and tangible situations—the advantage of this position is that it makes it less likely that the principle will be applied to prevent wise adaptation to subsequent social changes or to stymie future social inventions. Similarly, it is presumably to be desired that political scientists reiterate the wisdom of limiting and qualifying the unrestrained application of any given moral axiom by taking into account other axioms and the changing nature of empirical situations.

On this issue, there has not been a great deal of such qualification; and, so far as I know, there is not to be found anywhere a statement of the general considerations which ought to limit the applicability of "one-man, one-vote." One reason for such lack of general criticism is no doubt the fact that objections to the present position of the Courts on representation tend to be couched in rather narrowly legalistic terms or with reference to specific proposed reapportionments. Accordingly, although Mr. Justice Harlan's dissents, in the Georgia case in particular (*Wesberry* v. *Sanders,* February 17, 1964), suggest *some* of the general considerations which are, I believe, applicable, they are entangled in the specifics of particular cases and confused philosophically by irrelevant issues of constitutional history. Other general issues of equal importance are not, apparently, stated at all in the current discussions.

Since, so far as the recent decisions go, I suppose the net effect of specific reapportionments is favorable to causes I support—since I suppose that in several states, reapportionment will elect state legislatures more willing to adjust to Negro demands for equality of treatment and since, I suppose, there is a slightly greater chance under the current reapportionments of electing Congressmen who share my views on foreign policy[1]—I would not, if I could, reverse most of these decisions, once effectuated. But I fear the possible future consequences of "one-man, one-vote" as the sole determinant of representative districting and selection; and I am concerned as a social scientist by what seems to me to be the general willingness of our profession to accept rather uncritically currently fashionable emphases which happen to fit in with liberal preferences.[2]

[1] Because reapportionment, now, gives somewhat greater weight to suburban areas; and it is probable a higher proportion of people in suburban areas, active politically, share my particular foreign policy views.

[2] This article is one of several in which I have tried to present an antithesis

Accordingly, I am stating in general terms some principles which *also* ought *often* to be *explicitly* taken into account in consideration —whether judicial or philosophical—of apportionment and repre-

---

to a generally accepted position of the "liberal" social scientist, pointing out the danger that "one good custom, overemphasized, can corrupt the world." This is, of course, classically, the position of the Great Marquess of Halifax in his *Character of A Trimmer.* I have attempted to state this position in "On the Use and Abuse of Social Science by Practitioners," *American Behavorial Scientist,* 9:3 (1965), 25–29. I have tried to apply the approach to Congress in my "Check and Balance Today: What Does It Mean for Congress and Congressmen?" in A. de Grazia, ed., *Congress: The First Branch of Government* (Washington, D.C.: American Enterprise Institute for Public Policy Research, 1966; New York: Doubleday Anchor, 1967) (my article was originally issued as a separate pamphlet, 1965); I have also applied it to education in my *Tyranny of Schooling* (New York: Basic Books, 1964).

If there is any doubt that the prevailing view of the political science profession is uncritically accepting of the "one-man, one-vote" doctrine, it may be noted that most political science writings on reapportionment focus almost entirely on the technical, geo-arithmetical, question of how to get the "fairest" (most nearly even) equality of districts, rather than upon any other general issues involved; this literature is discussed critically by Alfred de Grazia in his valuable and incisive *Essay on Apportionment and Representative Government* (Washington, D.C.: American Enterprise Institute, 1963). (De Grazia's essay is basic for any criticism of contemporary theories of apportionment; but, because it exists, I have been able to refrain from the specific historical and polemic analysis which would otherwise be necessary and to concentrate on another job.) It may also be noted that de Grazia was the *only* dissenter out of sixteen political scientists of distinction, gathered by the Twentieth Century Fund, to the proposition stated in its pamphlet, "One-Man-One-Vote" (New York: Twentieth Century Fund, 1962), p. 4, that "the history of democratic institutions points compellingly in the direction of population as the only legitimate basis of representation today." *It is precisely to showing the limited and erroneous nature of this proposition that the current essay is addressed.*

It may also be noted that although I was on the platform during C. Herman Pritchett's Presidential address to the American Political Science Association in 1964 and made some effort to elicit criticism during the evening and the following two days of the convention, I found next to none; yet Pritchett declares that the Supreme Court through the reapportionment cases has "reminded us that judges who endeavor to speak for the constituency of reason and justice may truly represent the enduring principles of a democratic society . . . have taken sides in the crisis of our times . . . raised a standard around which men of good will might rally . . . [have shown] conscience, capacity, will to challenge scandal. . . ." This address was published as "Equal Protection and the Urban Majority," *American Political Science Review,* 58:4 (1964), 869–75. Listening to it confirmed me in the intention of suggesting that reason and justice are not quite as simple or simplifiable; as he indicates to me the real scandal lies in this very simplicity, so calmly accepted by our profession.

sentative selection. These principles may be discussed under the headings of:

a. Communications Area.
b. Culture and Social Group.
c. Interest.
d. Tradition.
e. Legislative Efficiency and Efficacy.
f. Social Invention: Improved Methods of Voting and Representative Selection.

II

Communications Area: The Sense of Efficacy and Competence. The most obvious (although perhaps the least important) of these important principles, overlooked in recent decisions and discussion, is that "one-man, one-vote" should, *other things being equal,* mean "one-man, one-subjectively-efficacious-and-meaningful-vote." All we know about political participation and political attitudes suggests that a sense of competence increases political participation and faith in a political system, other things again being equal. Ordinary common sense suggests that people who know something of candidates with whom they can identify are likely to have a greater sense of political competence and are less likely to feel that they are just picking names at random on a ballot. And ordinary common sense again shows that if people are part of a communications area in which politics is carried on, they are likely to experience identification. Perhaps equally important, they are actually likely to know more about candidates and less likely to fall for demagogues or slick advertising tricks or firm handshakes without any firmness of mind, if they are part of a communications area within which candidates are active—that is, if they know people who know the candidates.

Communications areas are not divided into equal arithmetic segments of the total population. Often arithmetically equal apportionment of populations does or would cut up communications areas. Take, for instance, this ecological situation: One small city has a newspaper, a radio station, and a community sentiment of its own, but it is not large enough to meet the minimum population size of a Congressional district. However, it is not far from a larger city, which is somewhat larger than the standard-sized Congressional district. Parts of the larger city would under such circumstances on the "one-man, one-vote" doctrine be cut off from their "natural" political area and be thrown in with the smaller city. Having, as it happens, voted all my life in an orphaned section of a Congressional district, I can from experience assert that in fact citizens of a cut-off area are far more psychologically remote from Congressional elections and somewhat more remote from their Congressional representative than would be the case if the big-city Congressional district were oversized. People in such a cut-off area typically trade, read, listen, work, make friends, have all their contacts in the big city; in my particular case, only a small proportion of our town's citizens have had any reason to know people in either of the two smaller cities with which we have been successively joined; trade and friendship patterns do not run that way; but if we were associated with any of the somewhat oversized Congressional districts on the other side of us, there would be numerous contacts, and the Congressional election would matter more to our citizens.[3] Add to this: In the most recent reapportionment, the particular precinct in which I live has, for reasons of arithmetical equality, been separated from the other seven-eighths of our town and joined with a formally contiguous area, which has little socio-ecological similarity, for purposes of electing a state representative! Since citizens of our precinct

[3] Consider this supplementary fact. I am particularly interested in Congress and Congressional elections—have taken part in eight Congressional campaigns in other states, have compiled a manual ("How Candidates Lend Strength to Tickets," privately printed, 1956) on voting by Congressional districts for other offices, have achieved some recognition as a writer on Congress (for example, Raymond A. Bauer, Ithiel de Sola Pool, and Lewis Anthony Dexter, *American Business and Public Policy* [New York: Atherton, 1963], dealing extensively with Congress), and have taken part in two recent Massachusetts statewide campaigns as speechwriter for gubernatorial candidates, and I know a dozen or so politicians who are active in the big city in our district including both the owner and editor of the only daily newspaper in it. Furthermore, in 1966 I kept my eyes and ears open to see if I heard anything about the Republican Congressional candidate (Republican candidates have received a majority in the district for other offices and the incumbent Democrat has no great personal strength, so it is not a hopeless situation for the Republican); yet, the only single thing I have heard, read, or seen from any personal acquaintance, in any campaign headquarters, or from the mass media (and I live in a town which is predominantly Republican) about the Republican Congressional nominee is his answers to a League of Women Voters questionnaire! (To make the record completely full, I should say that I was in the district thirty of the forty weeks before election.)

Similarly, I heard practically nothing about two of the three candidates for state representative during the entire period—although again, I am particularly predisposed, as a member of the Research Committee, Citizens' Conference on State Legislatures, to notice or remember any information about them.

do pay some attention to our town meeting and town affairs and in any case do know their neighbors in our town but have no real contact with this physically adjoining but economically rather different area, it takes considerable effort to find out about those who are legally our state representatives—particularly since the two people who represent the greater part of our town are always identified with it, whereas our precinct's legal representatives never are. Some of us would be more active participants in the state representative process if we had been left in an oversized district, consisting of the whole town.

In some other parts of the country, splitting counties in order to secure arithmetical fairness or throwing in a small rural section with a city district effectively disenfranchises a particular class of voters in regard to the office in question. At the Congressional level, where representatives are full-time professionals with a staff, citizens are not actually deprived of services by such apportionment; but in some states, where many representatives and state senators work at other jobs and themselves identify chiefly with their own neighborhood or class of people, people from such an orphaned segment of a district are in fact likely to find it more difficult to establish effective contact with their representatives at the State Capitol—partly because the representatives themselves will have less sense of solidarity with the minority constituents, partly because the citizens will be much less likely to know somebody who personally knows the representative. (In the particular case of our State representative district, it happens that having been active in statehouse politics, personally, I may know slightly one of our representatives; but, on the other hand, I know several dozen people who know the representatives from the major portion of the town, and I do not know anyone else in our legal district who knows our legal representatives in the General Court.)

Now, this kind of arithmetical and geographical disenfranchisement is sometimes unavoidable; I do not personally regard it as a sin against the True Spirit of Democracy that this sort of thing happens. But it seems to me it would be fairer and more democratic to decide that our precinct and our town take part in Congressional and State Representative elections on a fuller basis by putting us into oversized districts, than it is to give someone the satisfaction of sacrificing us to "one-man, one-vote." Nobody, unfortunately, to my knowledge has made a listing of such cases over the country; but I know of several and assume the existence of a number of others. Of course, they have existed anyway; but "one-man, one-vote" tends to increase their number. Incidentally, "one-man, one-vote," by cutting off orphaned districts, also tends to deprive citizens of such areas of the chance of competing for office; it would be quite difficult for citizens of our precinct to become known in the rest of our state representative district, still more difficult without some accidental factor to become known in our Congressional district; naturally our Congressional seat has been occupied for several generations by people from the big cities in the district, with which we have little contact.

I have chosen to discuss first this *less* important—from a moral standpoint—of the principles which should be balanced together with "one-man, one-vote," because it shows most clearly that the administrative and structural consequences of applying any one principle of "reason and justice" need to be thought out before it is adopted indiscriminately.

III

Culture and Social Group. The community area principle merges into another which could be—in some other countries *is*—of the greatest importance. Other things being equal, each cultural group of any size ought to have some legislative representation. In some of the newer nations, different tribes as such have rights to legal and political representation; for historical reasons, there has been an effort in India to provide representative rights to outcastes and certain lower castes. There probably are no large groups in the United States, taken as a whole, which are so different from each other in orientation and outlook and tradition as are different tribes in Africa or castes in India. There are, however, certain local situations where people of different cultures often do not get a fair hearing. I refer to the Indians in several states; some device should be worked out for permitting them to select representatives, familiar with *their* cultural practices and traditions, to speak for them in the state legislatures. Had the Cherokees had any such right, before the time of the dreadful Trail of Tears, perhaps the history of American oppression of the Indian would not have been so grim. The method of selection might not be—perhaps should not be—necessarily direct election in all tribes; it would have to be worked out by people familiar with and sympathetic to both cultures, the Anglo-American and the Amerindian; perhaps the ultimate result might turn out to be a little different from what we now think of as a legislator—perhaps the "aboriginal" groups should select a *Censor* with power to delay actions inimical to them and the right of appeal to some form of national ombudsman for a declaratory judgment or advisory opinion.

In the past, Spanish-speaking people certainly should have been permitted similar representation; whether this is still necessary or desirable is a matter to be considered by those in recent, local, intimate touch with their situation in different states. Part of the controversy about literacy in Spanish in New York State might have been avoided if the Puerto Rican population had been permitted for a time to select its own representatives in the New York State legislature and possibly in Washington. There is incidentally no reason why such situations should not lead to a few persons who actually live in two cultures having two votes, just as, until recently, university graduates in Great Britain could vote both for University M.P.s and for their own local borough representatives.

In the future, we may have to deal with some new group of immigrants of a quite different sort, and some way to permit them to be spoken for should be available rather than having to be devised ad hoc under pressure. Indeed, considering the numerous recent immigrants (Turks, Italians, Pakistanis, Portuguese, etc.) in Western Europe, this need may be recognized there before we ever have occasion to consider it.

IV

Interest. It will be noted, probably, that I have not spoken of Negroes under "cultural group." By and large, I do not consider American Negroes as markedly different in culture from other English-speaking Americans (although some allowance has to be made for internal migration and minor cultural differences between South and North, with many Negroes, of course, being Southern). But American Negroes do constitute an *interest* group of great importance; it so happens that the denial of residential equality to them means that in the North they can, do, and will elect plenty of public officials. However, were they to be scattered about the city, as they have been in a few Southern cities in the past, this would be difficult; yet, it would be important that they be able to elect representatives to speak for them. So, any insistence upon "one-man, one-vote" as a governing principle should be modified by awareness that such cases of special interest groups may exist, and no constitutional interpretation should prevent legislatures able to take account of these cases from doing so.

One interest group which perhaps should be taken account of on a national scale—which at least has a claim to be heard—is that of Americans living abroad. This group might again be entitled to select some sort of spokesmen regardless of its size, whether as full legislators or not.

Actually, and fortunately from this interest group standpoint, American government is, as Morton Grodzins often pointed out, "a system of multiple cracks," so most interests do in fact get heard, one way and another, save those (such as Negroes and the retarded) which are clearly discriminated against. But this complex system of multiple cracks does not exist to the same degree in most other countries and it does not necessarily exist (we really have little evidence on this point) to the same degree in all the fifty states, looked at in terms of their individual polities. There may be a case in certain states for minority labor or business or religious interests to be heard. (Supposing an Amish representative selected entirely by the Amish people themselves were to become a member of the Iowa legislature. Would that help to clear up the rather difficult situation involving their relationships with their neighbors?) Perhaps most important, "one-man, one vote" in several states will make cities dominant; will there be a case then for giving rural districts some disproportionate representation?

V

Tradition. Although the sweep of American developments is against tradition and the traditional, we know that there is an element in a good many places and cases of sentimental attachment to the old days, the old ways, the traditional pattern of doing things. If, for instance, a state has become accustomed to at-large election by counties, there is a certain patina of concern amongst the politically active which surrounds this tradition, similar on a small scale to the feelings people have for the flag, the White House, and Independence Hall. It may not be a better way of selecting representatives than some other way; but it seems unfortunate to challenge the feelings and sentiments which have developed around it. Indeed, in a few cases, particular Congressional districts or state senatorial districts have some feeling attached to them, because perhaps people have worked in a good many campaigns together or against the same foes (just as the Harvard-Yale game has some tradition attached to it). Since such sentiments and traditions and feelings are part of what makes political participation interesting and meaningful and worthwhile, mechanical reapportionment and arithmetical equalization to some small extent do make politics less worthwhile to the active participants. Of course, this is not in most parts of the United States a major argument against reapportionment; but it is one value to be taken into account against some proposed reapportionments and should not be simply forgotten.

VI

Legislative Efficiency and Efficacy. Obviously, also a major requisite of any constitutional provision for a legislative assembly is to ensure that it work and will continue to work in the future. It may very well be that dogmatic insistence upon the "one-man, one-vote" principle will make efficiency and efficacy more difficult. For instance, it has usually been the case that, due to gerrymandering, rotten boroughs, and other forms of malapportionment, a considerable number of experienced legislators have served from session to session, so that the inefficiencies and bother of starting off with new members, all of whom have to learn the ropes, is avoided. Anyone who wants to know how a legislature whose membership is nearly all brand new operates might study the Massachusetts legislature of 1853; due to the Know-Nothing sweep, the lower body had only six re-elected members, and it made more tragicomical blunders than could well be imagined.

I would be strongly in favor of providing that if, for some reason, either party in a legislature is largely swept away in a general election, the outgoing legislature may select a specified number of members from the defeated party to sit with the new legislature. The reason for this is that sooner or later the minority party is apt to come back and it is important that it have some experienced members who have been around the legislature continuously when it does. (I have discussed the arguments and procedures for this arrangement more fully as regards Congress in my essay in A. de Grazia, ed., *Congress: The First Branch, op. cit.*) For the same reason, I would provide that, if the minority party stays a small minority for several terms, some of its candidates, who have *not* had previous legislative service, shall be added to the legislative body. (A similar provision is actually made in the Puerto Rican constitution, chiefly with another objective—to avoid excessive one-party dominance.)

Some legislative bodies get into difficulties, particularly in organizing, from the reverse situation, when two parties are very close in numbers. (The very worst example of this was seen in the British Parliament in the first postwar Churchill and the first Wilson governments.) Under such circumstances, I would provide that the majority party could co-opt enough additional members (probably from its defeated candidates) to assure speedy organization and avoid the kind of thing that takes place when forty or fifty ballots may be needed to select a presiding officer. If the two parties were evenly balanced, I would specify that they should draw lots as to which could co-opt enough members to organize the body.

Such proposals as these of course run utterly athwart the "one-man, one-vote" principle; but they would make legislative bodies more dignified and more efficient.

VII

Practical Consequences: Social Invention. In the immediate short run, I suppose the chief consequence of acceptance of the arguments just made would be that courts (and perhaps some college professors) would become more modest and tentative about stating the application of the "one-man, one-vote" principle.

In the longer run, one might hope that awareness of such arguments as these would lead to something which has been rather lacking recently in American electoral discussion. It would be desirable to develop proposals and ideas which would help to realize the different values here stated—if possible, to reconcile them. This calls for systematic political inventiveness. Although American practice has demonstrated a certain amount of ad hoc political inventiveness, very few efforts have been made at the state or national level to develop procedures of election and selection which would enable us to realize the wide variety of relevant values. Obviously, at some point, values are apt to conflict; but equally obviously, it is possible that ways between the horns of apparent dilemmas can be found. But to find such ways, we need to focus our attention self-consciously upon the prospects and possibilities of invention, rather than to wait for inventions to occur by accident or chance. Obviously, again, other things being equal, the "one-man, one-vote" rule would be applied, but if possible it should be worked into schemes which take account of these other values—and, if not, weighed against them to see what is optimum in a particular situation.

I have here suggested a few ways in which I would think we might consider changing legislative bodies, election practices, and constitutional provisions. Any serious inventive effort, however, would involve taking a much more careful look at the assumptions I have made than I have done. My inventiveness is, to a certain extent, impressionistic and a wider awareness of relevant circumstances might check or alter some of my underlying assumptions.

Nevertheless, the emphasis upon inventions as an outcome of analysis in terms of political philosophy seems to me worth stressing. The present fashion for behavioral and empirical approaches to political science tends to lead only to naively descriptive generalizations. This was quite contrary to the hopes and intentions of the most influential founder of empirical American political science, Charles E. Merriam.[4] His intention and hope was that empirical political science would permit the development of a class of political inventors who would use empirical findings to develop means of solving political problems. But unless one self-consciously realizes that one is concerned with the critical clarification and analysis of political values, e.g., political philosophy, one takes for granted whatever the prevailing political orientation of the times is, and conceives "solutions" only within the framework of the fashionable and the conventional. It is for this reason, apparently, that recent professional and scholarly inventiveness on American electoral systems has been largely confined to arithmetizing or mathematizing or equalizing; my intention in this article has been to urge that real inventiveness demands going beyond the fashionable and conventional definition of problems.

[4] See Charles E. Merriam, *Systematic Politics* (Chicago: University of Chicago Press, 1945); also Harold D. Lasswell, *The Future of Political Science* (New York: Atherton, 1963); and Lewis A. Dexter, "Social Invention and Social Technology," *J. Lib. Religion* (1948), and "Sociology of Innovating Leadership," in A. Gouldner, ed., *Leadership* (New York: Harper & Row, 1950). I suppose Mr. Merriam must have spent altogether seventy hours talking to me about the need for self-conscious political inventors.

14

REPRESENTATION VALUES AND REAPPORTIONMENT PRACTICE: THE ESCHATOLOGY OF "ONE-MAN, ONE-VOTE"

ROBERT G. DIXON, JR.

Political representation, and its implementation in apportionment and districting practices, comes close to encompassing the full sweep of interests of democratic man. Its elements touch matters as diverse as the democratic tension between the power of majorities and the power of minorities, and the mathematical intricacies of weighted voting and multimember districting. It also relates in interesting ways to all that has gone before in the deliberations of the American Society for Legal and Political Philosophy, starting

The writer wishes to acknowledge the Rockefeller Foundation and the American Philosophical Society for assistance with this paper and his forthcoming book on representation and reapportionment.

with the initial program topic of Authority and running through such topics as Community, Public Interest, Rational Decision, and Equality. To extract every representation insight from the nine preceding Nomos volumes would be discursive and tautological, but three basic interrelations do merit brief mention.

Of crucial significance is the concept of "public interest" which takes us back to the interaction and conflict between the common will and the general will in Rousseau, and the difficulty of getting a "representative" expression of either. Eschewing the benevolent autocrat implications of the general will concept, and assuming a simple cancelling out process of the represented wills, does not a general will goal require a representation system whereby all interests will be brought forward into the assembly so that a grand cancelling out may take place?[1] Does not "public interest" then, in the sense of a purified general or community will, dictate both regular review of apportionment *and some consideration of minority representation?* The latter element, at least to 1966, has been almost totally lacking in recent judicial constructs of "one-man, one-vote" representation.

At the operational level Edgar Bodenheimer has noted the problem of weighting as well as identifying interests:

> Furthermore, if there should be wide divergences among the individual interests capable of being identified, should the numerical weight be the sole factor in deciding which of them should be given preference or at least priority? Should the desires voiced by a majority be entitled to greater consideration than those of a minority? How can we make sure in a situation calling for immediate action that the legislative will is in fact a faithful reflection of "the sum of the interests of the several members" who compose the community?[2]

And what of the related matter of the relative intensity with which differing views are held?[3]

[1] Indeed, a "fortuitous mutual cancelling out of irrational elements" has been said to be the kind of process relied upon by Rousseau for his argument that "the Will of All would *tend* to give expression to the General Will." J. Roland Pennock, "Reason in Legislative Decisions," in Carl J. Friedrich (ed.), *Rational Decision,* Nomos VII (New York: Atherton, 1964), pp. 98, 103.

[2] Edgar Bodenheimer, "Prolegomena to a Theory of the Public Interest," in Carl J. Friedrich (ed.), *The Public Interest,* Nomos V (New York: Atherton, 1962), pp. 205, 208.

[3] Robert A. Dahl, *A Preface to Democratic Theory* (Chicago: University of Chicago Press, 1963), pp. 90–123; James M. Buchanan and Gordon Tullock, *The Calculus of Consent* (Ann Arbor: University of Michigan Press, 1962), pp. 125–52.

"Public interest," however defined, needs a setting, thus leading naturally into the elusive concept of "community." Attempted definitions of "community," as noted by John Ladd, have a Scylla-Charybdis quality, tending to be so narrow as to exclude many types of community or so vague that any aggregation of individuals can be called a community. He does identify one essential feature of a community with which most may agree—its "organic character."[4] Clearly, legislative constituencies are aggregations of individuals. Whether they also are or should be "communities," with something of an organic character, or coincide with "communities of interest," is one of the central issues in representation theory and districting practice. By custom the apportionment of representatives even in a unitary state has not been rigidly mathematical, and, as Professor Elliott has observed: "Historically integrated areas are retained undivided to secure real areas of community."[5]

"Community" therefore leads directly into an analysis of constituencies: whether they are or should be fixed as in territorial systems or voluntary as in proportional representation systems; temporary or enduring; natural (organic) or amorphous. In reapportionment terms, the factor of community underlies consideration of federal plans, political subdivision representation, and the possible political artificiality of mathematically equal but frequently changing districts. If political representation is to be more than a formal consent structure, and more also than a close "PR-type" allocation of legislative seats according to party strength, then organic aspects of community and their relation to the shaping and functioning of legislative districts cannot be ignored. It was a sense of community factors, as well as a natural British distaste for running any principle into the ground, that underlay the 1948 and 1958 modifications in the English parliamentary constituency statute in order to permit the administrative reapportionment commission to deviate from the short-lived rule of a maximum 25 per cent deviation in constituency population in order to give greater recognition to local boundaries and "local ties."[6]

[4] John Ladd, "The Concept of Community: A Logical Analysis," in Carl J. Friedrich (ed.), *Community,* Nomos II (New York: Liberal Arts Press, 1959), pp. 269, 271.

[5] William Yandell Elliott, *The Pragmatic Revolt in Politics* (New York: Macmillan, 1928), p. 480.

[6] House of Commons (Redistribution of Seats) Act, 1944, 7&8 Geo. 6, ch. 41 (3d Schedule, Rule 4); House of Commons (Redistribution of Seats)

The reapportionment revolution is essentially a judicially imposed revolution. Hence the final interrelation with earlier Nomos materials is to ask if this revolution is the product of "rational decision." Apart from their feelings about the end sought, at least a few persons felt that the Supreme Court's Reapportionment decisions of 1964[7] were not so much reasoned decisions from conscious premises about the modes, purposes, and intrinsic limitations of representation systems as they were an "exercise in sixth grade arithmetic."[8] More charitably perhaps we could relate the decisions to a statement of Holmes: "In cases of first impression Lord Mansfield's often-quoted advice to the businessman who was suddenly appointed judge, that he should state his conclusions and not give his reasons, as his judgment would probably be right and the reasons certainly wrong, is not without its application to more educated courts."[9] After quoting this passage, Paul Freund has gone on to suggest a *caveat,* which still hangs over the reapportionment decisions: "The advancement of doctrine need not await an exposition of its full reach, so long as judges are reasonably satisfied that it will not prove to be intractable."[10] For the reapportionment cases this *caveat* still lives for several reasons, not the least of which are indications that freshly equalized districts may enhance the tendency for the district system of legislative election to overrepresent the dominant party, and indications in some states that reapportioners, freed by a tight mathematical mandate from compulsion to follow existing political subdivision boundaries, may have enhanced room for subtle but

---

Act, 1947, 10&11 Geo. 6, ch. 10; House of Commons (Redistribution of Seats) Act, 1958, 6&7 Eliz. II, ch. 26. The 1958 Act provides: "[The] Boundary Commission . . . shall take account, so far as they reasonably can, of the inconveniences attendant on alterations of constituencies . . . and of any local ties which would be broken by such alterations. . . ." *Ibid.,* p. 144.

[7] *Reynolds* v. *Sims,* 377 U.S. 533 (1964) and companion cases. More detailed discussion of these cases by the present author is found in *Michigan Law Review,* 63 (1964), 209; and *American Bar Association Journal,* 51 (1965), 319.

[8] 377 U.S. 713, 750 (1964), J. Stewart, dissenting in the Colorado case. *Lucas* v. *Forty-Fourth Gen. Assembly,* and in the New York case, *WMCA* v. *Lomenzo.*

[9] O. W. Holmes, Jr., "Codes and the Arrangement of the Law," *American Law Review* (1870), 1; reprinted in *Harvard Law Review,* 44 (1931), 725, as cited by Paul A. Freund, "Rationality in Judicial Decision," *Rational Decision, op. cit.,* pp. 109, 120–21, and n. 14.

[10] Freund, *op. cit.,* p. 121.

effective gerrymandering.[11] Whether the simplistic "bare population proportionality" rule which emerged from the reapportionment decisions of 1964 will prove flexible enough to support development of a sophisticated jurisprudence of representation responsive to some of the problems just mentioned must await the 1970 census.

In political philosophy, as in law, the grander issues form a seamless web.

REPRESENTATION GOALS AND "GRUNDNORMS"

Within the line of development of consensual systems of representation, analysis has tended to proceed on two levels: one concerns the nature and goals of an operating consensual system,

[11] For example, in the 1966 election in California the Democrats retained majorities of 42–38 in the Assembly and 21–19 in the Senate, although the Republicans polled a majority of *legislative election* votes on a statewide basis, in addition to the Reagan sweep in votes for the governorship. Democratic and Republican popular vote totals for Senate and Assembly respectively were 3,239,738 to 3,403,582 and 2,835,173 to 3,294,210. The drawing of a larger number of "safe" seats for the Democrats when the Democratic-controlled legislature reapportioned in 1965 operated to hold 1966 Republican gains to a minimum. Similarly, in the 1966 Congressional district races both in California and New Jersey the Republicans got a majority of the statewide popular vote for Congress, but Democrats won a majority of the House seats. (In New Jersey the new Congressional redistricting act had been nullified on federal constitutional grounds but was allowed to be used in 1966 on an interim basis. *John* v. *Folcey,* 222 A. 2d 101 [N.J. 1966].)

By contrast, in Michigan a suit challenging the 1964 Democratic-devised reapportionment plan on grounds, *inter alia,* of gerrymandering was not aided by the fact that in 1966 the Republicans' 51.4 per cent of the popular vote for the Senate and 53.2 per cent for the House enabled the Republicans to recapture the Senate (53 per cent of the seats) and gain a tie (50 per cent of the seats) in the House.

In a state like Michigan with large impacted pluralities for one party in one section, it may take a "benign gerrymander" (if such an animal can be conceived) to enable legislative seat gain to be roughly proportional to statewide legislative election vote. Conversely, however, an apportionment plan which in statewide perspective roughly proportionalizes legislative election votes and seats captured may contain individual district designs which achieve a desired political result at the expense of town or county-oriented communities of interest and representation needs. Creative use of bicameralism may be an answer to the problem of satisfying two instinctive feelings about representation: (1) some rough proportionalization of party popular vote strength and party seats; (2) a preservation wherever possible of political subdivision lines in districting regardless of adverse impact on parties whose pluralities are impacted in one area.

i.e., representative democracy or a thing called by that name; the other concerns the formalization of representation inside a democratic system.

A pervading problem in democratic political thought has been the attempted reconciliation of popular will with individual rights, in particular the problem of majority rule and minority interests. Difficulties in reconciling the two have involved those who have tried it in contradictions, e.g., Locke, Rousseau, Madison.[12] If Burke seemed to avoid a contradiction, it was only at the cost of substantially rejecting majoritarianism in favor of a tradition-based rational aristocracy which, anomalously, in his Bristol experience favored policies more liberal than the constituency majority would support. If the buoyant Jacksonians and Populists of the nineteenth century seemed to avoid contradiction, it was only at the price of elevating a majority infallibility which few minority-group-minded twentieth-century democrats can accept.

Tension between majoritarian impulses and minoritarian fears, and resultant yearnings for consensus, continue in postwar pluralist America. President Johnson, like President Eisenhower, seeks to preside over a national consensus, which even touches the Calhounian concept of concurrent majority. In an essay entitled "My Political Philosophy" a few years ago, the then Senator Johnson wrote:

> It is part—a great part—of my own philosophy that the Congress reaches a very dubious decision when its choices are made solely by head counts. . . . I do not believe we have arrived at an answer until we have found the national answer, the answer all reasonable men can agree upon, and our work is not done until that answer is found—even if the process requires years of our lives.[13]

The dominant overt forms of representation tend to be the *political parties,* the *legislative election process,* and the *legislative action process.* True, the executive plays an important role through

[12] See comments on Locke in Alfred de Grazia, *Public and Republic* (New York: Knopf, 1951); on Rousseau in G. D. H. Cole, *The Social Contract* (Everyman's Library edition, London: J. M. Dent & Sons, 1935); on Madison in Dahl, *op. cit.*

[13] The quoted material is derived from a *New York Times* story, December 30, 1964, p. 8, col. 1. For a further discussion on President Johnson's operating philosophy of government by consensus, see Louis W. Koenig, "The Hard Limits of Government by Consensus," *New York Times Magazine* (March 7, 1965), p. 26.

general leadership, veto, and party control. But even such an executive enthusiast as Charles E. Merriam also could write that: "The strength or weakness of the legislative agency is an index of the strength or weakness of the political community."[14]

The essence of the party system is that it be a system of two or more effective parties, providing not only the choice which vitalizes political action but also the consensus on which government rests. And yet, these two basic concepts of party purpose, if pushed to their extremes, vitiate the representation function and endanger the two-party choice system. Excessive stress on program (principle) makes the party an uncompromising "church with tenets."[15] Excessive stress on consensus yields a party with overwhelming numerical power but hobbled by its lowest common denominator. The resultant problem of representative government may be seen "as the issue between representation and effective government: representation understood as respect for variety, and effective government understood as following a consistent program set forth by a strong leader. . . ."[16]

The legislative election process is the crucial nexus between parties and legislative action. The goals to be achieved are several.[17]

An initial basic goal is maintenance of popular faith in the system. This goal is the core meaning of the slogan "consent of the people" and perhaps, as one critical study has shown, its only operative meaning. A second goal is really a twofold one, affecting the crucial role of parties as opinion-organizers and candidate selectors. In one aspect it is a goal of assuring continual existence of a power to govern in a majority party by avoiding a splintering multiparty

[14] Charles E. Merriam, *Systematic Politics* (Chicago: University of Chicago Press, 1947), p. 149.

[15] Walter Bagehot, *The English Constitution* (New York: Oxford University Press, 1900), p. 224.

[16] Harvey C. Mansfield, Jr., "Party Government and the Settlement of 1688," *American Political Science Review,* 58 (1964), 933, 934.

[17] Most of these rather generic goals may be consistent with the implications of such main bodies of representation theory as (1) the Madisonian separation and balancing of powers; (2) the nineteenth-century mass democracy approach of Jacksonians, Populists, and others; (3) the good government movement with its concern for executive power and theory of a representative executive (called "enlightened individualism" in De Grazia's *Public and Republic, op. cit.*); and emerging bodies of current thought either in the neo-Madisonian "consensus approach" of Dahl's *Preface to Democratic Theory, op. cit.,* or in the neo-individualist "consensus approach" of Buchanan and Tullock's *Calculus of Consent, op. cit.*

development. In its other aspect it is a goal of maximizing the effectiveness of the minority party as an opposition party potentially capable of leadership, and in any event capable of representing effectively the interests whose allegiance the majority party has failed to capture. A third major goal, in part reflective of the second, is that the legislative action process shall not be a mere process of rubber-stamping previously prepared positions, but shall be a deliberative process of compromise and adjustment in which the right to be *heard* is preserved to all, even though the right to *control* is reserved for those who can organize majority sentiment on the issue at hand.

As the vital nexus between effective parties on the one hand and deliberative legislative action on the other, a crucial and even determinative role is played by the legislative election process. This includes the whole range of apportionment and districting alternatives and practices. In this perspective the needs of fair and effective representation, which at bottom are what the reapportionment revolution is all about, entail a disposition to analyze critically our traditional legislative apportionment and districting practices, to assess their support of these goals, and to weigh critically in the light of these goals the merits of possible modifications or alternative devices.

Under such a goals analysis, significant deficiencies may appear both in traditional American apportionment-districting practice and in its diametric opposite, pure proportional representation. The former may be seen to involve a "fixed constituency extremism" which in many respects is as unsatisfying as the "voluntary constituency extremism" of pure proportional representation. Straight plurality election of legislators from single or multimember districts under our traditional "fixed constituency" system is causally related to such problems as the following: (a) the malapportionment-reapportionment problem of keeping districts relatively in step with population growth and shift; (b) the likelihood—because parties and interests are not rationally spread or rationally grouped geographically—that all apportionment-districting decisions, whether made by design or by chance, will have a crucial but arbitrary political effect on such matters as candidate availability, safe versus swing districts, homogeneous versus heterogeneous districts, and party competition; (c) the tendency to prevent rise of third parties but at the possible cost of overrepresenting the dominant party, of strengthening one-party system tendencies, and of blocking effective representation of minority interests including those centered in the second party; (d) the tendency to produce nonproportional and irrational relationships between the degree of party support in the electorate and the degree of actual party strength in the legislature.[18]

On the other hand, the "voluntary constituency" extremism of pure proportional representation has its own deficiencies, for: (a) it tends to encourage the development of a multiparty system with its instability of coalition government; (b) it minimizes the integrative process of compromise and adjustment at the citizen level which a choice confined to two parties tends to encourage, and which by minimizing opinion extremism tends to maximize forces of allegiance and stability; (c) it tends in short to pursue proportionality at the price of compromise, adjustment, and agreement.

A goals analysis may open the way to exploration of means to achieve an ultimate goal of fair and effective representation by devices which combine the virtues of fixed constituency systems and of proportional systems, while avoiding the representation deficiencies of each. The range of possibilities may run from a mere heightened sensitivity to gerrymandering, and to means of building more bipartisanship into initial apportionment-districting processes, all the way to adaptation of our traditional fixed-constituency system in the direction of formal hybrid systems such as cumulative voting, limited voting, or mixed formulae in a bicameral system.

EGALITARIAN IMPACT ON REPRESENTATION

What the courts seem to have had in mind in the recent reapportionment cases is something far less than the range of representation theories, goals, and operative problems suggested above. Specifically, what the Supreme Court seems to have had in mind in the reapportionment cases is an egalitarian ideal that as nearly as possible all men should count as one, politically, however different their other circumstances. Such an ideal has been one of the vital components of American political development. The strong persistence in actual practice of major elements of the Madisonian system of balanced factionalism has not been matched by overt respect for

[18] The exaggeration of majority party strength caused by the district system is common in British as well as American experience. D. E. Butler, *The Electoral System in Great Britain 1918–1951* (London: Clarendon Press, 1953).

it. After 1800 it became increasingly risky to profess it publicly[19] and a historian writing at the end of the nineteenth century could look back and say that "no capable politician has dared to place his cause on any other ground than the will of the people.[20] In this respect the ethos of American politics has been more French than English, placing greater stress, as Wolfgang Friedmann has observed, on equality of rights than on effective leadership.[21] De Tocqueville was expressing a distinctly French-American viewpoint when he wrote that democratic communities have "a natural taste for freedom. . . . they will seek it, cherish it, and view any privation with regret. But for equality, their passion is ardent, insatiable, incessant, invincible."[22]

The broadening of the franchise is one basic level in an egalitarian political ideal. It also may affect not only voting per se but also the apportionment base and hence the nature of an apportionment system. For example, in early Massachusetts property restrictions on the franchise for the upper house also dictated an apportionment of upper house seats on the basis of location of enfranchised property owners rather than on a population basis.[23]

A second level of egalitarianism is its application to voting rules concerning the filling of elective office once the breadth of the franchise has been settled. Practically, if not logically, the egalitarian ideal seems to be associated here with a simple numerical plurality or majority rule principle, because of the impossibility of getting unanimity and the likelihood that control of the many by the few could result from more complicated choice systems. In 1963 in the Georgia county unit case (*Gray* v. *Sanders*[24]), the Supreme Court made this principle a constitutional requirement for certain situations. (Of course, within this principle there are significant differences between requiring a majority and requiring a mere plurality as noted below.)

Gray involved not legislative representation but rather Georgia's system, applicable to such statewide offices as Governor and United

[19] De Grazia, *op. cit.*, p. 115.

[20] John S. Bassett, *The Federalist System* (1906), p. 296, cited in De Grazia, *op. cit.*, p. 115 and n. 5.

[21] W. Friedmann, *Legal Theory* (London: Macmillan, 1949), p. 452.

[22] De Tocqueville, *Democracy in America* (H. S. Commager, ed., New York: Oxford University Press, 1947), pp. 6, 7.

[23] Robert Luce, *Legislative Principles* (Boston: Houghton Mifflin, 1930), pp. 338–39.

[24] 372 U.S. 368 (1963).

States Senator, whereby a popular vote winner could lose if he failed to capture enough counties to yield a majority of the county unit vote—the unit votes in turn being allocated to counties on a non-population basis in such a way as to exaggerate the strength of the less populous counties. The political principle endorsed by the Court in *Gray* is that the most popular candidates should win. The prize of office in a given constituency should go to the man who has a majority or a plurality in the qualitatively equal votes cast by the politically equal citizens in the constituency to be served. Put another way, the question in *Gray* was whether an office-holder should be the most popular man in the entire constituency, or whether he should be the man with the maximum appeal to the maximum number of artificially weighted geographical units within the constituency. Of course, at the national level, we do continue to elect our President under a Georgia-type unit system, using state units rather than county units. There is, however, less unfairness, in population terms, in the electoral college state-weighting system than in Georgia's county-weighting system. In Georgia at the time of *Gray,* the disparity between the weight of a vote in the most populous county (Fulton—556,226 population, 6 unit votes), and the weight of a vote in the least populous county (Echols—1,876 population, 2 unit votes) was 99 to 1.[25] By contrast in the electoral college the equivalent disparity between a New York voter (16,782,304 population, 43 electoral votes) and an Alaska voter (226,167 population, 3 electoral votes) was 5 to 1.

The third level of attempted application of egalitarianism to political institutions is the difficult one, i.e., its application to the constitution of a bicameral representative assembly. Here a simple principle of egalitarianism becomes rather uninformative; it fuses, or should fuse, with corollary questions regarding the nature and problems of representative government. To take an obvious example, the common English and American practice of basing repre-

[25] *Sanders* v. *Gray,* 203 D. Supp. 158 (N.D. Ga. 1962). The court worked out a mere 10–1 discrimination against Fulton County by relating the population and unit votes of each of these two counties to the total of 410 county unit votes rather than by comparing the two counties in terms of voter status. It pointed out that Fulton, with 14.11 per cent of the state's population, had only 1.46 per cent of the total county unit votes, while Echols with .05 per cent of the population had .48 per cent of the total units. These different ratios illustrate the interesting gamesmanship of bare numbers analysis. All computations are based on 1960 census figures.

sentation on a district election system produces an obvious kind of vote weighting and vote forfeiture. Whether district populations be equal or unequal, there is in each district a plurality which elects its man or slate and thus is weighted as 100 per cent, at least for certain purposes. For these same purposes the minority becomes a zero minority, until the next election. Is this kind of vote-weighting irrelevant to the egalitarianism underlying the "one-man, one-vote" concept; or does it bear directly upon the basic purpose of the reapportionment plaintiffs which was to achieve political equity in the form of weight, i.e., seats, in the legislature roughly proportional to their *statewide* voting strength?

Were it not for our inheritance of the district system for creating legislative assemblies, and some corollary values, it would seem that "one-man, one-vote" applied to representative government would point either to pure proportional representation or at least to some modified form such as the mixed district-party list system in the West German Republic. In a sense proportional representation is simply the "one-man, one-vote" principle carried to its logical conclusion. Significantly our district system forebears, the English, came close after extensive consideration after World War I to adopting a modified PR form for parliamentary elections.[26]

It is unfortunate that the broader issues of representation theory and goals sketched in the preceding section, and the varied facets of the superficially simple egalitarian concept just suggested, have been ignored in the current reapportionment revolution. A careful analysis of egalitarianism and its relation to representation theory and problems was notoriously lacking in oral arguments presented to the Supreme Court in cases which led to the 1964 reapportionment decisions, and in the Court's opinions. Egalitarianism denotes an approach to the quantum of an *individual's power*. Representation in the special sense of fair representation denotes an *end result* in a system where not all can be winners but all want to be heard proportionately. Despite Chief Justice Warren's half-buried dictum concerning an ultimate goal of fair and effective representation, the Court invoked a formal egalitarianism of equal population districts to cure a representation illness, certain symptoms of which are not responsive to this treatment.

The basic difficulty is that representation itself is an elusive concept and can be approached from varying premises. Discussions of

[26] Butler, *op. cit.* pp. 38–47.

the theory of political representation often mention at the outset that at least two very different models exist, i.e., two very different ways of looking at representation. One is the "delegate model," which conceives of the representative as the agent of his constituency or at least a majority thereof. Under this model the task of the legislator is to record the will of his constituency; legislative representation becomes an additive process. Quite different is the "free agent model" under which the task of the legislator is to be guided by what he conceives to be the enlightened self-interest of his constituency. This is analogous to Rousseau's theory of a purified "general will," rather than the mere "common will" of overt group desire (although Rousseau deplored the use of representation as a device to achieve this purification).

The trouble with these models is that they push us into an either-or approach, which may be helpful for some purposes of mathematical model-building but obscures reality. Most legislators occupy both of the roles suggested by these models, and others in addition; and they do so concurrently in regard to different issues and in relation to different parts of the constituency.

A more helpful observation may be the following, focusing on the *quality of the "representation" received by the district minority,* particularly if it be a part of the statewide minority in a legislative election. In a broad way we can distinguish between what may be called, for lack of agreed terminology, "political organization representation" and "general or re-election representation."

Political organization representation may be viewed as maximum effective representation. It denotes membership in a party, group, or coalition which in a given election not only has elected its district candidate but also has captured control of the legislature. The members of this voter group are directly linked to the legislative majority which organizes the legislature and tends to dominate its committee system and other vital processes, both formal and informal. They are part of the governing group. (A citizen whose favored candidate loses in his own district but who belongs to or identifies with the party or coalition which controls the legislature shares in political organization representation to a degree, at least vicariously. A further qualification arises of course in the situation where the controlling wing of the dominant party, "liberal" or "conservative," shares and thus represents views widely held in the minority party.) Under our traditional plurality rule district system, it is mathematically possible, although unlikely, for the governing group, i.e., the possessors of political organization representation, to be a popular minority by winning a majority of seats by narrow pluralities and losing others by large margins.[27]

General or re-election representation may be viewed as minimum or automatic representation. It denotes the kind of representation most legislators give to all their constituents apart from considerations of party or faction. It rests on a legislator's desire to cultivate an image of local community service and concern with an eye to the next election when a vote is a vote from whatever quarter. General or re-election representation will be much more effective in close districts than in safe districts. This kind of representation may not benefit minority party voters in terms of the larger public issues but may be important on local and personal constituency matters. This kind of representation also may be bolstered by popular expectations, apart from considerations of party and faction, about how a "good" public-spirited legislator should act.

In a multiparty system with no party dominant, the quest for "majority rule" dictates party representation in proportion to popular voting strength so that each group may participate fairly and proportionally in the process of coalition formation. In the American two-party system (more recently a one and one-half, or one-party system), a clear party majority results in each legislative house, which can rule to the extent that it holds together. One might suggest then that if a group fails to obtain legislative control, and therefore fails to obtain "political organization representation," it does not matter much in our system whether the party manages to achieve its proportionate share of the seats, which will be minority seats anyway, or achieves substantially less than its proportionate share. Such a suggestion misses the mark for several reasons. One is that the American state party system is sufficiently loose so that in many times and places issues actually are resolved by a process of cross-party coalition formation analogous to the operation of a multiparty system. Thus each group can justly claim a vital interest in having its fair share of elected spokesmen to participate in this decision-making process. Another reason is that maintenance of the political vigor and competition associated with a two-party system

[27] See note 11.

requires that the current minority party and its voters receive something approaching their proportionate share of seats. Otherwise the party cannot maintain candidacies and leadership, and cannot hold itself in position to be an effective "loyal opposition" to the in-group and to be a potential governing party itself.

In this country both aspects of representation are the products of a system of election of legislators in districts under a plurality (winner-take-all) rather than a proportional division rule. In one aspect (political organization representation) the pyramiding effect of legislative district pluralities culminates in creation of a political power system which takes the form of organization of the legislature by the majority faction. In the other aspect (general or re-election representation) the district system does create a spokesman for at least some people, and on some issues for all the people, in a designated geographic area.

When it was stated earlier in this section that the majority or plurality in a legislative district may obtain "some 100 per cent representation," and the minority "zero representation," at least until the next election, obviously the context was possible representation in the sense of "political organization representation." It is also true that a district minority whose candidate has lost, and which thus may be zero-weighted from the standpoint of political organization representation, will have some of its concerns attended to by the incumbent because of general or re-election representation considerations. It seems, however, that the facet of representation most relevant to reapportionment and redistricting is the facet of "*political organization representation*." We are, after all, dealing with constitutional ground rules for the great game of politics and not for a Mad Hatter's tea party where the sole purpose is population form rather than political substance. The other facet, "general or re-election representation," is an automatic, universal, ongoing process under almost any conceivable electoral system. It is supported also by a legislative ethic of total constituency service even apart from concern for re-election, and cannot be related meaningfully to reapportionment and redistricting.

A concern for effectiveness of representation in the sense of "political organization representation," i.e., in terms of effective access to the halls where the compromise and adjustment process of decision-making occurs and in terms of proportionate legislative power, links conceptually with proportional representation and goes all the way back to John Adams.[28] It calls for interpreting the premise of *political equality* of men as including the concept of *political equity* at the operative level of allocation of political power (award of legislative seats), as well as the rule of district population equality at the initial level of citizen balloting. At least a trace of this thought is found in opinions rendered in two challenges to multimember district systems which reached the Supreme Court after the basic 1964 "one-man, one-vote" rulings. Rejecting a challenge in a case from Georgia for lack of proof, Justice Brennan for the Court wrote in *Fortson* v. *Dorsey:*[29]

> It might well be that, designedly or otherwise, a multi-member constituency apportionment scheme, under the circumstances of a particular case, would operate to *minimize or cancel out the voting strength of racial or political elements of the voting population.* [Emphasis added.]

This thought that the ultimate constitutional consideration turns on a fair handling of the difficult problem of *actual voting power,* rather than mere population equality (or population proportionality in the case of multimember districts), was re-emphasized in 1966. Rejecting, again for lack of adequate proof, a challenge to multimember districts in a case from Hawaii, the Court nevertheless reaffirmed the *Fortson* principle and added:[30]

> It may be that this invidious effect can be more easily shown if, in contrast to the facts in *Fortson,* districts are large in relation to the total number of legislators, if districts are not appropriately subdistricted to assure distribution of legislators that are resident over the entire district, or if such districts characterize both houses of a bicameral legislature rather than one.

[28] Adams, in a letter to John Penn, advocated that the representative assembly mirror, in miniature, the people at large. *Works of John Adams,* IV, 204.

The renewed focus on the problem of maximizing the effectiveness of votes and ensuring appropriate minority representation impelled by the reapportionment revolution has prompted a renewed interest in PR-forms among several scholars. See, e.g., James K. Pollock, "Considering all Angles," *Nat. Civ. Rev.* 55 (1966), 374. "Proportional representation has not caught on in the United States because it has been called un-American and unconstitutional; it has been tied too much to the single transferable vote system and has always been dubbed as 'foreign.' Nevertheless, a proper list system, with a single choice within the list, would not only be an easy system to administer but would also result in fairer representation."

[29] 379 U.S. 433 (1965).

[30] 384 U.S. 73 (1966).

A requirement of numerically equal districts (or proportional in regard to multimember systems) may cure "malapportionment of people"; it may not touch, or may touch in odd ways, "malrepresentation of parties and interests." Although the latter problem is recognized in dicta in recent cases from Georgia and Hawaii, the Court understandably is loath to lay down firm rules for this area.

Courts have created and directed—perhaps overdirected—the reapportionment revolution because the normal political forces were locked in by frozen malapportionment systems. But as we go forward, the problem of malrepresentation of parties and interests, and the intricacies and alternative models of legislative election systems, may transcend judicial capability. To solve these problems we shall need to devise, by combined judicial and extrajudicial effort, additional constitutional standards responsive to more clearly articulated theories of representation and ground rules of political equity. This task, which should engage the attention of both political theorists and constitutional lawyers, has barely begun.

Meanwhile mathematics, at varying levels of sophistication, is being used both by courts and theorists to justify or attack particular systems of apportionment. The concluding section of this essay is devoted to a consideration of some of these uses, and especially to an analysis of weighted voting, which is discussed also in Chapters 15 and 16.

THE "HIGHER MATH" OF WEIGHTED VOTING AND MULTIMEMBER DISTRICTING

Mathematics plays interesting roles in reapportionment litigation and in discussions of representation. Much reapportionment mathematics has been grossly unsophisticated. But there are signs that growing interest in testing political precepts by analyzing properties of simple mathematical models may be the threshold of a major breakthrough in social science at both theoretical and operational levels.[31] However, the necessary depoliticization in mathematical models to avoid making them too complicated to be manageable, coupled with their esoteric, unchallengeable quality to the un-

[31] One of the better examples of attempting to preserve some political sophistication while pursuing mathematical methods is Stuart S. Nagel, "Simplified Bipartisan Computer Redistricting," *Stanford Law Review,* 17 1965), 863.

initiated, poses a continual danger of misinterpretation and misuse.

Reapportionment cases culminating in the Supreme Court rulings of 1964 were fought through at a rather unsophisticated mathematical level using three so-called measures of malapportionment, none of which related necessarily or directly to the theoretical goals of political realities of effective representation. The two simplest measures were the "population variance ratio" and the "maximum percentage deviation" in district population.

The former measure compares extremes. Thus, if the one largest district is 10,000 and the one smallest district is 5,000, the population variance ratio is 2 to 1. The latter measure also can indicate extremes, but may be used more flexibly. If the ideal average district were 7,500, and we again assume two extreme districts of 10,000 and 5,000 population, each would have a percentage deviation of 33.33 per cent. If a ten per cent maximum deviation limit were imposed, no district could vary by more than 750 people, as of the last census, from the average figure of 7,500. The statement assumes, of course, an apportionment base of gross population. Alternatives include citizen population, adult citizen population, resident registered voters, or actual voters. A resident registered voter base avoids the distortion—possibly a large distortion if the tolerance is only 750—which may be caused by temporary presence in sizeable numbers of college students, institutional inmates, tourists, and military personnel.[32]

The third measure, fictional "minimum electoral percentage," purports to indicate the least percentage of the total population which theoretically could "elect" a bare majority of the legislature. However, there is a serious fallacy in the very term "electoral percentage" because the measure considers *only gross population* in legislative districts and *not voter behavior*. This measure is obtained by ranking districts in order of population and by cumulating district population and seats from the least populous district upwards until a bare majority (one half plus one) of legislative seats is accounted for. Thus this measure, which is a kind of raw population measure and not an electoral control measure, ignores such factors as multiple candidates, use of multimember and mixed districting systems rather than single-member districts, the actual party divisions in each district, etc.—in short, the essence of representation. In a

[32] See *Burns* v. *Richardson*, 384 U.S. 73, 90–96 (1966).

legislature with a sizable number of districts a "perfect" population score under the fictional "minimum electoral percentage" measure would be near 50 per cent.[33] However, in a perfectly apportioned system with two parties of near-equal strength in all districts, the minimum effective *control* percentage in terms of actual voter behavior never would be much more than 25 per cent. In other words, assuming single-member districts, and only two candidates, a party which gained one-half plus one of the popular vote in one-half plus one of the districts could control the legislature. Attempts have been made to achieve more sophisticated measures, but they are equally aseptic in concentrating on malapportionment of people in a gross sense, and in ignoring the politics and policies of representation and the group dynamics of a democratic party system.[34]

These three measures which dominated the mathematical discussions in the leading reapportionment cases—population variance ratio, maximum percentage deviation from average district population, and electoral percentage—all relate to the districts from which legislators come. A different range of mathematical inquiry arises from intralegislative weighted voting and fractional voting systems which have been suggested in some states in the wake of the "one-man, one-vote" ruling.[35] These systems also have a close relation to multimember districting.

[33] As a measure solely of the *number of people residing* in an artificially designated set of districts, disregarding legislative control and disregarding factors of agreement and disagreement among themselves and their legislators, the measure is actual, not fictional.

[34] Glendon Schubert and Charles Press, "Measuring Malapportionment," *American Political Science Review,* 58 (1964), 302; Alan A. Clem, "Problems of Measuring and Achieving Equality of Representation in State Legislatures," *Nebraska Law Review,* 42 (1963), 622; "Measuring Legislative Malapportionment: In Search of a Better Yardstick," *Midwest Journal of Politics,* 7 (1963), 125.

[35] In weighted voting, each legislator has at least one full vote, and legislators from overpopulated districts have a proportionally increased number of votes. In fractional voting no legislator has more than one vote, but the underpopulated districts are preserved by giving their representatives a properly proportioned fraction of a vote. Thus fractional voting necessitates giving the populous areas a "live body" for each legislative vote to which their population entitles them; weighted voting pyramids votes in the more populous areas without adding additional legislators.

In terms solely of "bodies" available for lobbying, weighted voting underrepresents the more populous areas; fractional voting overrepresents the underpopulated areas. However, in terms of effective citizen influence on legislative outcomes, weighted voting overrepresents the larger (more heavily weighted) districts at the expense of the smaller districts. Citizens

Weighted voting and fractional voting plans are products of desire to retain some unequal population districts for the primary purpose of preserving a voice in the legislature for the smaller units. "One-man, one-vote" equalization still rules, so the proponents claim. Equalization takes the form of allocating to each legislator a number of votes proportional to the unequal population of the represented districts, rather than of equalizing districts in order to keep them proportional to the single and equal vote cast by each legislator.

More than a century ago weighted voting for the Kentucky legislature was considered but rejected by a state constitutional convention. Its virtues were thought to be: (1) it would preserve separate and independent representation for each unit; (2) it would minimize gerrymandering; (3) it would prevent creation of communities of disinterest, which occurs when sections of different sentiment are placed together solely for mathematical quota purposes; (4) it would give every citizen a better voice in the councils of state; (5) by preserving separate representation for each county, jealousy and ill-will between counties would be minimized.[36]

Since *Baker* v. *Carr* weighted or fractional voting devices have been mentioned or attempted in regard to some state legislatures (Washington, New Mexico, New York), but have never been effected.[37] The primary recent area of experimentation with these

---

in multimember districts have a similar advantage over citizens in single-member districts. See text below and notes 40ff.

[36] Francis Newton Thorpe, *A Constitutional History of the American People 1776–1850* (New York: Harper & Bros., 1898), II, 107–09.

[37] *Washington:* In June, 1964, a federal district court intervened and ordered weighted voting as a temporary remedy unless reapportionment by a special session intervened (*Thigpen* v. *Meyers,* 231 F. Supp. 938 [1964]). Subsequently the court rescinded the weighted-voting remedy and substituted a requirement that no legislation except necessary housekeeping bills be enacted until the legislature had accomplished reapportionment (not officially published). See National Municipal League, *Court Decisions on Legislative Apportionment* (1964), XXII, 169.

New Mexico: A state court in New Mexico, although finding no problem under the federal Constitution, nullified a weighted-voting plan because it was thought to be inconsistent with state constitutional clauses providing that, for various purposes, specified percentages of "members" shall cast votes. *Cargo* v. *Campbell,* Santa Fe County District Court, Civ. No. 33273 (January 8, 1964). A subsequent attempt to amend the state Constitution to permit weighted voting failed on September 28, 1965. *Washington Post,* October 13, 1965, p. 7, col. 1.

New York: In New York, a fractional voting provision was included in two of three reapportionment plans nullified by a federal district court, but

devices has been at the local governmental level in New York state. Before Baker, weighted voting systems were found in New York in Nassau County and in the Board of Estimate of New York City.[38] Since *Baker* state courts in New York have split on the constitutionality of attempts to honor "one-man, one-vote" for the county governing body (board of supervisors) by adopting weighted voting plans.[39]

Depending upon assumptions one makes concerning the maximum disparity in number of votes allocated to legislators, several observations may be made about the practical utility and likely political effects of weighted voting. A range in weights not exceeding 1 for the "smallest" legislator and 10 for the "largest" legislator, with a

---

the court expressly reserved judgment on possible use of fractional voting for local government reapportionment. *WMCA* v. *Lomenzo,* 238 F. Supp. 916 (1965). One member of the three-judge federal panel subsequently indicated a preference for weighted voting as an interim measure, but it was neither enacted nor ordered. *WMCA* v. *Lomenzo,* 246 F. Supp. 935, 956 (1965.)

[38] Jack B. Weinstein, "The Effect of the Federal Reapportionment Decisions on Counties and Other Forms of Municipal Government," *Columbia Law Review,* 65 (1965), 21; Samuel Krislov, *M.U.L.L.* 37 (June, 1965).

Note: While this manuscript was in press, the United States Supreme Court took its first look at the question of applicability of the "one-man, one-vote" principle to local government. Without squarely deciding the issue of applicability, the Court in three ambiguous opinions by Justice William O. Douglas intimated that the principle did apply at the local level but with more flexibility than at the state level. *Moody* v. *Flowers and Board of Supervisors of Suffolk County, New York* v. *Bianchi,* 387 U.S. 97 1967); *Sailors* v. *Board of Education of County of Kent,* 387 U.S. 105 1967); *Dusch* v. *Davis,* 387 U.S. 112 (1967).

[39] See, e.g., *Graham* v. *Board of Supervisors,* 267 N.Y.S. 2d 383, *modified* No. 316 (N.Y. Ct. App. July 7, 1966); *Bianchi* v. *Board of Supervisors,* Civil Action File No. 62–C–821 (E.D.N.Y. August 4, 1966); *Town of Greenburgh* v. *Board of Supervisors,* Index No. 6859–1965 (N.Y. Sup. Ct. July 6, 1966). See also, State of New York Executive Department, Office for Local Government, "Reapportionment," Information Bulletin No. 6 (November 14, 1966).

Note: While this manuscript was in press, and subsequent to the United States Supreme Court's local government decisions (see note 38), New York's highest state court, the Court of Appeals, held that appropriate weighted voting plans could be a way of complying with the "one-man, one-vote" principle at the local level. However, the court said that the burden of proof was on the proponent in each instance to demonstrate that proposed weighted voting plans were mathematically acceptable. On this basis, the court refused to approve the plans under review. *Iannucci* v. *Board of Supervisors of Washington County, et al., The Saratogian, Inc.* v. *Board of Supervisors of Saratoga County, et al.,* 20 N.Y. 2d 244, 282 N.Y.S. 2d 502, 229 N.E. 2d 195 (1967).

fairly even distribution through the districts, may be quite different from weights of 30 to 1 in regard to such factors as adequacy of representation for the larger unit and effectiveness of voice for the smaller unit. In some situations use of weighted voting, fractional voting, or a combined system, may be able to provide minority spokesmen for the less populous areas and at the same time, if the range of weights is not gross, avoid two unfortunate side effects regarding the more populous areas: (1) creation of a winner-take-all monolith, i.e., the unrepresentative character of having one urban representative with 30 votes rather than 30 men better expressing the divergent views of the area; (2) loss of effectiveness in relying on one man instead of 30 for all urban voting, lobbying, and committee work.

Apart from these aspects of practicality, some persons have constructed abstract models to test whether or not weighted voting really does produce equal (i.e., properly proportionalized) *voting power* in the legislature, and equal voter influence in the constituencies from which the legislators come. In an article entitled "Weighted Voting Doesn't Work," John F. Banzhaf points out that where population disparities are large a shift to weighted voting may not equalize voting power effectively.[40] His approach involves an analysis of the frequency with which each weighted-vote legislator might be a member of a minimal winning coalition. He gives the simple example of a prereapportionment five-district legislature, each legislator possessing one vote, but with one district having 50,000 population and the remaining four having 10,000 each. Applying weighted voting as a corrective still yields a five-district, five-man legislature; but one man now has five votes, the remaining four each have one vote. The five-vote man now has all the voting power and the other four have no voting power. By contrast, if five seats are allocated to the largest district, whether on a subdistricted basis or on an at-large basis, the prospect of disagreement within this district's delegation preserves the possibility that the legislators from the other districts may on occasion have effective voting power. Simple analyses of voting combinations can be done by hand; analysis for large weighted-vote legislatures requires a computer because

[40] John F. Banzhaf, III, "Weighted Voting Doesn't Work," *Rutgers Law Review,* 19 (1965), 317. See also his "Multi-Member Electoral Districts—Do They Violate the 'One Man, One Vote' Principle," *Yale Law Journal,* 75 (1966), 1309.

of the large number of possible combinations of minimal winning coalitions. Additional illustrations are given by Riker and Shapley in Chapter 15.

The effect just described applies only to *legislator* voting power in weighted voting systems. There is a second effect, concerning *citizen* influence on legislative outcomes, which applies *both* to weighted voting and to those multimember district systems where there is a mixture of single and multimember districts for the same legislative house. (From the standpoint of pure mathematical analysis the effect is virtually the same whether one weighted legislator casts five votes or a five-man multimember district delegation act in unison.) This second effect is that it can be demonstrated that there is an exaggeration of the effective *citizen* influence on legislative outcomes in favor of the citizens in the larger districts.

A short digression may help to put the mathematics in perspective. A citizen in an unweighted district votes for a legislator with a single vote. The citizen in the larger weighted-vote district is a "smaller frog in a bigger puddle." But if it is assumed that legislators try to follow constituents' wishes on major issues (delegate model), the citizen in the larger district is in a position to influence a larger bloc of votes. Stated another way, the measure of effective citizen influence on legislative outcomes would be the frequency with which the citizen could be a member of a minimal constituency majority, which in turn was part of a minimal winning coalition in the legislature. From this standpoint it can be shown that the total or over-all influence on legislative outcomes of the voters in a weighted voting or mixed districting system is *proportional to the square root of the population of the district.* The influence thus varies with district size rather than being equal or uniform in different-sized districts, which have been superficially "equalized" by assigning weighted votes or extra seats.[41]

[41] The best references for guidance in this mathematical analysis are the two Banzhaf articles, especially the latter on multimember districting. The analysis is more sophisticated than the simple population equalization (or proportionalization) test of the Supreme Court in *Reynolds* v. *Sims* and the other basic reapportionment cases. It takes one part of *Reynolds* seriously and seeks to measure "effective representation," a matter which cannot be reached by gross population analysis.

A further comment may help in visualizing the concepts involved. Laying aside for the moment the number of weighted votes allocated to a district, it is true that voter influence has an inverse relationship to district population, i.e., voter influence goes down as district population goes up because

This line of "higher math" analysis of *legislator* voting power and of *citizen* influence on legislative outcomes yields several hypotheses, some of which are discussed by Riker and Shapley. One, of course, is that in weighted voting operation in legislatures there is a bias in favor of the more heavily weighted *legislators*. Another is that this bias will be only a "gentle bias"[42] to the extent the following conditions are observed: (1) large legislative size, i.e., more than 20 members; (2) many different weights; (3) no legislator awarded a weight close to a majority of the total votes; (4) simple majority voting. These conditions are deemed to prevail in the electoral college[43] and in most local legislatures for which weighted voting has been proposed.

Proceeding to the more complicated and abstract matter of *influence of district citizens on legislative outcomes,* they suggest two further hypotheses depending on whether one assumes a free agent or delegate model for the citizen-legislator relationship. Under a free agent model, and with the same four assumed conditions, again only a gentle bias emerges in favor of the residents of the larger districts. Assuming a delegate model, even with these four conditions, a "very large bias"[44] emerges in favor of the voting power of the residents of

---

each voter is competing with more voters. *But* as district population goes up, voter influence does not go down (i.e., vary inversely) in exact linear proportion to district population shift. Rather it goes down more slowly and decreases inversely to the square *root* of the district population. For example, if district population goes from 50,000 to 100,000, voter influence superficially would seem to be half; but this is not so because the square root of 50,000 is more than half of the square root of 100,000. Therefore, to preserve parity with the voters in the 50,000 district, the voters in the 100,000 district do not need to have twice the number of legislators (or weighted votes) of the 50,000 district. Nevertheless they do receive a doubled quota of legislators (or weighted votes) under the current apportionment practice, are thus overcompensated, and their citizens acquire exaggerated influence on legislative outcomes.

[42] Lloyd S. Shapley and William H. Riker, "Weighted Voting: A Mathematical Analysis for Instrumental Judgments." This reference, and all subsequent references, are to the paper delivered at the December 1965 meeting of the American Society of Political and Legal Philosophy, a revised version of which appears as Chapter 15 of this volume. The quoted phrase here is from p. 21 of that earlier manuscript.

[43] The constitutionality of the electoral college system was challenged on other grounds in a suit in which the present writer was special counsel, filed in the Supreme Court's original jurisdiction in July, 1966. *Delaware* v. *New York et al.* (The original suit was against all other states and D.C.; however, a substantial number of states promptly requested realigmnent as parties plaintiff).

[44] Shapley and Riker, *op. cit.*

the larger districts and against the smaller district residents' voting power. (Without a delegate model there would seem to be little reason to worry about the mathematics of district population regarding representation.)

These hypotheses are subject to some provocative interpretations. Shapley and Riker find it anomalous that in the face of their hypotheses it is the representatives of the more populous (larger) districts who oppose weighted voting, and the representatives of the less populous (smaller) districts who favor it. There are to be sure certain ancillary advantages to the citizens of the smaller districts, such as preserving their community integrity and obtaining a separate and independent voice in the legislature. But they find such advantages to be "petty when compared with the prospective loss of influence over policy."[45] Whether or not the loss is "petty" or whether there is any "prospective loss" at all, depends upon the available alternatives. There is no prospective loss for the residents of the smaller districts unless other systems are obtainable under which residents of the smaller districts would have greater power, not mere mathematical power but effective political power.

The matter may appear in a different light, making the position of the residents of the smaller communities more understandable, if the alternative to weighted voting is really no power at all—or no separate and effective power. Just this alternative may result from a "one-man, one-vote" induced reapportionment, which dissolves the undersized districts and joins their citizens to larger districts controlled by citizens with different values. In such a situation it would be anomalous for the citizens of the smaller districts not to seek weighted voting; conversely, it would make little sense for the citizens of the larger districts to oppose weighted voting because their gain in power would more than counterbalance the voice preserved for the smaller districts.

Despite these considerations some lower courts in New York state have deemed weighted voting to be intrinsically unconstitutional and have ordered that compliance with the "one-man, one-vote" mandate take the traditional route of district realignments.[46] Granted

[45] *Ibid.*

[46] See, e.g., *The Saratogian, Inc.* v. *Bd. of Sups. of Saratoga County,* N.Y.S. 2d (1966); *Orlando* v. *Bd. of Sups. of Genesee County,* N.Y.S. 2d (1966); *Dickinson* v. *Harris* (Albany County), N.Y.S. 2d (1966). Also see a memorandum opinion of New York's highest court approving weighted voting for Erie County as a temporary expedient, *Graham* v. *Bd. of Sups.,*

the pro-large-district biases of weighted voting and multimember districting, the critical question often may be this: Is it really a "solution" to make a strictly mathematical correction of these biases by the all-too-common tactic of dissolving smaller districts and absorbing them into larger districts; or is the possible loss of power *and* voice stemming from such a solution a counterbalancing factor?

Is this not a realm of policy where views may differ legitimately, and where conclusions may differ depending on such "real" factors as the range and weights which a weighted voting system would entail, the composition of districts facing dissolution, the composition of districts to which they could be attached, the balance of party competition in the area, the role of parties, the nature and importance of committees, the governmental policies at stake, and so on? One can hypothesize either ridiculous examples of weighted voting, or situations where the weight spread is small, the factor of "voice" for the less populous districts is meaningful, and the weighted representatives neither create a monolith nor find themselves unable to discharge their own "constituency lobbying" and committee work effectively.[47] Considerations of this sort seem to underlie suggestions

---

274 N.Y.S. 2d 256 (1966), and not thoroughly airing the question of the validity of weighted voting as a permanent plan in situations where the range of weights and distortion would be minimal.

Note: While this manuscript was in press, New York's highest state court, the Court of Appeals, clarified its position by ruling that permanent weighted voting plans could be constitutional if the range of weights and voting disparities were not too great and placed the burden of proof on proponents to make this demonstration. See *Iannucci* v. *Board of Supervisors of Washington County, et al., The Saratogian, Inc.* v. *Board of Supervisors of Saratoga County, et al.* (note 39).

[47] Because of the population spread and the small number of legislators, Nassau County's system of weighted voting, which antedates *Baker* v. *Carr,* has been shown by mathematical analysis to produce zero voting power for the representatives of three of the six municipalities. John F. Banzhaf, "Weighted Voting Doesn't Work," *op. cit.,* p. 339. Under the weighted voting system disapproved for Herkimer County, by a court which relied on the kind of mathematical analysis outlined here, the distribution of votes was such that a voter in one town had, in abstract mathematical terms, 260 per cent more voting power than a citizen in another town. *Morris* v. *Bd. of Sups. of Herkimer County,* 273 N.Y.S. 2d 453 (1966).

By contrast a weighted voting system was judicially approved for Westchester County, subject to popular referendum, under which the population variance ratio, under conventional gross population analysis, was only 1.08 to 1 and the minimum percentage of the population needed to elect a majority of the board was 49.6 per cent. *Greenburgh* v. *Bd. of Supts. Westchester County,* 266 N.Y.S. 2d 998 (1966). Subsequently, however, further hearings were held.

of two commentators that the constitutionality of weighted voting, at least as applied to local government, should remain an open question governed by the facts of each case.[48]

When weighted voting is presented to a court the issue is not one of the wisdom of the policy but of its constitutionality on a given set of facts. That courts would differ under varying sets of facts might be expected. But in practice little evidence has been adduced concerning the operating realities of a given weighted voting system. New York's courts, insofar as they have given the matter more than casual attention, have differed not on empirical proof grounds but because of their different reactions on the one hand to the intrinsic uncertainty of the "one-man, one-vote" principle, and on the other hand to differing sets of mathematical abstractions. With so many variables and so much uncertainty, and there being as yet no agreed constitutional tests of fair and effective representation, it would seem that a Holmesian sense of the virtue of experimentation should leave such devices as weighted voting within the area of constitutional permissibility—however "unwise" the devices may be considered. The proviso of course is that the devices be aimed at achieving such legitimate corollary goals mentioned by the Supreme Court as preserving the integrity of various political subdivisions for party and community-of-interest purposes, and that the devices neither upset majority control nor underrepresent the more populous areas.

On the issue of constitutionality, one can make a most provocative comparison of weighted voting systems and multimember districting systems. As noted above, the square root factor regarding distortion of citizen influence in favor of the citizens in the larger districts applies to each system. A weighted voting system is really a multimember district system plus a requirement of delegation unity; and the degree of distortion caused by the unity factor adds only slightly to the rather gross distortion caused by the size factor (square root analysis) itself. Many state multimember district systems have passed muster in lower courts and been left undisturbed by the Supreme Court, although in no instance was the kind of "higher math" analysis suggested here made. Figures from selected states indicate the degree of overrepresentation (citizen influence on legislative out-

[48] Riker and Shapley, *op. cit.*, p. 14, where they say: "Thus it appears that for bodies like the electoral college and most local legislatures for which weighted voting has been proposed, the system of weighting does not greatly distort the influence of citizens." See also Weinstein, *op. cit.*, p. 41.

comes) possessed by the citizens in multimember districts compared to citizens in the single-member districts for the same legislative house. For the Texas House there are 52 single-member districts of substantially equal population whose citizens would be in parity (mathematically) regarding influence on legislative outcomes. But there also are several multimember districts, some of whose overrepresentation percentages would be: 145 per cent in two 6-member districts; 216 per cent in one 10-man district; 274 per cent in one 14-man district. For one 22-man district for the Florida House (Dade County–Miami) the overrepresentation is more than 350 per cent and approaches a ratio of five to one (100 per cent overrepresentation yielding a ratio of two to one).

For this reason, in a memorandum prepared for New York State (Office for Local Government) on weighted voting, the present writer suggested the following conclusion: "Wholly apart from the theoretical wisdom of weighted voting as a representation device, it cannot be viewed as intrinsically unconstitutional at the local governmental level until: (1) there is a ruling that use of multi-member districts of varying sizes, or mixed use of multi-member districts and single-member districts in one legislative house, is unconstitutional; or (2) there is a *documented* finding (burden of proof on the challenger) that such aspects of a legislator's work as committee activity and general lobbying are so important at the local governmental level that use of a weighted voting plan for ultimate decision-making of county boards or city councils is inadequate to provide citizens their due under a developed 'one man-one vote' concept."[49]

The essence of the matter is that in mathematical analysis made at the level of the Supreme Court's "sixth-grade arithmetic" of 1964, on which the reapportionment revolution was based, weighted voting (or a multimember system with varying sizes of districts) may satisfy the simple "one-man, one-vote" proportionality principle. If analyzed at a more sophisticated mathematical level, unexpected (disproportional) variants appear in abstract measures of *citizen* power to influence legislative results. Further, if such a focus on equality (i.e., proportionality) of power to influence *actual* legislative results becomes important—which some have argued was the root issue all

[49] Robert G. Dixon, Jr., "Memorandum on Implementing 'One Man-One Vote' With Special Emphasis on Weighted Fractional Voting," October 11, 1966, p. 56. See also my forthcoming *Democratic Representation: Reapportionment in Law and Politics* (New York: Oxford University Press, 1968).

along anyway, rather than the single question of equality of district populations—a further anomaly appears. We are then seeking a goal which cannot be achieved under the traditional American single- and multimember district system, no matter how much the district lines and district populations are tinkered.[50] Despite the apparent contrary premise of *Reynolds* v. *Sims,* a district system, and citizen equality in affecting legislative *outcomes,* cannot coexist.

We face a rich field for analysis. Both the Supreme Court's characterization of the nature of the reapportionment issue, and the derivative reapportionment mathematics, must come to terms with party government weak or strong, with policy alignments that transcend party, in short with the group dynamics of American politics, else we may create a new scholasticism, proceeding with an assurance of method equalled by its confusion in goals.

[50] The well-known tendency of district systems to overrepresent the dominant party has been expressed in a mathematical formula. If all the districts are single-member, if at least 90 per cent of the popular vote is distributed among no more than two parties, and if the popular strength of the two parties is equally distributed throughout the state, it can be shown that the ratio of the seats won by the parties is approximately equal to the cube of the statewide popular vote each receives. M. G. Kendall and A. Stuart, "The Law of Cubic Proportion in Election Results," *British Journal of Sociology,* 1 (1950), 163.

WEIGHTED VOTING AND THE THEORY OF REPRESENTATION

15

WEIGHTED VOTING: A MATHEMATICAL ANALYSIS FOR INSTRUMENTAL JUDGMENTS

WILLIAM H. RIKER and LLOYD S. SHAPLEY

The purpose of this essay is to clarify a particular question of political justice by means of a mathematical analysis and thus to demonstrate the utility of such inquiry for political philosophy. Traditionally political philosophy has had two tasks: one is to determine what justice is; the other is to determine whether or not particular instruments are appropriate for realizing given conceptions of justice. Except for a modern Pythagorean who seeks justice in formal symmetry, mathematics is not likely to be useful in the former task. But it can be useful in the latter because of the clarification it permits.

The particular subject of this volume, representation, is well suited for the demonstration of this utility because representation is not an end-in-itself, but a means to achieve some other goal. The system of representation creates a policy-making body. But, since any relatively small body—whether representative or not—can make policy, the purpose of representation is not primarily to create a body, but rather to create one that involves a large electorate in the policy-making process. And the way the electorate is involved expresses some conception of justice, e.g., preference for hereditary aristocracy, preference for equality, and so on. Whether the system of representation expresses the given conception of justice well or badly is an instrumental problem. If a mathematical analysis can be shown to clarify it, then the utility of formal methods will be demonstrated for that case and by analogical inference for other instances of instrumental judgment as well.

The particular subject of this essay, weighted voting in legislatures, is also well suited for a demonstration of the utility of mathematical methods inasmuch as the consequences of weighted voting are not immediately obvious. Until the recent efforts at reorganization of the representative system as required by the rulings in *Baker* v. *Carr* and *Reynolds* v. *Sims,* the United States had had very little experience with weighted voting, and hence scholars have had no occasion to analyze its consequences. Recently, however, we have had some experiments with weighted voting and, if the analysis in this essay is correct, the social circumstances suggest that the legislators involved completely misunderstood its consequences. Paradoxically, those who its advocates say are its main beneficiaries are in fact those who are probably hurt by it, while those who its opponents say are its main victims are in fact those who probably benefit from it. To the elucidation of that paradox we now turn.

AN INDEX OF INFLUENCE

The moral proposition expressed in the Supreme Court's insistence on "one-person, one-vote" is that each citizen ought to have—through the medium of his representation—the same chance as every other citizen to influence the outcomes of the legislative process. The technical problem of realizing this moral proposition in institutions is that of finding a device that preserves the equality of citizens when their influence is funneled through their representatives.

It has been assumed that legislative technicians have two variables they can adjust to retain this equality in spite of the funnel: the size of districts and the vote of representatives. One alternative is to make both districts and votes exactly equal. In this case, if there are n legislators, then each legislator's district has the same number of citizens as each other district, and each legislator has $1/n$ of the total votes in the legislature. This is the system we have heretofore supposedly used almost exclusively in local, state, and national legislatures, despite some gross variations in the size of districts and a surprisingly frequent occurrence of multiple-member districts. The other alternative, so-called weighted voting, is to make both districts and votes unequal but proportionate to each other. Thus, if there are s votes in the legislature, if there are m citizens in the area for which the legislature sits, and if a specific district contains a given fraction, $k\,m$, of the citizens, where $0 < \mathrm{k} < 1$, then the legislator from that district has $k\,s$ of the votes in the legislature. It is on the basis of the assumption that these alternatives are equivalent that weighted voting is advocated.

The difficulty with this assumption is that what counts in the legislature for preserving the equality of citizens' influence is not the weight of the legislators' votes but the actual influence a given weight has over the legislative outcomes. If it turns out that weight and influence are different things, then weighted voting cannot preserve the equality of citizens as influence is funneled through the legislators.

In order to discover whether or not weight and influence are the same, we need a measure of influence that is independent of weight. Such a measure is immediately at hand in the form of the Shapley-Shubik power index, which is a specialization of Shapley's value for n-person games.[1] This index is based on the following considerations:

1. For each weighted vote, one wants to know what chance the legislator who casts it has of influencing an outcome of the legislative process.

2. Influence over an outcome involves, at the very minimum, membership in a winning coalition, i.e., being on the winning side

[1] L. S. Shapley and Martin Shubik, "A Method for Evaluating the Distribution of Power in a Committee System," *American Political Science Review* 48 (1954), 787–92; L. S. Shapley, "A Value for n-Person Games," *Annals of Mathematics Study No. 28* (Princeton: Princeton University Press, 1953), pp. 307–17.

on a division. Certainly one who is on the losing side is not ordinarily thought to have much influence.

3. Membership of a given legislator in a winning coalition is significant for influencing the outcome only if the coalition is *minimal,* or if it has a winning subcoalition that is minimal and contains that legislator. Here a minimal winning coalition is defined as a coalition that would cease to be winning if any member were subtracted from it. The rationale of this consideration is obvious: If a given legislator could have voted the other way without affecting the ability of the coalition, or of any subcoalition, to win, then his influence is nil.

4. The uniquely influential position in a minimal winning coalition is that of the member who was added last, in a chronological sense. This is conventionally known as the *pivot* position. The paramount importance of this position may not be completely obvious, but the following model may make it clear: Let there be both supporters and opponents of a bill and some members who are undecided. Let the manager of the bill persuade by various inducements (such as rewriting the bill, promising votes on another bill, etc.) enough of the undecided to support the bill so that the supporters become a minimal majority. In such circumstance, when the vote occurs, some of the undecided who were not approached by the bill's manager may nevertheless vote for the bill, perhaps because they have concluded that their vote will make a good impression on their constituents. One can say that the original supporters and especially those undecideds who become supporters for a consideration have influenced the outcome. But it is very hard to say the same thing about the undecideds who become supporters without solicitation, i.e., those who joined after the pivot. These latter have not influenced the form of the bill which passes, nor have they traded influence on this bill for influence on another one. All the unsolicited supporters have gained is, if anything, some personal advantage for themselves, which can hardly be regarded as the transmission of voters' influence. So we shall assume that their support is without significance for our purpose.

Similarly, we may discount the influence of the supporters who preceded the pivot. Typically, the main inducement the manager of a bill offers to the undecideds is a modification of the bill into something they can support. Presumably the original supporters were satisfied with the bill as originally introduced, so that each modification lessens the desirability of the bill for them. Hence the undecideds who have become supporters after modification are more satisfied with the modified form of the bill, while the original supporters are less satisfied. Carrying this argument to extremes, the single legislator most satisfied is the last one added to the minimal winning coalition, that is, the pivot.

This argument holds, of course, even if the currency used to pay the undecideds is promises about votes on other bills, promises about patronage, or the like. Arrange the undecideds on a scale of hostility to the bill as originally introduced and consider the problem of the manager of a bill who is soliciting their support with promises and so on. Presumably the least hostile will become a supporter for the lowest price (i.e., the smallest promise), the next least hostile for the next higher price, and so forth. Since we can assume the manager of the bill has limited resources, we can assume also that he will buy the least hostile undecided first, the next least hostile second, and so forth. Thus, clearly the highest price he must pay goes to the legislator in the pivot position. This is not to say that only the pivotal legislator is influential. Rather it is that the pivotal legislator is significantly more influential than any other on a given roll call.

The model on which this conclusion is based may seem unrealistic if one looks only at the outcomes of roll calls as they appear in the printed record with its alphabetical list of yeas and nays, for the pivot is not labeled, and one cannot tell which voters on the winning side were original supporters, persuaded undecideds, or unsolicited undecideds. But in the actual history of the formation of the coalition of original supporters and persuaded undecideds on any important roll call, there is always a manager for each side, and managers seldom seek more votes than their count of the house tells them is necessary to win. And it is in that more historical sense that one affirms influence to be concentrated at the pivotal position.

In many cases, of course, the legislators' decisions will not be so precisely ordered in time, nor their views on the legislation so precisely ordered in a "scale of hostility," that an exact identification of the pivotal man would be possible, even if the full history of the bill could be known. But this is not a serious drawback, since we are ultimately concerned not with votes on individual bills, but with the distribution of power inherent in the voting system itself. Those legislators who are assumed to have just missed the pivot position, in a doubtful case, will nevertheless be recognized in the power index, to the extent that other, equally likely arrangements (in time or in viewpoint) exist in which they would be pivotal.

5. Adherents may come to a coalition in any order, and all orders

are equally probable.[2] This is admittedly a *ceteris paribus* assumption but there is a strong reason for adopting it when one is analyzing a constitutional provision like the method of legislative voting. After a legislature is elected, and the political viewpoints, personal groupings, and even the bargaining abilities of the members are known, one *might* be able to make a fairly accurate forecast of what minimal winning coalitions will occur and which legislators will be pivots—i.e., hold the "balance of power"—on the important bills. But before elections, the expectation of any particular winning coalition or of any particular losing coalition is quite uncertain.[3] Furthermore, in any particular session, legislators are faced with diverse issues, each of which in a poorly disciplined system is likely to produce a different set of supporters and opponents and to arrange the opponents and undecideds differently on a scale of hostility. And when one is writing an apportionment statute which is expected to last through many elections, the uncertainty is compounded.

The Shapley-Shubik index embodies all these considerations. It is a measure of the chance that a legislator with a given weight, w, has to influence the outcomes of the legislative process when the outcomes are visualized as influenced by the means described in the foregoing model. Naming this chance the *power*, ϕ, of w (i.e., ϕ_w), the index is:

$$\phi_w = \frac{p\,(w)}{n!}$$

where n is the number of legislators and where "$p\,(w)$" signifies the number of permutations of n in which some particular legislator having weight w is the pivot.

To show that this index embodies all the previous considerations, we observe that the denominator on the right side, $n!$ (read: "n

[2] A variant assumption could be adopted at this point, in which all divisions between yeas and nays are considered as equally probable, rather than all orderings of members. Although the numerical values obtained are slightly different, we know of no significant qualitative differences that would arise from defining the power index in this way. See John F. Banzhaf III, "Weighted Voting Doesn't Work: A Mathematical Analysis," *Rutgers Law Review,* 19 (1965), 317–43.

[3] In large bodies with a relatively low degree of party discipline (such as most legislatures in the United States), it is not possible to predict coalitions and pivots even after the election. See William H. Riker and Donald Niemi, "The Stability of Coalitions on Roll Calls in the House of Representatives," *American Political Science Review,* 54 (1962), 58–65.

factorial," that is, $1 \cdot 2 \cdot \ldots n$), includes consideration 5, inasmuch as $n!$ is the number of possible permutations of n. Thus it takes equal account of all possible ways in which the legislators might be ranked in order of hostility to, or support of, a measure. The numerator, on the other hand, reflects consideration 1, 2, 3, and 4, which successively narrowed the meaning of influence from influence over outcomes (1), to membership in a winning coalition (2), to membership in a minimal winning coalition (3), to holding of the pivot position (4). In words, the power index might be expressed thus:

Power of a legislator of a given weight = the ratio: (Number of possible pivots for that legislator) / (All possible arrangements of legislators in historically distinct coalitions)

Since we are primarily concerned with the question of whether or not influence and weight are different things, it is also important to construct a measure of the relationship between "power," as it has just been defined, and the nominal voting strength, w. To this end we define the *power ratio* ρ_w associated with the weight w, as

$$\rho_w = \phi_W \div \frac{w}{W},$$

where W is the total weight of all members. Thus, the power ratio is the power index of a legislator divided by his *relative* weight in the assembly. We note that the power indices of all the members must add up to 1, since there is exactly one pivot associated with each arrangement. Since the relative weights also add up to 1, we see that, when weight and influence are identical, the power ratio for each weight will be equal to 1. When weight and influence are different, however, some of the power ratios will exceed 1, and others will be less. Thus, the power ratio gives a quick indication of the "bias" inherent in a given weighted voting system.

It would be well to emphasize here that for a system that includes well-disciplined and long-lasting political parties, the foregoing discussion is inadequate. Not only would the cohesiveness of each party's voting behavior have to be measured, but we should have to inquire into the process whereby the party reaches its decision on how to vote on a bill, whether to press for modifications, and so on. The decisive battles, if the parties are few and large, would be fought in the caucus rooms, or in party councils far removed from the formal law-making machinery. The theoretical tools of pivot analysis and the power index might still be applied, in principle, to such strong-party situations. The practical difficulty lies in the fact that the mathematical model of the process is no longer given to us ready-made in the Constitution or by-laws of the legislative body, and we are confronted with the problem of translating an informal or semiformal system of partisan procedures into formal terms.

Even with weak or unstable parties, there are, of course, some kinds of legislative influence that the power index does not directly reflect, e.g., the influence of legislative officers who are more likely to be managers than pivots. Yet officers are agents of members, and at the time of election of officers, members transmit some of their constituent's influence to officers. The index may be interpreted therefore as attributing to back-benchers (though perhaps not in a precise way) some of the influence they have by election transmitted to house officers. One kind of influence it does not reflect, however, is the influence of nonelected leaders (e.g., committee chairmen in the House of Representatives, who achieve their special influence mostly by seniority).

This failure aside, however, it seems that the Shapley-Shubik index embodies the decisive source of influence in voting bodies. It would give us added confidence in this assertion if we had some empirical evidence that this was the case. Unfortunately, such evidence is hard to come by. One of the authors has attempted to assess whether or not members of the French Assembly who moved from party to party in 1953–54 displayed an effort to improve their influence as measured by the index (applied in this case to parties, not individuals). The outcome of the test was equivocal, although it was apparent that the smaller parties, which have typically less power than weight, were more unstable than the larger ones.[4]

In spite of the absence of hard evidence on its adequacy, the index seems to capture, better than any other available measure, our intuitive notions of power.[5] Consideration of simple numerical examples, where all the possibilities can be seen and kept in mind,

[4] William H. Riker, "A Test of the Adequacy of the Power Index," *Behavioral Science,* 4 (1959), 120–31.

[5] William H. Riker, "Some Ambiguities in the Notion of Power," *American Political Science Review,* 58 (1964), 341–49.

tends to reinforce the intuitive appeal of the model, by providing many instances where the power indices satisfactorily straighten out the distorted picture given by the raw weights.

RELATION BETWEEN POWER AND WEIGHT

The interesting feature of the power index for the present consideration is that influence as measured by the power index is often, indeed usually, quite different from weight. One extreme and dramatic example often repeated in the literature is this: Assume a three-person committee with 50 votes for *A*, 49 votes for *B*, and 1 vote for *C*, wherein 51 votes are required to win. There are three voters and hence $1 \cdot 2 \cdot 3 = 6$ possible arrangements, which are here listed with the pivotal member indicated by a superscript of an asterisk:

AB^*C	BCA^*
AC^*B	CA^*B
BA^*C	CBA^*

In this case the power indices are $\phi_{50} = 4/6 = 2/3$, $\phi_{49} = 1/6$, $\phi_1 = 1/6$. Here *A* and *C* have more power than (relative) weight, and *B* has less, the power ratios being $\rho_{50} = 1.33$, $\rho_{49} = .34$, $\rho_1 = 16.67$.

In the previous example, the least-weighted member gains influence at the expense of the medium-weighted one. More frequently, however, the least-weighted loses. An extreme example is the five-member committee weighted (12, 6, 6, 4, 3), in which 16 can win. Here, the least-weighted member, 3, is a dummy, since he could not figure in any minimal winning coalition. For this member to pivot, some combination of some of the other four members must sum to 13, 14, or 15 so that, when 3 is added, a minority becomes a majority. But no subset of (12, 6, 6, 4) sums to 13, 14, or 15. So the three-vote member is powerless and the indices are $\phi_{12} = 1/2$, $\phi_6 = 1/6$, $\phi_4 = 1/6$, and $\phi_3 = 0$.

Most real weighted voting systems that have been examined do not display quite these extremes, but in few of them are power and weight identical. In Nassau County, New York, some of the members of the Board of Supervisors are actually dummies who never pivot.[6] In the Electoral College, the most heavily weighted states have a power ratio of about 1.05, which means that they have about 5 per

[6] Banzhof, *op. cit.* The 1964 weights are given as (31, 31, 28, 21, 2, 2); the corresponding indices are 1/3, 1/3, 1/3, 0, 0, 0.

cent more chance to pivot than their weight would indicate, while the least-weighted states have a power ratio of about .97, or about 3 per cent less power than relative weight.[7] These are not startling variations, although they may have some practical significance. In the French National Assembly in 1953–54, among approximately sixty distributions of weights of parties for which the indices were calculated, four showed that the smallest parties had power ratios of less than .80, and in one instance the ratio was less than .60.[8]

Of course, power and weight can turn out to be exactly proportional (that is, exactly equal for each legislator so that all power ratios are 1), although it seems that such cases are relatively rare. In a marginal note we list all the exactly proportional systems we have discovered or had brought to our attention.[9] Although we do not know a general rule to construct such systems and therefore cannot estimate their likelihood, we do know that they must meet at least one highly restrictive condition. A necessary condition for power and weight to be proportional is that the *sum* of the weights, when they are expressed in whole numbers without a common factor, must be a divisor of $n!$. (If fractional weights appear, then their least common denominator multiplied by the sum of the weights must be a divisor of $n!$. Thus, in the case (1, 1, 1, 2 1/3, 2 1/3, 2 1/3) the sum is 10 and the LCD is 3; the product of these numbers is 30, which is a divisor of $6! = 720$.) The reason for this condition is that the indices are expressible as ratios of integers of which the denominator is $n!$. If, therefore, weight is to equal power, relative weights must also be expressible as a ratio of which the de-

[7] Irwin Mann and L. S. Shapley, "The *a priori* Voting Strength of the Electoral College" in Martin Shubik (ed.), *Game Theory and Related Approaches to Social Behavior* (New York: Wiley, 1964).

[8] William H. Riker, "A Test of the Adequacy of the Power Index," *Behavioral Science,* 4 (1959), 120–31.

[9] Particular cases are (5, 3, 3, 1), with seven votes required to win; (9, 9, 4, 4, 4) with 16 to win; (43, 43, 43, 43, 43, 20, 20, 20, 20, 20), with 158 to win. There are also the following classes of examples, in each of which n denotes the number of members: $(x, 1, 1, \dots, 1)$ where $x = b + [(b^2 - b)/(n - b)]$ and b is any whole number less than $\sqrt{n}$ (for example, (2 2/3, 1, 1, 1, 1) with 3 to win); $(1, 1, 1, y, y, \dots, y)$ where $y = 2 + [1/n - 3)]$ and n is even and greater than 4 (for example, (1, 1, 1, 2 1/3, 2 1/3, 2 1/3) with 5 to win); and $(1, 1, 1, z, z, \dots, z)$ where $z = 2 + [1/(n - 1)]$ and n is odd and greater than 3 (for example, (1, 1, 1, 2 1/4, 2 1/4) with 4 to win). In all these classes the terms in brackets [ ] do not affect the outcome but serve only to equalize the power ratios. Finally there are all cases generated from these particular cases and classes of cases by multiplication of each weight by a constant.

nominator is $n!$. This necessary condition is in itself quite restrictive, but the actual number of cases of identical power and weight is even smaller than this condition indicates, for it is not a sufficient condition. This is easily shown by the counterexample of the set of weights (3, 2, 1) which sums to $n!$ but has the following indices: $\phi_3 = 2/3$, $\phi_2 = 1/6$, $\phi_1 = 1/6$.

It seems clear, therefore, that power and weight are not usually identical and are often quite different. This fact indicates that the assumption on which weighted voting is built is false. It is not the case that unequally weighted legislators (whose weights are, however, proportionate to the sizes of their districts) always or even occasionally funnel citizen's influence into legislation without distortion. Hence one might conclude that weighted voting cannot satisfy the Court's insistence on "one-person, one-vote." Such a conclusion would be somewhat premature, however, because it may well be that the distortion induced by weighting is less than the distortion which courts will come to allow as a result of variations in the size of districts which are supposed to be equal.[10] We therefore turn to an examination of the degree of bias generated by weighted voting.

DEGREE OF BIAS IN WEIGHTED VOTING

For large bodies (e.g., over twenty members) with weighted voting, in which there are many different weights and no weight close to a majority, a good approximation to the power indices is that they are proportional to $w/(W-w)$, where w is the weight of a given member and W is the total vote. The constant of proportionality is somewhat less than 1, being at most $(n-1)/n$ where n is the number of members. Since $(W-w)$ is close to W when w is small, the smaller members will have power ratios approximately equal to that constant of proportionality, and hence power indices slightly less than their relative weights. The larger members will have power ratios correspondingly greater than 1. This indicates a general bias in favor of the more heavily weighted members. But it also places an

[10] Just how much variation in district size the Supreme Court will allow is now uncertain, for in *Reynolds* v. *Sims,* 377 U.S. 533 at 578, the Court announced its intention of proceeding on a case-by-case basis rather than of laying down guidelines. In that same case, however, Mr. Chief Justice Warren frequently observed that for one voter to have twice the influence of another was "inconceivable."

upper limit on the degree of bias, for it means that the *spread* between the power ratio of the largest member and that of the smallest member is about equal to the difference between their relative weights, and hence will seldom exceed the relative weight of the largest member. (In the Electoral College, which is the largest weighted "legislature" for which the actual computations have been carried out, this spread amounts to about 8 per cent, as already remarked. This proves to be a rather small bias when compared with the intentional advantage given the smaller states by the framers, in the form of two extra votes to each state regardless of population.[11])

TABLE 1

Weight	*Power Index (%)*	*Power Ratio*
32	6.43	1.023
31	6.22	1.021
29	5.79	1.016
28	5.58	1.014
27	5.37	1.012
24 (4 seats)	4.74	1.006
23 (3 seats)	4.53	1.004
21	4.12	0.999
20 (2 seats)	3.92	0.997
17	3.31	0.991
13 (2 seats)	2.51	0.984
10	1.92	0.978
9 (2 seats)	1.73	0.976
8	1.53	0.974
7 (3 seats)	1.34	0.972
5 (2 seats)	0.95	0.969
4	0.76	0.967
3 (6 seats)	0.57	0.965
2	0.38	0.963
1 (2 seats)	0.19	0.962

An analysis of a recently proposed system of weighted voting for the New Mexico State Senate yields similar results, as shown in Table 1. Thirty-seven districts were proposed, with votes in the Senate ranging from 1 to 32 in proportion to population, the total vote being 509. The power ratios reveal a small but systematic bias in favor of the larger districts. The total "spread," however, is only 6.1 per cent, which cannot be considered a very serious distortion of the intended allocation of power among the senators.

[11] Mann and Shapley, *op. cit.*

Flukish exceptions do exist to the general rule just described for obtaining the indices approximately. For example, the case (12, 6, 6, 4, 3) previously discussed can be generalized to any number of members, thus: (... ... ..., 6, 6, 4, 3). If the unspecified weights are all multiples of six, and if their total is a multiple of twelve, then the smallest member will always be a dummy: $\phi_3 = 0$. Moreover (as the reader can verify in the five-member example), the four-vote member is as powerful as a six-vote member: $\phi_4 = \phi_6$, which makes for a considerable spread in their power ratios. Though possible, a gross distortion of this kind is extremely unlikely to occur in a real situation.

Such exceptions aside, it is safe to assume that the bias given by difference of the weights of the members is not very great so long as one considers only the weights and powers of the members. But the Supreme Court asks us to look beyond the legislature, and to consider also the influence of the citizens.[12] And this introduces complications.

The Supreme Court seems to ask that each citizen have the same chance as each other citizen to influence legislative outcomes. This suggests that power indices should be calculated for citizens rather than legislators. And for this calculation we have two quite different models available, according to whether the representative is regarded as a Burkean legislator, who acts for the whole area represented without consideration of the particular interests of his constituency, or as a delegate, who on each issue acts only on behalf of his constituency. We will call the first model the "free agent" representative and the second model the "delegate" representative.

In the free agent case, where representatives supposedly seek to satisfy the general interest, it is difficult to say that the citizens have any power at all, for they have abdicated to their legislators. But, since citizens do elect legislators, we can conventionally assume that each citizen has a power index of ϕ_w/d where w is the weight of his representative in the legislature and d is the size of his district. In this case, therefore, the power of citizens can vary only as much as the power *ratios* of the legislators, provided that the weights are assigned in proportion to district size. And, as we have already indicated, this is not usually a great variation.

12 "And the right of suffrage can be denied by a debasement or dilution of the weight of a citizen's vote just as effectively as by wholly prohibiting the free exercise of the franchise." Mr. Chief Justice Warren in *Reynolds* v. *Sims*, 377 U.S. 533, at 555.

At the other extreme, where legislators act simply as "funnels" for their constituencies' decision, as, for example, in the Electoral College, the calculation of citizens' power indices is much more complex, but the result is quite startling. In general, the citizen in a small district proves to have a much smaller power index than the citizen of a large district. Without involving ourselves in excessive mathematical detail, let us see why this must be so.

Consider the following model: An election in which there is a single, overriding issue—e.g., which party is to rule—is held for a weighted-vote legislature with weights proportional to the sizes of the different districts. The process of coalition-formation—i.e., campaigning—may be thought of as assembling supporters for a "platform," which can be modified and reformulated to attract increasing numbers of supporters. (It is easy to visualize this in the Electoral College, where the platform, in the present sense, is essentially just the Presidential candidate and his running mate. In the kind of legislative system we are now imagining, where the legislators are mere ciphers transmitting the popular will, the analogous thing to the Presidential ticket is not so much the several legislative candidates, as the bundle of opinions they carry, or the program that they advocate.) The election is decided by the fact that one of the competing bundles of opinions obtains the support of a winning coalition of the whole electorate, that is, more than 50 per cent of the voters in enough districts to make up a weighted majority in the legislature. For simplicity of exposition, we are assuming a unicameral system, without executive veto.

In the process of building up a coalition, the citizens are assumed to join (i.e., decide to vote for it) in random order. But the order in which majorities in the various districts occur will not be purely random. To see this, suppose at some point exactly 30 per cent of the population supports a coalition. Since its supporters join in random order, each district will have about 30 per cent of its population in the coalition. But this will not be exact. The larger districts will, usually, have closer to 30 per cent than the smaller, simply because they represent larger samples of the total population. In other words, whatever the over-all percentage is at any one time, the district percentages will be dispersed around that number, with the smaller districts having the larger standard deviation.

Thus, as the coalition approaches winning size, adding citizens drawn at random from the population, the various districts will begin to swing over and give the coalition majority support, but not all at once. Because each district is a unique sample of the total population, some districts will come in sooner than others. And they do not do it in purely random order because of the differences in standard deviation. The big districts will tend to come in near the middle of the list. This definitely enhances their chance of pivoting. In consequence, a big district has distinctly more power than the power index of its delegate in the legislature would indicate. A new bias, under the delegate representative model, is therefore superimposed on the bias already discussed; both favor the larger districts at the expense of the smaller.

The magnitude of this effect is surprisingly large. An estimate using techniques of probability theory, supported by numerical computations for some particular cases, indicates that the citizens' power indices are multiplied by a factor proportional to the square root of their district populations when we pass from the free agent model to the delegate model. For example, if district *A* has 10,000 citizens and its delegate has one vote in the legislature, and if district *B* has 40,000 citizens and its delegate has four votes, then a citizen of *B* has roughly twice the chance of being pivotal in an election as a citizen of *A*. If district *C* has 250,000 citizens, then its citizens are individually five times as powerful (under the assumptions of the delegate model) as those of *A*. A very considerable advantage accrues to the citizens of large districts.[13]

The principle behind this "square root" bias in such two-step voting systems can be expressed in a few words independently of our detailed definition of power. The influence of the citizens is most strongly felt and exercised in close elections. But if the over-all election is close, then all other things being equal, a large district is more apt to be closely divided than a small district because the larger district is a better sample of the total population.

To compare the effects of the two models—free agent and delegate representative—we present in Table 2 an example of a ten-seat

[13] This conclusion can be supported by an independent argument (which is closely related to the variant described in note 2). Let each citizen assume that all other citizens vote purely at random, and let him ask what the chance is of his vote deciding the outcome. This number is of course very small, since it requires essentially a tie vote in his district, coupled with a nearly evenly divided legislature. However, this small number again proves to be approximately proportional to the square root of the size of the citizen's district.

TABLE 2*

		Powers of legislators			Powers of citizens		
1.	2.	3.	4.	5.	6.	7.	8.
Size of district	Votes in assembly	Ideal case	Free Agent case	Delegate case	Ideal case	Free Agent case	Delegate case
400	4	.04	.0333	.0178	.0001	.0000833	.0000445
400	4	.04	.0333	.0178	.0001	.0000833	.0000445
400	4	.04	.0333	.0178	.0001	.0000833	.0000445
400	4	.04	.0333	.0178	.0001	.0000833	.0000445
900	9	.09	.0921	.0737	.0001	.0001023	.0000819
900	9	.09	.0921	.0737	.0001	.0001023	.0000819
900	9	.09	.0921	.0737	.0001	.0001023	.0000819
1600	16	.16	.1504	.1606	.0001	.0000940	.0001003
1600	16	.16	.1504	.1606	.0001	.0000940	.0001003
2500	25	.25	.2897	.3866	.0001	.0001159	.0001546

* Columns 6, 7, 8 are columns 3, 4, 5 divided by column 1. Column 4 gives the calculated power indices of the legislators in the assembly. (Their power ratios may be found by multiplying column 7 by 10,000.) Column 8 gives the approximate power index of a typical citizen in each district, in the two-step voting model. It was obtained by mlutiplyng column 7 by the square root of the district size and then rescaling, so that the sum of the powers of all citizens would total 1.

assembly, in which the legislators have one vote for each 100 citizens represented. (We have purposely made the total population a round number and the district sizes perfect squares, in order to make the relationships among the numbers in the table more apparent.) In this example, there are 10,000 citizens, so that under the ideal of equality embodied in the phrase "one-man, one-vote," the ideal power index for citizens would be .0001. It is apparent that neither interpretation of weighted voting achieves this ideal, and that in the delegate case it departs from it widely and consistently. In the free agent case, the irregularities that appear are due to the small size of the assembly and the even smaller number of different weights. A larger example would show a more consistent pattern, as in Table 1, with only moderate departures from the "ideal" case.

A few comments on this example are in order. Columns 3 and 6 are what the advocates of weighted voting think (or at least say) they are establishing, and column 6 is what would be achieved by equal districts with equal votes in the legislature. Columns 4 and 7 are what weighted voting actually establishes, if one accepts the free agent model, while columns 5 and 8 are what is established if one accepts the delegate model. Note in column 8 that the power of a citizen in the largest district is more than three times as great as the power of a citizen in one of the smallest districts.

We do not presume to decide whether the free agent model or the delegate model, or something in between, is preferred for American legislatures. Apparently sometimes one, sometimes the other, fits the situation better. We note only that the free agent model is peculiarly attractive to legislators and less attractive to citizens. Burke first set forth the free agent model in a speech to the electors of Bristol, *after* he had been elected to a seat which he *never* thereafter contested. Wahlke *et al.* found that in the four states they studied state legislators viewed themselves as free agents (or "trustees" in Wahlke's terminology) much more frequently than as delegates.[14] Unfortunately, Wahlke *et al.* had no independent way of observing their behavior so we do not know that their own role conceptions were actually carried through into action. And internal evidence in the findings suggests that the preference for the free agent model is simply a consequence of the conventional culture of legislatures in which the creative role of trustee is more highly valued than the more or less mechanical role of delegate. Contrasting with these data, Miller and Stokes found by interviewing congressmen and constituents simultaneously that congressmen in 1958 conformed to the delegate model on issues such as civil rights and to our formulation of the delegate model on social welfare issues, but that they tended to be free agents in foreign affairs.[15] This evidence suggests that neither model is entirely satisfactory in general but that on some occasions one fits and on other occasions the other fits.[16] We conclude, therefore, that if weighted voting occurs in large legislatures and if the free agent model is appropriate, then weighted voting introduces a mild bias in favor of the larger districts. On the other hand, for large legislatures, if the delegate model is appropriate, weighted voting introduces a very large bias in favor of the citizens of larger districts. At least in this latter circumstance, therefore, weighted voting is entirely inappropriate for achieving the ideal of "one-person, one-vote."

[14] John Wahlke, Heinz Eulau, William Buchanan, and LeRoy C. Ferguson, *The Legislative System* (New York: Wiley, 1962), p. 281.

[15] Warren E. Miller and Donald E. Stokes, "Constituency Influence in Congress," *American Political Science Review*, 57 (1963), 45–56.

[16] This is the conclusion reached also in Lewis A. Froman, *Congressmen and Their Constituencies* (Chicago: Rand McNally, 1963).

In the beginning of this essay we suggested a paradox: that those who its advocates say are its beneficiaries are probably those who are hurt by weighted voting, while those who its opponents say are its victims probably gain from it. This paradox can now be easily explained.

Typically, the reason (whether publicly stated or not) for advocating weighted voting has been that the advocate wishes to save the seats of representatives from small districts which are likely to be consolidated under reapportionment into districts of equal size.[17] Furthermore, it has almost invariably been the citizens of large districts who have brought suits against the adoption of weighted voting in legislatures, presumably because they feared that their influence would be less under a system of weighted voting than under a system of districts of equal size. If the analysis in this essay is correct, however, both advocates and opponents have been wrong and each have taken positions contrary to their own best interests, which is the paradox we set out to explain. And the explanation appears to be quite simple: Both parties to the dispute have apparently assumed that the citizens and legislators from the smaller districts would have more power than citizens and legislators from larger districts simply because the former have more legislators than the latter. If, as we have argued, this assumption is false, then the paradox is explained.

Reverting to our initial purpose of showing the utility of mathematical analysis for political philosophy, we observe that the paradoxical behavior of both advocates and opponents demonstrates that our mathematically arrived-at conclusions are not immediately obvious to common sense. In this circumstance at least a mathematical analysis has made possible a complete reversal of judgment on the appropriateness of a particular instrument for realizing a given conception of justice. We believe it is quite likely that mathematical analysis might similarly clarify many other problems of political philosophy especially when (as with the notions of equality, representation, freedom, liberalism, etc.) both the ideals and the instruments have some quantitative elements.

[17] In the report of the Mulligan committee, which proposed weighted voting in the New York legislature, it was argued that such voting "would provide the people in the less populous counties . . . an independent voice in the Assembly." Citizens Committee on Reapportionment, *Report* (New York, 1964), p. 38.

16

WEIGHTED VOTING AND "ONE-MAN, ONE-VOTE"

ROBERT NOZICK

Except for isolated cases of election fraud, and the systematic exclusion from voting of some group, each eligible voter can, if he wishes, cast one vote. We are here not concerned with the number of votes someone casts, but with how much weight or power his vote has. Ignoring the considerations which the Supreme Court says might justify deviations from equal weight (e.g., maintaining political subdivisions as the basis for electoral districts, achieving compact districts of contiguous territory) and ignoring some practical difficulties, one wants to equalize,[1] given appropriate

My comments refer to the paper by Riker and Shapley given at the 1965 meeting of the Society for Political and Legal Philosophy. Their essay here differs from that version, so that some of my remarks may not be relevant and some of my questions already answered.

[1] "One wants to equalize" shall in this paper mean "one must equalize in order to conform to one reasonable interpretation of the Court's decisions."

measures of power, some function of the power of the legislator and of the power of the person to choose the legislator. If each person eligible to participate in choosing a given legislator has equal power in determining that choice, then one wants to equalize, for each i,

$$\frac{\text{Power of legislator } L_i}{\text{Number of persons eligible to participate in choosing legislator } L_i.}$$[2]

If, furthermore, each legislator has equal power, then one wants to equalize the number of persons eligible to participate in the choosing of each legislator.

I shall assume that the representative systems under discussion are based upon a system of legislative districts. Professor Paul Freund has mentioned the possibility of a representative system without legislative districts, in which there are n representatives, persons' names are arranged in alphabetical order, and the first nth of the people are eligible to vote for one representative, the second nth for another, and so on. Such a system can easily bring about the equalization discussed above, but since no one seems prone to suggest such a system, this shows (and, I believe, was intended by Professor Freund to show) that we are concerned that our legislative system satisfy conditions in addition to equalizing the weight of the voters' votes. (And perhaps we would countenance some deviation from the latter condition in order better to satisfy the former ones.) It is of some importance for a theory of representation to state what purposes are served by representation by geographical districts.[3]

If in each legislative district, each eligible voter has equal power

---

I shall not here be concerned with the desirability of this equalization, and shall not discuss whether in constructing a system of representative institutions one should, under all circumstances, build into it such equalization. Nor shall I discuss the question of under what circumstances one should reconstruct an existing system of representative institutions in order to achieve such equalization.

[2] The situation is somewhat more complicated, as is pointed out in John F. Banzhof III, "Multi-member Electoral Districts: Do They Violate the 'One Man, One Vote' Principle?" *Yale Law Journal,* 75 (1966), 1309. Questions paralleling those I raise arise for the more complicated formulation.

[3] To say that important purposes are served by representation by geographical districts is not to say that one never should want to modify such a system. For example, if persons working in New York City but residing elsewhere must pay some income tax to New York City, and one takes seriously the slogan "No taxation without representation," then one may think it desirable to give such persons some vote (weighted less than one) for the representatives in the New York City Council of the districts in which they work.

in selecting the legislator, then in the legislature, one wants each legislator to have power proportional to the number of eligible voters in his district.[4] But it also seems that there are persons other than eligible voters residing in his district whom the legislator is to represent, whose interests he is to care for; for example, recent immigrants who are not citizens, and also nonadult citizens. And we want a legislator's power to be proportional to the number of persons in his district whom he is to represent (in this wider sense). It follows (assuming that in each legislator's district there will be persons whom he is to represent who are not eligible voters) that a legislator's power should be proportional to the number of persons in a set which has as a *proper* subset the set of eligible voters in his district. Thus it seems that there are two conditions to be satisfied: (1) A legislator's power is to be proportional to the number of eligible voters in his district; (2) A legislator's power is to be proportional to the number of persons in his district whom he is to represent. It is possible to satisfy both of these conditions together only if there is some positive number n (which need not be an integer) such that, for each legislator, the number of persons he is to represent $= n \times$ the number of voters eligible to select him. And it seems very unlikely that this will be the case. Having mentioned this difficulty, I shall ignore it in the remainder of my comments.

The standard proposal about weighted voting in a legislature, and the one discussed by Professors Riker and Shapley in Chapter

[4] Interesting questions arise about whether in this situation the legislator's power should be proportional to the number of eligible voters, the number of registered voters, or the number of actual voters in his district. I shall not pause to discuss these questions, nor shall I discuss the claim that the legislator's power should be proportional to the number of votes he has received, which presumably would require something like a system of proportional representation. Though I shall not discuss systems of proportional representation, I should mention that they seem to me to raise very important questions for and perhaps about political philosophy. I conjecture that one can list conditions on representative institutions which are jointly satisfied only by a system of proportional representation, and which are such that each seems reasonable and desirable and indeed required by justice. But political science books tell us that systems of proportional representation work out terribly and so we reject such systems. Still, it may be that when we go back to our conditions, though we see which must be rejected to avoid a system of proportional representation and keep (an idealization of) our current system, we will feel that these conditions, which must be rejected if we are to avoid proportional representation, are conditions of fairness and justice. Yet we are reluctant to conclude that we should sometimes choose unfair and unjust institutions over fair and just ones. I do not claim that there can be no adequate theory of justice to resolve this difficulty, but merely that it poses a problem for and perhaps about a theory of justice.

15, gives to each legislator a number of votes proportional to the number of eligible voters in his district. If we assume that each legislator will on each issue cast his votes as a bloc,[5] then it can be shown, as Professors Riker and Shapley point out, that such a weighted voting scheme does not guarantee equalization of

$$\frac{\text{Power of the } i\text{th legislator}}{\text{Number of persons eligible to vote for the } i\text{th legislator}}$$

where the power of the legislator is measured by the Shapley procedure. (Henceforth I shall refer to this fraction as $\frac{P_i}{N_i}$.)

If one supposes that Shapley's procedure gives a reasonable measure of the power of a legislator,[6] this result is unfortunate, since it looked like such a weighted voting scheme would both perfectly satisfy the Supreme Court decisions[7] and avoid tricky redistricting problems.

Professors Riker and Shapley go on to investigate the questions of whether, in large legislatures, the deviations from equalizing $\frac{P_i}{N_i}$ will be great, greater than is compatible with court decisions, and investigate in what direction one can expect the deviations to go,

[5] A legislator might wish to split his votes on an issue, if this is permitted by the system, to reflect deep divisions within his district.

[6] As I understand it, there are two (related) rationales for the Shapley power measure:

(1) The three conditions which only the Shapley measure satisfies. For a statement and discussion of these conditions, which raise some questions about the adequacy of the third condition, see R. Duncan Luce and Howard Raiffa, *Games and Decisions* (New York: Wiley, 1957), pp. 245–50.

(2) The rationale in terms of random coalition formation.

Does the Shapley measure yield intuitive results for all systems of voting, e.g., for the system in which the legislators are ordered, and each may vote for a bill, against it, or abstain. If a legislator votes for (against) a bill, and all legislators before him in the order abstain, then the bill passes (is defeated). If no one votes for the bill, it is defeated. Under this arrangement, it seems that (a) each legislator has more power than anyone who follows him in the order, and (b) the first legislator could not have more power. I believe the Shapley measure cannot yield both (a) and (b), and it would, I think, lead to the rejection of (b), thus not giving the first legislator the maximal amount of power. This may lead one to question the imposition of Shapley's second condition (that the individual values of the game from an additive partition of the value of the whole game) in measuring the power of legislators in legislative bodies.

[7] If one ignored everything but voting power on the floor of the legislature, e.g., that some districts would be represented on committees less than proportionally to their size.

given the size of a district and of the other districts. What I should like to do is raise some questions about whether, assuming that the districts are satisfactory and that there aren't gerrymandering-type objections to them,[8] *some* system of weighted voting will equalize $\frac{P_i}{N_i}$. Given the result which Professors Riker and Shapley mention, a system of weighted voting which equalized $\frac{P_i}{N_i}$ would have to be a system which did *not* give legislators a number of votes proportional to the number of eligible voters in their districts.

The most general question is: For every legislature with any number (>1) of legislators, such that each legislator may have associated with him (as eligible voters) any number of persons, is there some assignment of numbers of votes to each legislator (these numbers of votes need not be integers, and need not be proportional to the number of persons associated with the legislator) such that $\frac{P_i}{N_i}$ is equalized? The answer to this question is "no." For example,

1. Suppose there are two legislators in the legislature who are associated with different numbers of persons. If the legislators are given the same number of votes, their power will be equal and hence their fractions will be different. If the number of votes the legislators have differs and it is a system of majority rule, then the one with more votes will have all the power (and his fraction will be positive); and the one with fewer votes will have no power (and hence his fraction will be zero). Hence the fractions will differ.

2. Suppose the legislature consists of an odd number of legislators having the same number of persons associated with them, and one legislator with fewer persons associated with him. Each of the odd number of legislators must get the same number of votes (or something equivalent). If the remaining legislator gets this number of votes, he has the same power as they do, and the fractions are unequal (his is greater). (Similarly his fraction is at least as great if he gets more votes than they do.) If he gets fewer votes than they

[8] It is of some interest to formulate the conditions which a gerrymandered system of districts violates. If the *intention* of the person forming the districts isn't relevant (but rather the effects of certain districting) and the geographical and population density conditions formulated by political scientists are not desirable in themselves but are meant to make unlikely the violation of further conditions, then one wants to know what these further conditions are. One suspects that these further conditions may naturally tie in with systems of proportional representation.

do, he has no power, and his fraction is zero (while theirs is greater than zero). Hence the fractions cannot be equalized.[9]

The Shapley power value will always be a fraction whose denominator is x, the total number of possible permutations of the legislators' (bloc) votes[10] and whose numerator will be some integer less than x. Since it will usually be the case that a legislator does not have associated with him exactly some integral xth of the total population,[11] it will often be impossible to have a legislator's power be that fraction of the total power which the persons associated with him are of the total number of persons associated with all of the legislators. Whatever fraction of the total population is associated with a legislator, this fraction will fall between $\frac{n}{x}$ and $\frac{n+1}{x}$ for some integral $n > 0$ (where x is as before.). Let us say that $\frac{n}{x}$ and $\frac{n+1}{x}$ surround the fraction.

The first questions we want to raise are:

1. What are the conditions under which it is possible, by a system of weighted voting (where the number of votes a legislator has need not be proportional to the number of persons associated with him), to get, for each legislator j, $\frac{P_j}{\sum_{\text{all } i} P_i}$ equal to one of the fractions which surround the fraction whose denominator is the total number of persons associated with all the legislators, and whose numerator is the number of persons associated with the jth legislator.[12] That is, under what conditions is it possible to get, for each legislator j, $\frac{P_j}{\sum_{\text{all } i} P_i}$ equal to one of the fractions which surround $\frac{N_j}{\sum_{\text{all } i} N_i}$ where N_i is the number of persons associated with the ith legislator.

2. Do current legislative districts (and the ones which would

[9] For this example, I assume that all the legislators must vote, and that each must cast his votes as a bloc.

[10] When m is the total number of legislators, $x = m!$.

[11] Where $x = m!$.

[12] One actually wants something more than this; namely, that a legislator's power be between zero and one (excluding the endpoints) if he has associated with him some though not all of the persons associated with the legislators.

result from foreseeable population changes) satisfy these conditions?

If current legislative districts do satisfy these conditions, then *some* system of weighted voting, which does not assign votes to legislators in proportion to the number of their constituents, will serve the purposes that the standard system of weighted voting was designed to serve.

But suppose that current legislative districts do not satisfy these conditions. Must one redistrict in order to get, for each j, $\frac{P_j}{\sum_{\text{all } i} P_i}$ to one of the fractions which surround $\frac{N_j}{\sum_{\text{all } i} N_i}$?

There are various alternative weighted voting schemes which *may* enable one to achieve this goal without redistricting. It is worth mentioning some such alternative schemes, since some of them would be rejected even if they achieve *this* goal, and hence raise questions about what further conditions one wishes an electoral scheme to satisfy.

In standard legislatures, all legislators, if they wish to do so, may vote on each bill which comes before the house of the legislature of which they are members (though they may not be able to vote in legislative commitees of which they are not members). An alternative scheme might assign to each legislator some probability (not necessarily the same for each legislator) of being allowed or entitled to vote on any given issue, with random devices being used to determine if he actually does get to vote on the issue. Once the different probabilities of voting are assigned to each legislator, a generalization of the standard power measures can be used to compute the power of each legislator. This system might be combined with one of weighted voting whereby legislators who get to vote (after the random device determines that they may) may be entitled to cast different numbers of votes. This scheme raises the second question:

For any number, > 1, of legislators, each having any finite number of constituents, is there some assignment of weighted votes and probabilities of getting to vote to the legislators so that, for each j, $\frac{P_j}{\sum_{\text{all } i} P_i}$ is equal to one of the fractions which surround $\frac{N_j}{\sum_{\text{all } i} N_i}$? If there is not always such an assignment, what conditions must be satisfied for there to be one, and do current legislative districts satisfy these conditions?

Even if such a scheme could achieve the stated goal, many would find it objectionable. (For, it would be said, it *might* turn out that some legislators would almost never get to vote, and some might not get to vote on some bills of great importance to their districts.) Almost all would find objectionable a system wherein only one legislator gets to vote on any given bill (thereby determining whether or not it passes during that session of the legislature), and each legislator has some probability, for any given bill, of being the one who decides. Even if, given current legislature districts, there is a probability assignment which achieves the stated goal, such a system would be rejected. It is worth mentioning such legislative systems, since they make clear that we are not concerned *only* with $\frac{P_i}{N_i}$ and suggest the task of stating the specific additional conditions which we wish to impose upon an electoral and legislative system.

Alternative systems could be proposed which might achieve the stated goal. For example, legislators might be divided into blocs whose votes are weighted. Each bloc must vote as a bloc, and how a bloc votes is determined by how its members, with weighted votes, vote in a caucus of the bloc. So the power of each legislator is a function of the power of the bloc of which he is a member, and of his power within the bloc. (A more complicated scheme would have some legislators being members of more than one bloc.) Given current legislative districts, can such a system achieve the stated goal?

I should briefly mention one qualm about Riker and Shapley's interesting result, about the model of the delegate representatives who "act simply as funnels for their constituencies," that in general the citizen of a small district has a much smaller power index than the citizen of a large district. It seems that the authors assume that each legislative district is (roughly) a random sample of the total population with respect to political beliefs; hence their claim that smaller districts will deviate more than larger ones from the national percentage on an issue. The large (in population) districts which we now have are urban districts, and it is not obvious that the political beliefs found in these districts are a random sample of the political beliefs of the total population, or more representative of the political beliefs of the total population than are those of the small districts.

(It is a commonplace that large urban districts generally elect more "liberal" representatives than do other districts.) This is especially clear for counties containing some large urban districts, though most of their population is in small (in population) agricultural districts. The large urban district is not, I think, more likely (than its population justifies) to be in a pivot position. Thus, though Riker and Shapley's result about large and small districts follows from considerations about probability and random samples, one would hesitate to apply it to actual political situations where the large urban areas are known not to be a random sample of the total population with respect to political beliefs. It might be said that the *structure* of the legislative system favors large (in population) districts. But even if we grant that facts about the distribution of political beliefs are not part of the structure of a legislative system,[13] we may not worry about a bias the structure imposes since it is counterbalanced by general conditions likely to continue, and indeed we may desire a biased structure to compensate for certain nonstructural biases.

[13] It is not, I think, clear what facts may legitimately be included in the relevant structure for determining measures of power. Should one include the fact that certain methods of election make it more likely that the two representatives of a multimember district will vote in the same way than that two randomly selected representatives will, that the number of political parties and the degree of party discipline affects the likelihood of different permutations, that some representatives look to others for guidance on specific sorts of issues, that some legislative committees' recommendations are rarely rejected, and so forth.

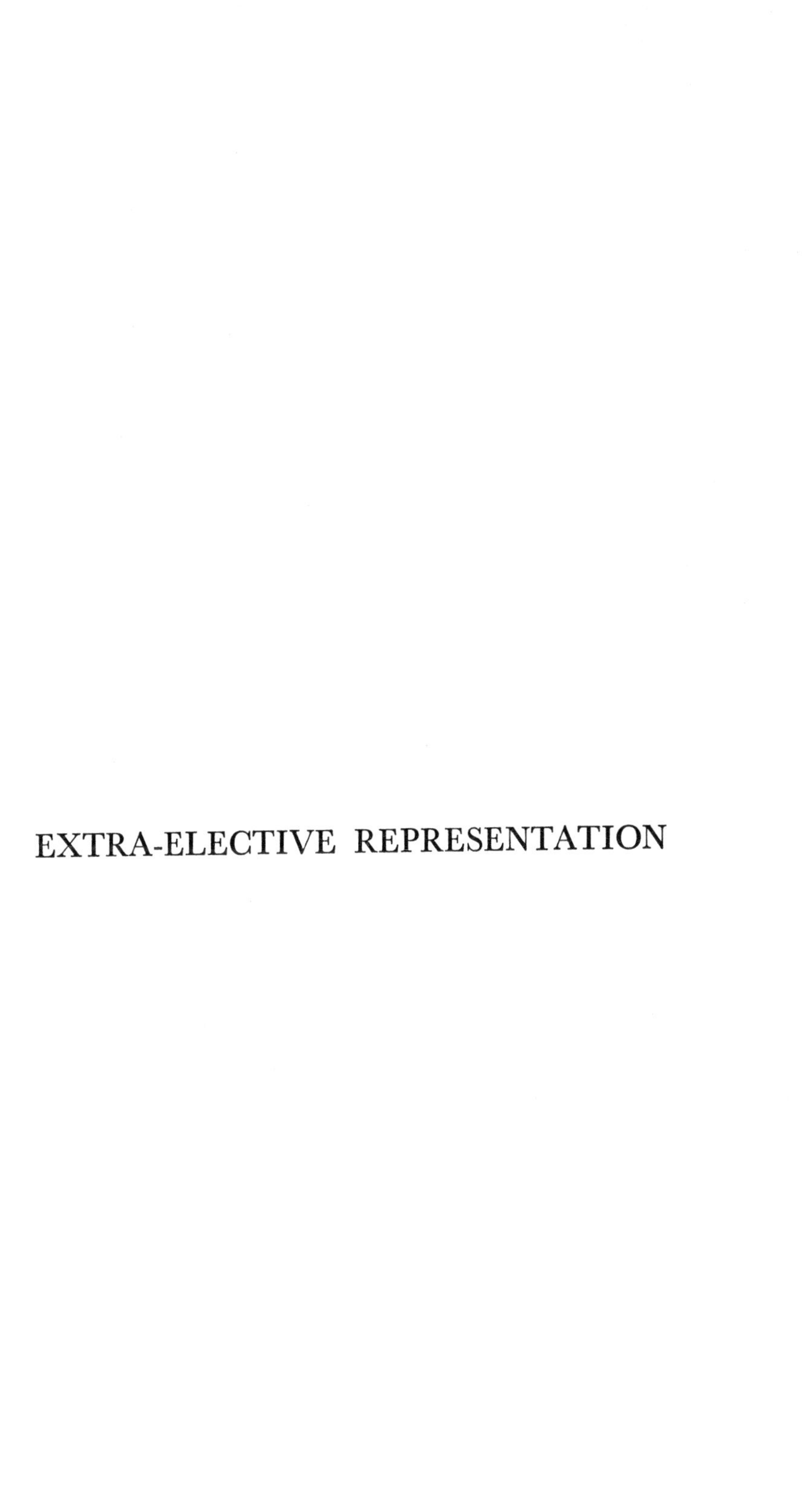

EXTRA-ELECTIVE REPRESENTATION

17

THE BUREAUCRACY AS REPRESENTATIVES

JOSEPH P. WITHERSPOON

Some scholars have suggested that the most important current problems of representation arise within groups rather than government.[1] With this assessment the author is in fundamental disagreement. However currently significant the problem of representation relating to groups, the perennial importance of the problem of representation concerning government has not decreased in the United States but rather increased. This is particularly true, as we shall see, with regard to extra-elective representation by administrative officials.

One difficulty with the suggested distinction between group and governmental representation problems is best highlighted by ref-

[1] Charles E. Gilbert, "Operative Doctrines of Representation," *American Political Science Review,* 57 (1963), 604.

erence to the continuing civil rights revolution. The Negro, the Mexican-American, and the Puerto Rican, for example, like the Indian, the poor generally, the very old, and many other classes have enormous difficulties with representatation that relate as much to government as to groups. Inadequate representation of a population element by organized interest groups inevitably affects the quality of the representation of the former by government authorities. On the other hand, the practical solution of this latter problem cannot await, and is not even necessarily related to, resolution of the former. There may even be the necessity for emergence of solidarity within an inadequately represented group and formation of organizations by it in order for adequate representation of it to begin on the part of other groups and government. Perhaps some will say that this is what the civil rights revolution is all about. But this is hardly the problem of representation as it is generally understood.

As in all cases of representation, the problem of extra-elective representation by administrative officials is a problem, of course, of what is to be represented by them and how this is to be assured in light of the purposes underlying a doctrine concerning representation and the circumstances in which representation must occur. Political scientists have distinguished in American thought six doctrines of representation: the idealist, the utilitarian, the rationalist, the pragmatic, the participatory, and the populist.[2] These doctrines are primarily normative rather than descriptive and involve different approaches to broad normative problems of politics.[3] Participants in this discussion have recognized the problem of extra-elective representation by administrative officials, sometimes characterizing it as a problem of developing a "representative bureaucracy."[4]

Important as this particular discussion by political scientists is, it does not provide us with an adequate vantage point from which to engage in a study of what may properly be designated as the jurisprudential problem of representative government and particularly of extra-elective representation by administrative officials. In the first place, it does not provide us with knowledge of the concrete setting or context in which this problem has existed and continues to exist. A knowledge of this context is essential for one who wishes to assess

[2] *Ibid.*

[3] *Ibid.*, p. 617.

[4] Edgar Lane, "Interest Groups and Bureaucracy," *The Annals of the American Academy of Political and Social Science,* 292 (1954), 105.

the kinds of actual problems for the resolution of which representative government has been devised and which have confronted it as a way of government in actual operation. Through this knowledge we are enabled, to some extent, to assess the way in which representative government, as concretely conceived at an earlier point, has subsequently responded to those problems and, in light of that response, has been changed in significant respects for certain reasons. We are also enabled to examine the justifications for these changes and their effectiveness as well as to probe for better solutions of the problems to which earlier ones were addressed. In the second place, the discussion by political scientists in question has not primarily focused upon the decision-making process *in actu exercitu* by which administrative officials resolve the problems committed to their care. This process has its inherent structure, dynamism, requirements, and limitations that present enormous implications for the effectuation of representation. Discussions of the *what* and *how* of representation that fail to take account of the problem concerning assignment of statutory meaning, for example, neglect what is probably the most difficult aspect of representative government in the twentieth century. This essay will focus upon the first of these approaches to the problem of representative government. The author has treated the second aspect elsewhere.[5]

THE CHANGING ROLE OF ADMINISTRATION IN GOVERNMENT

John Stuart Mill, the philosopher of democracy, in elaborating a theory of representative government,[6] sharply distinguished between the proper function of the people's representatives in the legislature or parliament and the proper function of administrators selected by them.[7] The representatives' principal function was to deliberate and decide relative to legislation, although they also had important secondary functions related to choice of administrative officials, oversight of their administration, removal of corrupt officials, and expression and testing of opinions concerning the public

[5] Joseph P. Witherspoon, "Administrative Discretion to Determine Statutory Meaning," *Texas Law Review,* 35 (1956), 63; *Texas Law Review,* 38 (1960), 372, 392; *Texas Law Review,* 50 (1962), 751.

[6] J. S. Mill, *On Liberty and Considerations on Representative Government* (Oxford: Blackwell, 1948), p. 161.

[7] *Ibid.,* pp. 163–74.

interest offered for general acceptance. The administrative function, by way of contrast, was to administer and to act under law made by the people's representatives. The latter, owing to their equal and numerous nature were, in Mill's view, unfit to administer law. This nature precluded the possibility of their exercising a due responsibility for what they might do in administration of the law they enacted. It also made it unlikely that they could attain the professional skill and impartiality essential to the performance of the administrative function. Administrative officials, in contrast to the representatives, should ordinarily not be subject to removal from office except for personal misconduct and they certainly should not be required to stand for election in order to obtain or retain their office. Their selection should be made by the professional representatives of the people strictly on the basis of professional fitness to administer rather than to make law or policy.

The American form of representative government, as carved out by our federal Constitution, by and large preserved the classic notion of representative government with regard to administrative officials as later elaborated by Mill. The principal exception was the provision for election of the President. The principal concern of the framers was to place responsibility in a proper way for achieving good administration by officials. "The true test of a good government," they stated, "is its aptitude and tendency to produce a good administration."[8] To achieve this goal they relied upon "the sole and undivided responsibility of one man,"[9] the President, who through being subjected to the electoral process would have "a due dependence on the people."[10] They realized the value of continuity among subordinate administrative officials who had given satisfactory evidence of their fitness for office and sought to promote this result upon the election of a new President by requiring the Senate to participate in appointments of officials.[11]

Immediately following the American Revolution, state and local governments established their legislatures in a position of supreme authority while reducing their chief executives to a position of little more than ceremonial importance.[12] The latter had no authority for

[8] Alexander Hamilton, *The Federalist* (Heritage ed., 1945), No. 68, p. 458; No. 76, p. 507.

[9] *Ibid.,* No. 76, p. 508.

[10] *Ibid.,* No. 70, p. 470.

[11] *Ibid.,* No. 77, p. 513.

[12] For a general exposition see Herbert Kaufmann, "Emerging Conflicts in

administration of law and little control over it. This situation continued for well over a century at the state and local level. In the first half of the nineteenth century two additional developments intruded upon the classic conception of representation as it was worked out in practice. One was the election of numerous state and local officials. In addition, the absence of a strong chief executive caused a fragmentation in administration of law at these levels and greatly hindered the rationalization of administrative policy. Another development was the spoils system, a result of unregulated party government and political short-sightedness. This brought about lessened competency and increased partiality on the part of administrative officials who were frequently appointed only as a reward for service to their party rather than for their special competence to administer law. This development extended also to federal officials. Both these developments presented some aspects of the modern problem with extra-elective representation. Nevertheless, one further development in modern government involves the major aspects of this problem.

This later development has been the most fundamental change in the operation of modern government—the emergence of administrative process and its institutions in the twentieth century as a major facet in the making and administration of governmental policy. A part of this change has been the enormous increase in authority and significance of the President in our federal government, a change somewhat paralleled by some state chief executives. Also, a part of this change has involved the competition for control of administrative process and institutions—the fourth center of crucial authority in our government—a competition at once between the legislature and the chief executive, between private special interests and administrative agencies, among special interests, and often among the administrative agencies themselves.

Before assessing the meaning of this change for the problem of extra-elective representation, it will be profitable to examine the reason for and nature of the change. The central reason has been the vast increase in the business of government, a business demanding a strong center of official power capable of dealing wisely, vigor-

---

the Doctrines of Public Administration," *American Political Science Review,* 50 (1956), 1057; and Fritz M. Marx, "Administrative Regulation in Comparative Perspective," *Law & Contemporary Problems,* 26 (1961), 307.

ously, continuously, and flexibly with problems created by or associated with the emergence of private centers of economic power. Large corporations, major railroads, big industrial concerns, financial tycoons, high political bosses, secret rebates and other discriminatory practices in transportation, watered stock, interlocking directorates, monopolies and conspiracies to restrain trade, unfair competition, reckless and inhumane treatment of workers, poisonous and adulterated foods, alternating booms and depressions—these were the institutions, practices, and conditions following in the wake of the industrial revolution that created the problems first necessitating modern forms of administrative process. During the past eighty years these and similar major public problems have become more and more complex and numerous as additional big institutional centers of private power and their practices and conditions requiring regulation in the public interest have come into being. The consensus has been that Congress and other legislatures could not deal with them adequately by formulating laws to regulate the conduct of persons and organizations through fairly precise rules and by providing for their administration, where voluntary compliance is not given, through case-to-case adjudication in the courts. Instead, most of the very important laws enacted in this century have either established or designated an agency to administer a legislative policy.

These laws have conferred upon administrative agencies a variety of administrative functions to be performed pursuant to legislative directives involving large measures of discretion in decision-making. Only in this way was it judged possible to provide for expert administration of law that could affirmatively and continuously promote, supervise, and ensure the realization of legislative policy directed to economic and social matters. Only in this way was it deemed possible to provide for the adequate adaptation of legislative policy to problem areas, the nature of which was originally difficult to foresee and which, indeed, might be in the process of changing. This new kind of legislation has called for employment of many new administrative functions such as promotion of voluntary action, negotiations, conciliation, publicizing, insuring risks, and production of goods. It has also called for a considerably greater emphasis upon older administrative functions such as rule-making, investigation, testing, licensing, adjudication, contracting, allocation of benefits, and rendering of services rather than upon the traditional function of courts.

The more general form of statutory law creating and empowering administrative agencies must usually be further elaborated in order for it to have a particular meaning or bearing for individual persons and organizations subject to administrative action. This general statutory law, perhaps the finest product of the legislative art when well formulated, now largely overshadows the common law and other forms of judge-made law. The latter continue to serve the vital functions in our society they have always served, but they simply cannot respond, even by the most enlightened administration, to the major public problems of this century. The function of the courts is still a vital one to free government in administering statutory law, but it is now largely one of "backstopping" the work of administrative agencies. This function is designed to ensure that the agencies stay within the authority granted to them, that there is a reasonable basis in law and in fact for their action, that their decision-making procedures are lawful, that their authority and exercise of it are constitutional, and that their lawful regulations and decisions are obeyed.

The phenomenon of modern government described above simply means that the administrative agencies have become major policy-makers within the over-all framework. Policy-making, or more correctly, its crucial directions, are today in large measure administratively determined. Legislation by the legislature is but the beginning of law-making in the resolution of a public problem. This is especially true when legislative directions to the administrative agency are to be carried out through rule-making, licensing, contracting, and other largely discretionary functions. One need only mention the price- and wage-fixing functions exercised in wartime by the defense mobilization agencies and the rate-making functions exercised at all times by public utility and similar commissions to appreciate the great significance of the legislative decisions of administrative agencies. Moreover, the licensing functions of these agencies determine the very life and mode of operation of many businesses such as the communication, transportation, and oil and gas industries.

A major development with regard to administrative agencies has been their separation from the chief executive as organs for administration of law.[13] At the state and local level this separation was a

[13] See Robert E. Cushman, *The Independent Regulatory Commissions* (New York: Oxford University Press, 1941); and Emmette S. Redford,

concomitant of several forces: (1) a weak chief executive, (2) the election of a number of key administrative officials, and (3) the deliberate action of the legislature in separating administration of law by officials from the function of the chief executive. This latter factor has been the operative one at the federal level. Beginning with establishment of the Interstate Commerce Commission in 1887 Congress has created a considerable number of large independent commissions to which it has committed final responsibility for decision-making free from direction of the chief executive or from influence of his ordinary removal power. Congress has also accomplished much the same result with many departmental executives who hold office at the pleasure of the President. The separate character of administrative process greatly increases the significance of that process and its institutions relative to government policy-making. It also greatly complicates realization of the goals of representative government.

Students of administrative process are inclined to overlook a major institution of public administration that is even more separate and independent than independent regulatory commissions. They are undoubtedly preoccupied with public administration that is oriented overtly and formally to regulation of human action. This major institution is the public corporation set up to utilize the technique of private management in operation of a public enterprise designed to be self-supporting or productive of revenues.[14] Typically called a public authority, such as the Port of New York Authority or the Massachusetts Parking Authority, these public corporations operate outside the regular framework of federal, state, or local government and are not subjected to the procedures and restrictions of governmental operations. For this reason they are a form of administrative process far more separate and independent than the independent regulatory commissions. Originated at the state level for the purpose of evading debt limitations placed upon government, they have come into very extensive use since 1921.[15] The governing body of these authorities is usually a board of directors whose members are appointed by the chief executive. Sometimes the governor, a finance

---

"The President and the Regulatory Commissions," *Texas Law Review,* 44 (1965), 288.

[14] For an excellent description see Robert Gerwig, "Public Authorities in the United States," *Law & Contemporary Problems,* 26 (1961), 591.

[15] *Ibid.,* p. 597.

officer, and the attorney general are ex officio members of the board in statewide or regional authorities. The policies developed by these agencies can have enormous effect upon direction of economic activity. Often consequences of authority policies are not brought home to the public. Usually these consequences become so well embedded in the economic fabric before they become generally apparent that public action to modify or reverse them cannot be effectively mounted until long after the policies responsible for them have been elaborated and effectuated. It is generally recognized that public authorities tend to accumulate power that is difficult to justify and to remain in operation long after completing their originally assigned project. While there has been a leveling-out in creation of public authorities, they represent a continuing institution of independent public administration that is likely to endure. With their freedom from direct administrative, legislative, or electoral control, they present one of the great problems relative to the representativeness of government.

Another development within administrative process that should be noted is the fact that its institutions are increasingly making and executing major governmental policy through means that differ fundamentally from the formal means of government such as rule-making, adjudication, or licensing. To this extent these agencies are performing roles in policy-making that legislatures have always been incompetent to perform. The means being utilized are directed toward persuading or inducing persons to conform their conduct to administratively developed programs of proposed action or patterns of conduct. The most dramatic instance of this new administrative tool in recent years has been the action of the President of the United States in opposing price increases by certain segments of industry and taking or directing administrative action in buying goods designed to discourage these increases. The mediation and "program proposing" roles of modern human relations commissions is another example.[16] Through performance of these roles these commissions are enabled to push integration on broad fronts or sectors of the business community rather than to rely upon slow and largely ineffective case-to-case complaint investigation and adjudication. It seems likely that much of our governmental process in future decades

[16] See Joseph P. Witherspoon, "Civil Rights Policy in the Federal System: Proposals for a Better Use of Administrative Process," *Yale Law Journal*, 74 (1965), 1205–17.

will be concerned with eliciting or inducing reasonable patterns of conduct by large groups of persons and institutions. This technique of government, however, is largely one that the legislature cannot effectuate through legislative directives. For this reason, its use inevitably heightens the importance of administrative process in over-all governmental policy-making.

In addition to formulating governmental policy in the course of administering legislation, administrative agencies have become very significant for their role in the legislative process itself. Probably most important federal legislation has either been originally prepared by a federal agency or submitted to it by the President for evaluation and comment on the position he should take. With the vast increase in complexity of modern public problems, this agency function relative to proposed statutory programs has evolved into a function of giving legislation the definitive form in which it is both proposed and adopted. The legislative winnowing of statutory proposals still remains an important part of representative government, of course, but it is also clear today that the nonlegislative official formulator of proposed legislation makes the essential determinations as to form and content of most major legislation. This means that legislative process does not begin in the legislature but in the offices of administrative agencies.

The function of administrative agencies just noted is fully as important as the others previously noted regarding governmental policy-making. All together they make the administrative agency a center of power in the operation of our society exceeded by no other element of our governmental system. While Congress still passes upon and to some extent formulates basic legislative policies and the courts still contribute to delineation of those policies and their enforcement, administrative agencies have ushered in the governmental age of administration. Like Big Business, Big Unions, Big Foundations, Big Parties and their counterparts in state and local political societies, administrative agencies represent a major and independent force in giving content to the form of American life. If they are not the principal part of Big Government, they loom very large within it indeed. Policy-making, it has been said, is and must be a political process. Even if that must be very carefully understood with regard to administrative policy-making, administrative agencies engaged in this process are subject to the same kind of natural and reasonable interest in their work that is directed toward legislation by state and local legislatures and the Congress. Industries, unions, Congress, the President, governors, state legislatures, cities, associations, particular individuals and business concerns, and the public at large may all be vitally concerned with the content of a policy-making decision of a federal or even a state administrative agency. They are similarly interested in the legislative proposals which agencies prepare for submission to the legislature or review on request of the chief executive.

ADMINISTRATIVE PROCESS AND REPRESENTATION

In light of what administrative process and its institutions have come to be in modern government, what are the goals with respect to representative government that should be realized concerning it, what problems have arisen with regard to realization of these goals, and what should be done to resolve these problems? These are some of the principal questions involved in the jurisprudential problem involved here.

A careful student of representative government has recently summarized the functions of this system of government as they have been evolved in actual operation.[17] These were stated with reference to the electoral process to be the following:

1. To give a special kind of legitimacy to the administration that is made up of members of the party winning a general election;
2. To give citizens an opportunity to express their views, as voters, upon the behavior of incumbents belonging to the majority party and their opposition;
3. To provide a permanent channel for the communication of opinions and complaints from people to their government;
4. To provide a counterbalance to the influence of organized pressure groups upon the making and administration of public policy.

Each of these considerations has relevance to the problem of extra-elective representation by administrative agencies. Obviously, the consensus is and long has been that election of the heads of administrative agencies at the national level, other than the President, is improper. Moreover, extension of the electoral principle to state and local administrative officials has long since passed its high-

[17] Anthony H. Birch, *Representative and Responsible Government* (London: Allen & Unwin, 1964).

water mark. Most of them are today appointed to their offices with a few key officials being elected. Nevertheless, the considerations relative to providing for "legitimacy" in governmental authorities to make policy, citizen expression of views relative to governmental policy-making, permanent channels for communication of opinions and complaints, and a counterbalance to influence of organized pressure groups in the making and administration of policy provide a good basis for exploring the status of representative government today. If there are functions that representative government should serve and in fact serves when operating at an optimum, it is important to examine how their performance is affected because administrative process now marks the location of a powerful center of government policy-making.

Is any process available for legitimating the membership of administrative agencies analogous to what goes on when legislative representatives have been put to the test of an election? The answer must be that there is no necessary relationship under our existing institutional arrangements between the holding of a key position in an administrative agency and the expression of judgments of voters about their existing government. It seems inevitable, if we would respond to the representative principle, that we establish a connection of this sort. The interests in impartiality and expertness would not necessarily be disserved by establishment of such a connection. The question is how to establish the connection without disserving these and other interests that underlie good administrative process. Let us assume the propriety of having an administrative agency whose head is a board consisting of several members. Let us also assume the validity of any existing process for selecting membership of this board. The latter assumption, as we shall see, is a doubtful one at the state and local level. Implementation of the principle of "legitimacy" underlying representative government in this situation would appear to call for, at a minimum, the selection after regular elections of some new board members or the continuation in office of old members whose term had come to an end, with selection to be by appointment by the chief executive and subject, where appropriate, to confirmation by the upper house of the legislature.

Numerous problems are involved in introducing the principle of legitimacy into administrative process. They are neither as simple as advocates of leadership by the chief executive in administrative process have asserted nor as impossible as supporters of the independent regulatory agencies have claimed. Undoubtedly, reflection of elections in appointment of administrative officials should be tied to election of the chief executive. This policy has several good points. One is that a good case can be made that rationalization of administrative process depends to a considerable extent upon insertion of the influence and control of the chief executive over policy-making. Another is that the term of office of the chief executive is longer than the term of at least some members of the legislature and this provides some greater degree of continuity in office. Still another is the new leadership role of the chief executive in matters of public policy that has emerged in this century.

Another problem is the number of members of a multimember board whom a chief executive should be privileged to appoint after his election or re-election and whether he might replace one of his appointees at will. The principle of legitimation would seem to call for the right of the chief executive to appoint a sufficient number of members of a board to influence its policy-making product. What this should be from one board to another necessarily must call for a judgment based upon familiarity with the particular board. With this once settled, the principle calls also for according the chief executive the right to keep that influence intact. If his appointees do not measure up to his conception of an adequate performance, the chief executive should be privileged to replace them. Still another problem relates to what should be done with the single head of an agency. Since the principle of legitimation under our approach demands minimal satisfaction with regard to any agency engaged in policy-making, this official must be appointed by each chief executive and subject to replacement by him.

There are positive benefits in building into administrative process a principle of legitimating it in relation to the electoral process. It recognizes the responsibility for rationalization of administrative process in its policy-making aspects and indicates that this responsibility is squarely upon an elected chief executive and the party group in the legislative saddle that confirms his appointments. Moreover, it creates an indirect accountability of administrative officers to the electorate for the quality of administrative policy-making and procedures utilized by them. Inevitably administrative agencies will be rendered somewhat more sensitive to the less organized interests of the electorate. These two gains are sufficiently important that any disadvantages possibly created by recognizing the principle of legitimation should be dealt with by special arrangements likely to overcome them. Some of these arrangements have already been mentioned. Others are examined below.

Undoubtedly where an agency is assigned adjudicative functions, it would be necessary to subserve the interest of impartiality by an appropriate provision. Where the principal function of the board is adjudication, and policy-making is achieved almost exclusively through performance of that function, as in the case of the National Labor Relations Board, the function of legislative rule-making should be given that agency if it does not possess that authority and a maximum effort made by it to channel the making of its policy into the performance of that function. The adjudicative function of the agency should then either be allocated to specially designated adjudicative members of the board who are not subjected to the representation principle here advanced or should be given to subordinate adjudicative officers pursuant to a delegation of authority by board members. There will always be instances of new agencies that must develop the foundational administrative policy through case-to-case adjudication. These perhaps must be treated as temporary exceptions to the proposal made here. There may even be old agencies, such as the Federal Trade Commission, that can make a case for the necessity for making much new policy adjudicatively. The answer to these situations is the same as the one earlier proposed, either specially designed adjudicative members of the commission or subordinate adjudicative officials designated by the commission. It is likely, however, that agencies of this kind, and in particular the Federal Trade Commission, would greatly increase the effectiveness of the statutes they administer through more extensive use of the rule-making power.

There remains the problem of independent commissions having a licensing function, particularly where the granting and renewal of licenses have a great intrinsic value in the marketplace wholly apart from the person obtaining them. The handling of this function has come under severe critical fire in recent years on two principal counts. One urges the incompatibility of the adjudicatory approach with the underlying administrative task to be performed.[18] The solution often urged is adoption of a technique resembling that of business management. Another criticism of the great licensing agencies

[18] See, e.g., James Landis, "Air Routes Under the Civil Aeronautics Act," *Journal Air L. & Com.*, 15 (1948), 295.

assumes that the adjudicatory approach is essential and that it can be so modified in structure and procedures and so supplemented by other techniques as to make it satisfactory and effective.[19] The theory advanced in this essay is that so long as our government participates in or controls the economic decisions of an industry, whatever the administrative device ultimately selected—departmental executive, independent regulatory commission, government corporation, or public authority—the representation principle must be satisfied in a substantial way due to the extraordinary grant of policy-making authority to these agencies. The great controversy over our licensing agencies has focused upon almost everything else but the representation principle as a reason for changing from the present independent commission approach. Its implementation, as suggested in this paper, would have no necessary implications adversely affecting exercise of good judgment by administrators. Indeed, in increasing their ultimate responsibility to the people for performance of their tasks, it adds a missing dimension to the administrative calculus that has worked well in other contexts. It is also important that it leaves room for choice of administrative techniques, which is denied by the present commitment to the independent commission form. The continuing conflict between the legislature and the chief executive over control of independent regulatory commissions should be recognized for what it is—a competition between institutions in our government for an adequate share in the making of policy.[20] It is an unseemly and unfortunate conflict in representative government, due to its resulting in isolation of these commissions from responsibility to the people for policy-making. Both the chief executive and the legislature have appropriate roles to perform relative to the making of this policy. Implementation of the representation principle will better set the stage for allocation and performance of these roles.

Just as the first two functions of representative government previously noted have been closely associated in the foregoing proposal, so too are the remaining two functions closely associated in the proposals made below. These are the functions of providing a permanent channel for communication of opinions and complaints from people

[19] See, e.g., Louis J. Hector, "Problems of the CAB and the Independent Regulatory Commissions," *Yale Law Journal,* 69 (1960), 931.

[20] See Hugh Hall, "Responsibility of President and Congress for Regulatory Policy Development," *Law & Contemporary Problems,* 26 (1961), 261.

to their government and of providing a counterbalance to influence of organized pressure groups upon the making and administration of public policy. These two functions are being unsatisfactorily responded to by our present structure of administrative agencies. If the first of these demands some degree of direct communication between governmental policy-makers and the people, we must say that our administrative agencies in their policy-making frequently fail to get across to the public the nature of the problems they are handling and to provide the public with a realistic opportunity to voice their opinions and complaints to the agencies. This is especially true at local and state levels. However inadequate the electoral process for engendering discussion of opinions and complaints of people about their problems to government, it is nevertheless true that this discussion does in fact occur in a substantial way. The people who express these opinions do expect that the persons they elect will respond to them at some later point. After the election, the elected representative becomes the first person the voter—or even the nonvoter—thinks of when he has a problem concerning government. He feels he can get a sympathetic hearing of his problem and perhaps some directions as to what he might do and what he might expect from government. Now that the administrative agencies have become major policy-makers in government, it is utterly essential that they become permanent channels for communication of opinions and complaints from the people to their government. Given the existence of so many one-newspaper cities and towns in the country and the refusal of newspapers to provide a forum for the discussion of public issues, it will be difficult for administrative agencies to go to the people through newspapers. Moreover, radio and television services are in many ways even less well adapted, owing to their present methods of programming, than newspapers for accomplishing this purpose. Also, neither the individual legislator nor the whole legislature can satisfy the needed contact between administrative agencies and the people. The most obvious reasons for this fact are the tremendous tasks of legislation and oversight concerning administrative process already being performed by them. Another is the fact that legislative process is to a considerable extent an adversary one with positions already having been taken, argued, and promoted. The contact between the people and the administrative agencies needs to be engendered frequently prior to any position-taking and in a spirit of investigation and research looking to a determination of what is an appropriate solution to a public problem. Legislative committee process serves many useful purposes in the operation of government but it usually does not promote this purpose. The individual legislator is also subject to many pressures from those who have provided him with needed political support during campaigns; therefore he is prone to promote their interests uncritically before administrative agencies when pressed to do so rather than to investigate each request for obtaining administrative action and determining whether the request is one that should be supported in light of the public interest.

THE USE OF ADVISORY COMMITTEES

If administrative agencies are to be in contact with elements of the population who are affected by their policy-making, it is essential that a new structure be built into the operation of government. One device that has come into more frequent use for accomplishing this purpose is the advisory committee. These committees have been utilized both by chief executives and administrative agencies, frequently at the direction of the legislature through statutory provisions, and even by legislatures, particularly at the local level. The basic thought in organizing these committees has been to get a representative group of people to study and advise with regard to a public problem with which a chief executive, an administrative agency, or a legislature is faced. Congress, for example, recently provided for the establishment of Advisory Councils on Social Security.[21] It directed the Secretary of Health, Education, and Welfare to appoint twelve members to each of several councils with the requirement that they "shall, to the extent possible, represent organizations of employers and employees in equal numbers and represent self-employed persons and the public." Under this directive each council is to review the status of one of the various social security funds in relation to the long-term commitments of the old-age, survivors', and disability insurance programs and the adequacy of coverage and benefits under these programs. Each council appointed is directed to report its findings to the Secretary within a certain period of time, with copies of these to be sent to Congress and to the Board of Trustees of each affected fund.

[21] 79 Stat. 339, 42 U.S.C.A. 907 (1965 Cum. Supp.).

Similarly, the President by an executive order in August 1966 established a National Advisory Commission on Selective Service to study the fairness, adequacy, and proper goals of the selective service system and to make recommendations to the President regarding certain specified matters.[22] The twenty-five members appointed were required to be "broadly representative of the various aspects of our national life." With the enactment of an amendment to the National Housing Act in 1954[23] relating to a workable program in connection with urban renewal efforts, a great impetus was given also to the formation of advisory committees at the local government level.[24] It was hoped that implementation of the requirements involved in the workable program concept would lead to a high degree of citizen participation in urban renewal during the past twelve years. These committees have afforded great assistance to city officials on general goals of planning programs, on attitudes and desires of citizens relevant to execution of urban renewal programs, and on popular reactions to government proposals. These committees have frequently served the function of a sounding board for the tentative ideas of government officials for dealing with a public problem. In this way officials are able to elicit able assistance in molding their programs before deadlines are set and political pressures present limiting factors. In addition, committees may even arrange forums and meetings before which city officials appear and exchange ideas with interested citizens concerning a given program. Closely associated with this function is the positive function of helping to educate a community to the need for a program. Finally, an advisory committee can serve to move an administrative agency or city council to take action essential to the integrity or forward movement of a particular program such as urban renewal. It can become a pressure group representing the interests of displaced persons in adequate provision for their relocation and better housing. The danger involved in the last role mentioned is that the advisory group may seek to seize control of or pervert an administrative program. It has even been suggested that this is an inherent characteristic of the possession of power even of an advisory sort. This is especially the

[22] Exec. Order No. 11289, 31 Fed. Reg. (No. 30) 9265 (1966).

[23] National Housing Act, 42 U.S.C.A. s 1451(c) (1965 Cum. Supp.).

[24] For a general discussion see Lyle E. Schaller, "Is the Citizen Advisory Committee a Threat to Representative Government?" *Public Administration Review,* 23 (1963), 175.

case with advisory committees that have not been constituted so as to be truly representative of the people. Usually few persons from the central city areas are selected to sit on advisory committees appointed by local government officials. This feature is much less a danger at the federal level.

Sometimes the advisory commitee is made an integral part of the agency machinery for processing regular administrative business. The experience with these committees is especially instructive about the potentialities and limitations presented by them. One of the early examples of this type of advisory committee is found in Section 9 of the Fair Labor Standards Act of 1938.[25] Under this section as amended, the Wage and Hour Administrator is required to appoint an industry advisory committee with equal numbers representing employees and employers in the industry and with due regard to the geographical regions in which the industry is carried on. This committee is directed to review at least once during specified biennial periods any prescribed minimum wages for certain workers that are not equal to the maximum statutory minimum wage rate with a view to determining whether these prescribed rates should be increased. The committee is then to recommend to the administrator the highest minimum wages for the industry that it determines to be compatible with certain statutory standards. Upon receiving the recommendation the administrator is required to approve it and to carry it into effect if he finds it to be in accordance with law, supported by evidence, and calculated to carry out the purpose of the section.

Another example of the use of advisory committees as an integral part of the policy-making process occurred in conjunction with maximum price regulation in World War II and the Korean War. Since the committee technique utilized in the latter was redesigned in light of difficulties with its use in the earlier, it is profitable to examine the differences between them and the reasons for these differences.[26] The Director of the Office of Price Administration (OPA) under the Emergency Price Control Act of 1942[27] was required to appoint an industry advisory committee when any sub-

[25] Fair Labor Standards Act, 29 U.S.C.A. 208 (1965).

[26] For an extensive and enlightening discussion see Robert V. Faragher and Fritz F. Heimann, "Price Controls, Antitrust Laws, and Minimum Price Laws," *Law & Contemporary Problems,* 19 (1954), 650–63.

[27] 56 Stat. 24 (1942).

stantial portion of a regulated industry requested it. While the act required members of the committee to be "truly representative" of the industry for which it was appointed, in fact the larger and more influential members of an industry received most of the appointments to many committees. When appointed, a committee could by filing a request with the administrator require him to advise and consult with it and in that way initiate consideration of regulatory problems. These committees often received extensive delegations of policy-making authority and acted beyond the scope of their delegated functions, according to a report of the Attorney General of the United States.[28] These committees could elect nonmembers as their secretary or treasurer and in fact elected trade association officials to these positions; could receive contributions from the industry represented for staff salaries and expenses; could, through their chairmen, call meetings; could meet without government officials being present; could, through their chairmen, make up their own agenda; could meet off government premises and did in fact meet in hotel rooms and on trade association premises; and could file representations, recommendations, or petitions relative to any official action of OPA as they saw fit.

The statutory authority of OPA advisory committees and the administrative procedural regulations under which they operated raised the very great possibility of an undercutting of our federal antitrust policy. These statutory structures inevitably promoted the practice of cooperation and agreement between elements of each industry that could become destructive of vigorous competition between them in the market place. It was true, of course, that OPA was able to obtain information and advice from 652 committees that it could not obtain through government surveys and otherwise available data.[29] This information and advice enabled OPA to construct fairer and more workable regulations than otherwise would have been possible. The committees identified trouble spots and unanticipated problems, stated industry positions likely to be taken on OPA actions, and corrected factual misapprehensions. These advantages, however,

[28] Cited in Faragher and Heimann, *op. cit.*, p. 651, n. 6.

[29] For a general discussion see Harvey C. Mansfield, *A Short History of OPA* (Washington, D.C.: U.S. GPO, 1947), pp. 310–12; and Nathaniel L. Nathanson and Harold Leventhal, *Problems in Price Control: Legal Phases* (Washington, D.C.: U.S. GPO, 1947), pp. 75–76.

were obtained at the cost, under the statutory and administrative authority of these committees, of creating the difficulties previously mentioned and many others. One of these stemmed from the practice of OPA officials in discussing in detail with committees proposed regulations and amendments to regulations. With this information in hand businessmen could profit personally at the expense of competitors or customers by temporarily delaying or expediting shipments or by making changes in production or distribution in anticipation of a regulation. Sometimes this information was leaked by committee members to competitors. Another difficulty was the role assumed by these committees of vigorously proposing and pursuing changes in the pricing program desired by the industries they represented. This role made these committees in effect an organized group of lobbyists for administrative price actions and legislative oversight relative to them, a function heavily reinforced by their institutional recognition as part of the administrative process.[30]

An attempt was made to avoid these difficulties by Congress in enacting two provisions of the Defense Production Act of 1950 under which the Office of Price Stabilization (OPS) operated.[31] By Section 404 of the Act appointment of the committees was committed wholly to the discretion of the President who delegated his authority to the Director of Price Stabilization. Section 701 (b) (ii) sought to avoid the nonrepresentativeness of the OPA committees by specifying that on industry advisory committees there be "fair representation for independent small, for medium, and for large business enterprises, for different geographical areas, for trade association members and nonmembers, and for different segments of the industry." Under a price procedural regulation the industry advisory committees were confined solely to an advisory capacity. The director could disband committees and only he could call a meeting of them. A meeting also could only be held in Washington, D.C., under the director's supervision. Only the director or his designated representative was authorized to serve as chairman of a committee and to preside over its meetings. Similarly, preparation of the agenda for a

[30] See, e.g., the review of the work of the OPA Pig Iron Industry Advisory Committee in Harvey C. Mansfield, *Studies in Industrial Price Control* (Washington, D.C.: U.S. GPO, 1947), pp. 101–20.

[31] Sections 404 and 701 (b) (ii), 64 Stat. 807 (1950), 65 Stat. 1381 (1950).

meeting was wholly within control of the director. Trade association representatives, as such, were not permitted to attend these meetings either as members or as observers. The Department of Justice had insisted on this to preclude creation of an atmosphere in which interests of special groups would prevail rather than those of the public. In short, the statute, regulations, and practices under them by OPS confined industry advisory committees to an advisory role with regard to matters presented to them by the director. Determinations to take any official action with regard to prices were made solely by governmental officials. In this way most difficulties presented by earlier OPA committees were resolved satisfactorily.

The OPA-OPS experience with advisory committees as an integral part of administrative process suggests that, carefully handled, these committees enable administrative agencies to serve better the representative government function of being a permanent channel for the communication of opinions and complaints to government. Proper selection of committee members and proper regulation of committee procedures can preclude their acting as lobbyists for a special interest. Like many of the local urban renewal advisory committees, however, neither OPA nor OPS committees had persons sitting as members to represent the general public or consumers, workers, dealers, minority groups, and others having interests affected by the particular policy-making involved.

A similar problem is presented when statutes place regulatory authority in a commission or board whose members are required to be appointed, either solely or principally, from persons who are and remain active in the regulated industry, occupation, or profession.[32] Prior to this century only a few occupations or professions—law, medicine, and the ministry—were subject to regulation through a licensing system. Today the opposite is true. A 1950 survey by the Council of State Governments revealed that there had been an extraordinary increase in this form or regulation during this century.[33] It showed that by 1950 over seventy-five different occupations and professions were subject to licensing regulations in most of the states. Since that time many additional licensing systems have been created. In most instances commissions exercising licensing authority are

[32] See Walter Gellhorn, *Individual Freedom and Government Restraints* (Baton Rouge, La.: L.S.U. Press, 1956), pp. 105–51.

[33] The Council of State Governments, *Occupational Licensing Legislation in the States* (Chicago: 1952), p. 2.

required to be manned by members who are or have been practicing or working in the regulated field.[34]

Licensing legislation establishing industry-manned commissions has been sought by the regulated industries rather than by the public

[34] State licensing systems affect industries of the greatest importance to the public and to operation of the economy. An example is the Texas Finance Commission, consisting of a banking section of six members and a building and loan section of three members. These members—as in the case of most state commissions with licensing authority relative to trades, occupations, and professions—are appointed by the governor pursuant to statutory requirements concerning the qualifications of appointees. Each of four appointees to the banking section must not only be "active bankers" with several years of experience as a high-ranking bank official. In addition, each must be from banks having a certain range of capital and certified surplus. A similar requirement of active engagement in the savings and loan industry is made with regard to two appointees to the building and loan section. Two appointees to the banking section and one to the building and loan section may be selected on the basis of recognized business ability. In practice, however, the governor has appointed members of the regulated industries to these positions so that the commission does not in fact differ from most state commissions with licensing authority whose members are required to be drawn wholly from the regulated industry or trade.

The commission elects a banking commissioner and a savings and loan commissioner, each of whom has primary responsibility for administration of the statute and administrative regulations. Each commissioner is required to have been at the time of appointment a high-ranking official of a bank or association for a specified number of years. Administrative rules covering numerous operations of state savings and loan associations are promulgated by joint action of the savings and loan commissioner and the building and loan section of the Finance Commission. In addition, the commissioner passes upon applications for a charter as a savings and loan association and upon alleged violations of law by these associations. It is obvious, therefore, that under this statutory system and its practical administration the crucial administrative rules applying statutory policy are made by active members of the industry sitting with the commissioner as official administrators. Beyond this, expenses of the state savings and loan department administered by the building and loan section and the commissioner are paid for, not by governmental funds, but by the regulated industry itself.

No system could be better calculated to cause administration of the statute to be industry-oriented. Both the power of appointment of the administrator and the power of the purse, traditional checks over administration retained by the chief executive and the legislature, have been discarded. Of course, the judiciary, as is usually the case, can have little effect upon rule-making and licensing action of the agency and only limited impact upon its adjudications. This way of organizing the agency does not mean that its administration will necessarily be against the public interest but rather that it is designed to be representative primarily of a special interest, that of the savings and loan industry. The people as a whole are not being represented in the agency's decision-making process. Tex. Rev. Civ. Stat. Ann. articles 342–103, 342–104, and 852a (1964). Also see, "Comment, Statutory Control of the Texas Savings and Loan Industry," *Texas Law Review,* 44 (1966), 966.

affected by their operations. The same has been true of the regulated trades, occupations, and professions. Recent studies indicate that a principal reason for their seeking formation of these commissions manned by their peers is the desire to protect themselves against competition.[35] In addition to regulating access to a field of work or business, licensing boards in exercising their authority develop policies calling for imposition of severe sanctions upon persons who engage in practices normally left in our society to private decision-making because they relate to ethical or economic matters. These boards, like the medieval guilds, are frequently given authority to fix prices for services rendered the public by licensees. Sometimes after a licensing system is established, licensees having larger operations and access to more financing move their commission to establish restrictions concerning modes of operation calculated to drive out of the field those licensees having smaller operations. Minorities also find it difficult to enter fields governed by commissions whose members are drawn from the majority group.

Five major steps must be taken in order to assure that the representative principle is realized with regard to industry-manned commissions having licensing, regulatory, and other authority.

1. Any statutory requirement that a commissioner be drawn from the regulated industry, trade, or occupation must be eliminated. Instead, appointment must largely be left to the discretion of the appointing authority. The one exception to discretionary authority should be the proviso that no commissioner may continue to pursue his private activities in the regulated field, or be associated with any person or organization active in that field. The appointing authority should strive to select persons as commissioners who have ability to be good administrators of law.

2. The appointive power should be in the hands of the chief executive and he should be able to appoint a majority of commission members after his election as well as to replace them when he deems this appropriate. Of course, the limitation mentioned earlier with respect to handling of the adjudicative function by these boards should apply.

3. In the interest of increasing responsiveness of these boards to the public interest, their work should be allocated, as far as possible,

[35] See, e.g., Lynn W. Eley, "Michigan's Professional and Occupational Boards: Organization and Powers," *University of Detroit Law Journal,* 41 (1964), 349.

to one department of licensing. This should especially be possible with regard to the various occupations, trades, and professions. Experience at the state and federal levels also shows that it is feasible to allocate regulation of related industries to a single commission. The expedient of consolidating the work of licensing boards for occupations, trades, and professions has been recommended by several studies and adopted in some degree by several states.

4. Advisory committees should be established similar to those set up by the Office of Price Stabilization. The members of an advisory committee should consist in part of persons drawn from the regulated occupation, trade, profession, or industry. Other members should be drawn from the general public, consumers of the services or goods of the regulated group, persons dealing with the group through contractual transactions, and any other classes having interests substantially affected by the operations of the regulated group.

5. Any licensing system where the predominant purpose or effect of that system is protection of licensees from competition should be eliminated. The reason for this last measure is that one cannot, despite implementation of the foregoing suggested steps, avoid the impact of the nonrepresentative purpose of such licensing systems upon their administration. While the free competitive market may not technically be classified as a democratic or representative institution, it is clearly one of the most desirable alternatives in a democracy to government control clearly destructive of the representative principle, a factor always involved in licensing boards manned by members of the regulated group.

DECREASING DISCRIMINATION THROUGH ADMINISTRATIVE PROCESS

The final topic of this essay concerns the breakdown of representation in a part of a federal system and the extraordinary usefulness of administrative process, when properly organized, for restoring operation of this principle. The framers of the Constitution of the United States foresaw the problem and attempted to deal with it in Section 4 of Article IV: "The United States shall guarantee to every State in this Union a Republican Form of Government. . . ." In actual administration this has been largely a dormant part of our constitutional framework. We have, however, had a widespread breakdown in representative or republican government, one especially evident in this century in the South and Southwest. Despite decisions of the Supreme Court of the United States relating to state action denying Negroes or Mexican-Americans equal protection of the laws and due process and despite federal legislation culminating in the Civil Rights Act of 1964 and the Voting Rights Act of 1965, these and other minority groups are still subject to widespread discrimination due to their race, color, religion, or nationality both by government and private persons and organizations. Discrimination against minority groups relates to voting rights, public education, government services, public employment, private employment, apprenticeship training, union membership or privileges, public and private housing, hospitalization, and many forms of public accommodation. Members of these groups have been excluded from the holding of public office and effective participation in official decision-making processes. The same has been true with regard to membership in significant community organizations and their decision-making processes.

The principal device being utilized under recent federal legislation to deal with some forms of discrimination against minority groups is a suit in equity by the federal government to obtain an injunction against their continuation. This device, however effective it is in the individual case, is a very slow and cumbersome one for dealing with discrimination in gross. Experience has demonstrated during the past twenty years that, properly adapted, our modern administrative process and its various institutions can be extraordinarily effective in opening up various kinds of needed opportunities to members of minority groups.[36] What is really needed to deal with discrimination against these groups is the device of the human relations commission. Undoubtedly, discrimination of this sort is both engendered and operative at the local level. Some commissions have been particularly effective when operating at this level, depending on their being adequately staffed by professional human relations specialists, well financed, equipped with strong regulatory authority, and conducted on the basis of an effective program for opening up opportunities for minority groups. State human relations commissions have on the whole been less effective than well-organized local

[36] See Joseph P. Witherspoon, "Civil Rights Policy in the Federal System: Proposals for a Better Use of Administrative Process," *Yale Law Journal,* 74 (1965), 1171; and Norgren and Hill, *Toward Fair Employment* (1964).

commissions. The former have usually not embarked upon community relations and similar programs. They have also failed in most instances to decentralize their administration. Local commissions, by way of contrast, have sought to involve the local leadership in their work. Perhaps the most effective tool used to open up opportunities has been a series of methods directed toward getting wide sectors of business and government to adopt programs for facilitating integration proposed by personnel of the local commissions.

Unfortunately, there can be little hope in the immediate future that effective local commissions will be established in the South or, for that matter, in the Southwest. There is, perhaps, even less hope that state human relations commissions will be established in these areas. Thus, if the breakdown in the representation principle in these areas is to be met, it must be bypassed by the federal government through some kind of effective expedient. The author has proposed elsewhere the establishment by the federal government of what might be called federal-local human relations commissions.[37] These would be full-fledged commissions of the federal government. They would, however, operate at the local level in the various cities, counties, and larger towns of the South and Southwest, and elsewhere as needed. The commissioners of these federal-local agencies would be appointed by the President so as to be properly representative of the various ethnic groups in the locality served by the commission. They would administer at the local level any federal law proscribing discrimination on the basis of race, color, sex, religion, or national origin. The commissioners would use the typical steps of administrative process: receipt of complaints of discrimination, investigation, conciliation, formal hearing of complaints where necessary, and issuance of cease-and-desist orders where appropriate. These orders would be enforceable by the commission in actions brought before a federal court of appeals.

Beyond the technique of processing individual complaints of discrimination, the federal-local human relations commissions would utilize the most modern techniques in getting wide sectors of the government and business to adopt programs for opening up needed opportunities to minority groups as proposed by their commissioners and staffs. They would also seek to assist both the majority group

[37] Witherspoon, *op. cit.*, pp. 1223–25.

and minority groups to develop a leadership that would begin to deal positively and effectively through private action with local human relations problems. They would move toward developing and involving a leadership in each city that eventually would get that city to take the necessary official and private steps to eliminate the very notion of a second-class citizenship. The commissioners, drawn from the city in which they sit, would have the whole weight and protection of the federal government behind them. Their operation would be completely funded by the federal government and a highly expert staff of human relations specialists would be provided them. In time, it would be expected that these commissions, having dealt effectively with human relations problems through an administrative agency thoroughly representative of the community and oriented toward subserving the common good of the state and the nation, would cause the representative principle to be built back into the public life of the South and Southwest. It is hoped that they would set models of official performance that would be imitated in time by local and state government. In any event, they would serve to preclude and ameliorate the almost certain conflicts and explosions in future years as the Negro, Latin American, and other ethnic groups seek to throw off the chains that have so long enslaved them.

CONCLUSION

This essay has attempted to illustrate some of the major problems in administrative process regarding extra-elective representation. I have tried to show the potentiality for realization of the representative principle in this realm of government. I have suggested that perhaps the greatest problems of representative government—and, indeed, of representation—are concerned with administrative process. This major new source for policy-making in modern governments makes it necessary to re-examine the goals and purposes of representative government. The nature and conditions of administrative process also make it necessary to discover new means of realizing these goals and purposes. Upon the success of these two efforts the practicability and meaningfulness of representative government depend. Finally, as with all major developments in governmental structure, administrative process provides us splendid new resources for dealing with breakdowns in representative government within a part of a federal system.

REPRESENTATION UNDER NONCOMPETITIVE PARTY SYSTEMS

18

THE MECHANISM OF POPULAR ACTIVITY IN THE EXERCISE OF STATE AUTHORITY IN PEOPLE'S POLAND

WITOLD ZAKRZEWSKI

To discuss the influence of the people on the exercise of state authority, we have to take into consideration at least three questions:

First, the basic principles of our Constitution, which form the fundamental rules relating to the exercise of the sovereign rights of

The Polish Academy of Science, Institute for Law, has organized a research group active under the direction of Prof. S. Zawadzki, which investigates fundamental problems of the activity of People's Councils. Some of its studies, published in *Problemy Rad Narodowych* [Problems of People's Councils], and others still in manuscript form, were used in the preparation of this essay. Many materials pertinent to the problems discussed appear also in the periodicals *Państwo i Prawo* [State and Law], *Gospodakra i Administracja Terenowa* [Regional Economy and Administration], and *Rada Narodowa* [People's Council].

the nation; second, the legally provided mechanism of the institutions developed to carry these principles into effect; and third, the development of the practice determining the real use made of those institutions.

BASIC CONSTITUTIONAL PRINCIPLES

According to the Constitution, all state authority is vested in a system of representative assemblies, elected by the people and empowered to direct by appropriate means state activity at all levels of territorial division. That means that the people have to exercise their power primarily through the Sejm (Parliament) as supreme organ of the state power, and by People's Councils elected for every province (*województwo*), district (*powiat*), town, and town districts in larger towns (*miaste*), and rural community (*gromada*).

The representatives elected both to the Sejm and to the People's Councils are responsible to their constituents, and may be revoked by them. They are obliged to maintain close relations with the population and the social organizations active in different spheres of social life.

All public authorities, the representative assemblies as well as the administrative bodies, are obliged to work in close touch with the people and their organizations in order to take into consideration popular demands, and also to explain to the people the aims and principles of state policy and other grounds for their decisions.

If the first of these principles allows Poland to rank among representative democracies, the latter two give to our system of representation a special, popular character. They open channels for direct participation and direct influence of the people on state activity.

PEOPLE'S COUNCILS

Social scientists from outside the Socialist camp seldom understand that the system of the People's Councils is hardly comparable with the institutions of local or self-government. These forms have in common only that they both furnish people with organized institutions, provided to allow their representatives to take an active part in public life and to influence the determination and realization of tasks lying within the scope of their competences. Regarding the differences, two are of utmost importance for our problem:

1. The local-government bodies are legally limited in their competences. The fundamental tasks to be realized by the state belong traditionally to the competences of governmental agencies acting independently of local-government bodies. Outside the scope of the latter are many fields of governmental and administrative work of major importance. On the contrary, the People's Councils have general competence to direct the economic, social, and cultural life within the boundaries of their territory. All administrative and economic tasks not legally exempt and transferred to other authorities are to be carried out by offices directed in their work by People's Councils and acting under their supervision. According to the principle of dual subordination, these authorities have to conform not only to the directives received from the government and appropriate ministers, but also to the resolutions of the People's Councils; and People's Councils are legally competent to exercise control over their activity.

Acts voted by Parliament in 1958 and in 1963 have substantially enlarged the powers of People's Councils. Even in the case of tasks legally transferred to independent authorities, the People's Councils have received important powers for coordinating their activity with the work done by bodies under the competence of the councils.

2. The local-government bodies do not form one interconnected system of organs of state. Each acts independently according to the powers transferred to it by law. On the contrary, the Sejm and the People's Councils form one interconnected system of representative authorities. These legally determined interconnections serve to realize uniform state policy by all People's Councils. At the same time, these interconnections serve to provide opportunities to adjust state activity to peculiar territorial or local needs and other particular circumstances and factors determining the due course of development of each territory.

The mechanism of these interconnections is very flexible and may in practice be used in many different ways. The practice may stress the subordination of local bodies to central directives, leaving insufficient scope for popular influence on the territorial levels of the administration. These bureaucratic tendencies appeared with certain strength in the years 1950–56. The process of decentralization may result in the drastic reduction of central directives, in diminishing the help provided to People's Councils by governmental agencies. In that case there appears the danger of false decisions, striving at aims disproportionate to really existing means, and causing dangerous tensions between the tasks resolved and possibilities of implementation. At the same time other authorities may accept an easy-going attitude resulting in the waste of means and marked slowing down of the development of services provided. This danger appeared in practice immediately after 1956.

This mechanism may also be used in a proper way by reasonable decentralization within a framework of tasks set in national plans of development according to centrally determined directives of state policy, on the basis of means and resources distributed centrally with discernment of real needs and possibilities. From past experience, the goal at which both changes in legal system and practical experiments are striving appears in efforts to develop real influence of the people and their representatives on the process of shaping the policy of state activity in different spheres of social life and on its implementation by appropriate measures taken at different levels of the state structure.

The influence of the people's representatives active at the lower levels of the hierarchy of People's Councils is not limited to the sphere in which they are competent to decide and instruct subordinate units by their own resolutions.

Each People's Council, both by its own resolutions and by the orientation which it gives to the work of subordinated bodies, is empowered to influence the projects of fundamental acts of state policy: statutes and major statutory instruments, budgets and plans of development, basic decisions established by appropriate bodies at higher levels. Among many ways open to them in this connection, the following are of greatest value:

1. The active participation in drafting projects in those parts which touch directly interests of the territory represented;

2. Sending up resolutions of their own initiative regarding services to be provided or developed, establishments or undertakings to be organized, administrative measures to be taken—to satisfy needs, to take advantage of the existing resources and to stimulate the economic development and also the social and cultural life of the population.

3. Giving opinions regarding projected measures with substantial influence on the conditions of life of the population represented or in any other ways important for the social situation of their territory.

Each People's Council is also empowered to supervise the execution of state policy and the carrying out of measures taken at higher levels. In this respect they may use their competence to coordinate all state activity in their territory, as well as to point out shortcomings in the work done by institutions dependent on the government or on the People's Councils of higher levels.

Because of these powers, and because of the ever-growing use made of them in practice by the deputies, the influence of the people on state activity is exerted not only through a few hundred members of Parliament, but through many thousands of representatives.

POWERS OF COMMITTEES

It might be said quite frankly that these large powers would be formal if the representatives were reduced to expressing their views at council meetings, if they were not provided with means to exercise real control over the work done by subordinate bodies. There ought to be real opportunities to decide which problems are of basic importance and are to be decided by the councils themselves so as to influence directly the process of drafting the proposals to be presented at the council meetings and to control the execution of the resolutions voted.

Because the importance of providing the representatives with appropriate organization to work effectively was clearly understood, great weight was put on the development of the powers of committees. Many efforts are made to stimulate these committees to do productive work.

Each council is empowered to elect as many committees as it believes necessary to cover all essential fields of its competence. The committees are free to elect not only their own members, but also other active citizens whose participation may be useful—but not more than half of the whole number. (These are elected either because of personal aptitudes and qualifications, or because they are valuable as links with particular groups of the population or with particular social organizations.) In other words, to the active participation in the work done by the councils are called, in addition to the representatives, many other thousands of people.

The data show that more than one per cent of the adult population directly take part in the work of the People's Councils. This by itself gives popular character to our representative system, further strengthened by the obligation of committees to work in collaboration with social organizations and to develop the direct activity of the people.

It is not possible at the moment to describe in detail the powers and the mechanism of work of the committees. Generally, the committees deliberate and take stands on reports and information presented to them by authorities active in the field of their competence and by territorial units of the office of state control. They may send out their own members to see for themselves the working of controlled institutions and to gather the necessary information regarding the problems under consideration. They may also, if necessary, organize consultations with appropriate social organizations and between the committees working at different levels of the structure of the People's Councils.

It is possible to criticize the committees for sometimes leaning too much on information received from administrative bodies; as a result, they are not penetrating enough in their work. Sometimes they do not develop well enough their own controlling activity and forms of social intercourse with interested groups of people and their organizations. In this respect they are sometimes satisfied with formal representation of appropriate organizations; with the fact that some members of the committee were elected to represent them. On the other hand, it would be interesting to note changes that are appearing recently, especially in the practice of the district and town councils' committees. It appears that they are taking greater pains to gather varied information by sending out their own groups to form personal observations and direct contacts with the people. At the provincial level, some steps are being taken toward using information and opinions gathered and formulated at the lower levels.

The committee may influence the state activity in three basic forms: (1) through opinions, motions, and recommendations directed to administrative bodies and other institutions; (2) through collaboration with the "presidium of the council"—an administrative organ of general competence established to control and direct the execution of the competences of the council according to the laws and the legally binding directives and policy expressed by resolutions of the council (the presidium is obliged to help the committees in the discharge of their functions; it must consider their opinions before taking decisions of greater importance; each committee is empowered to present to the presidium motions to issue dispositions or orders believed to be necessary to direct the work of the subordinated bodies); (3) the last channel of influence appears in the work done for the council itself. Each committee may present its own motions and draft resolutions, collaborate in the preparation of the drafts of resolutions, express its opinions, and propose amendments to projects from other sources.

At the moment it is generally believed that the powers of committees are large enough, and that what matters most is to organize their work to stimulate their efficiency. In this respect several obstacles appear.

One of the hindrances is that the deputies—as working people—have limited possibilities to offer their time and effort for discharge of their duties. This difficulty occurs especially when their opinion has to be formulated in a short time, according to a timetable set in advance for the process of drafting projects of the most important measures (budget, national plan, etc.).

Another real hindrance is also that too often information and papers presented to the committees are formulated in a complicated and technical form not easy to understand for people having no special knowledge, and without a clear distinction between problems on which their opinion may determine the decision and other questions regulated by law or by directives and decisions from higher levels. This distinction is of the highest importance to organize effective work. Even if sometimes it appears necessary to present postulates to higher authorities in order to change their attitude, the appropriate forms of action are different, and motions should be supported by very convincing arguments.

It would be misleading to assert that all the powers granted by law to the councils and their committees are fully used to direct and to influence the activity of the state according to the ideas, evaluations, and wishes of the people truly represented by their deputies. In fact, professional public servants employed in offices subordinated to the councils take part in no small degree in the work of the councils. But at the same time it is necessary to remember that they are acting with the agreement of the councils and their committees with full knowledge of their attitude evidenced at the discussions at the meetings, with good information regarding the people's wishes, sometimes further informed by motions presented by appropriate political and social organizations and by direct contacts with deputies acting individually on behalf of their constituencies.

If we stress principally the organized means of influence provided for collective action of representatives, it is also necessary to point out possibilities open to each one of them acting individually. Each deputy is empowered to present motions not only at the meetings of the councils and their committees, but to all authorities and institutions able to decide on questions submitted to them. He is empowered by law to be informed on steps taken in the process of deciding upon the matter submitted by him, and to intervene if he has any doubts about the proper attitude of the officials concerned. The most efficient means of such intervention is his right to submit to the presidium of the council interpellations which oblige this body to consider the question put and give him a reasoned answer. If he disagrees with the answer, he may present his case through an appropriate motion to the council itself. This allows each deputy to act in every question which he personally believes to be of importance, even if it has no connection with the topics on which the actual work of the council and its committees is concentrated.

In many councils, the use made of the interpellations has developed in recent times. This fact proves, in our opinion, that the deputies have experienced the usefulness of this means.

SELECTION OF CANDIDATES

Around a quarter of a million men and women participate in the Polish People's Republic in the work of People's Councils and their committees. Their position as representatives of the people allows them to exercise greater influence than other citizens on state activity. It may be of some interest to ask: how do they reach that position?

The formal answer is simple. Deputies are elected in general elections. Members of committees are chosen by the councils. But it would be interesting to go beyond that and to probe the question not from a formal, but from a sociological, point of view. How do they get to be presented as candidates on the lists?

There is no doubt that the answer is not simple, that many factors may influence the committees of the Front of National Unity to take into consideration some persons and to decide to accept them as candidates. Various studies organized at the time of the last elections have thrown some light on this subject and allow us to formulate at least some tentative hypotheses.

These hypotheses apply to the process at all levels, the picture appears most clearly in small rural communities and in small towns. There the people know each other and the selection of candidates by the local Committees of the Front of National Unity takes the most concrete forms. At higher levels, beginning with the districts and larger towns, the process of selection becomes more complicated. But the general pattern is in principle the same.

As the first step we find everywhere a process of scrutiny into the activity of previous members of the council and its committees during the last term. This scrutiny aims at maintaining or even promoting those who have distinguished themselves by their work, and at eliminating those who have not fulfilled expectations.

The mandate of a representative offers a position of some relative eminence in social relations, opens possibilities to exert influence on social and state life. To maintain this position it is necessary to be considered a person whose participation serves some useful purpose, and to fulfill these expectations by the proper exercise of the duties accepted. If a person neglects his duties, has no time or no abilities to perform properly the functions pertaining to his mandate, he ought to be replaced by a new candidate.

Each election opens, therefore, possibilities of promotion. This promotion may take different forms. The best people from those who were chosen by councils to participate in the work of committees and who have gained some esteem because of their activity are the first to be considered as candidates for mandate. The process of selection goes on all levels at the same time, and the committees of the Front and the political organizations at all levels consult each other. The people who have achieved some success in their work with local councils, who have gained some social standing in the eyes of their constituents, who have learned how to perform duties pertaining to their mandate, are naturally among those who are considered for selection to more responsible functions. In this way, for every council at a higher level there appear candidates whose claim to election is supported by distinction in work done in the previous term at lower levels of the People's Councils hierarchy.

There is no doubt that the higher the level of a representative authority, the greater the possible scope of influence of those who participate in its work. Accordingly, a mandate to the Sejm is not comparable in public esteem to the mandate of a deputy to a provincial council. Therefore, it is possible to speak of a promotion when somebody is selected to a higher authority than that to which he had been elected in the previous term.

On the other side, it might be appropriate to observe that even the scope of competence of a district council is large enough to allow the deputies to exert real influence on state activity and on the economic, social, and cultural development of their territory. At higher levels, the ability to think in abstract categories, to summarize observations and information into general propositions appears fundamental for exercising any real influence on the process of decision-making. Because of that, a promotion may be of very relative value. Not everybody gaining in social status gains at the same time in real influence.

At this second stage in selecting the candidates, while the committees work on filling the vacancies, previous activity within the representative authorities is not the only asset which is taken into consideration. Another one, no less influential, is participation in other forms of social activity. One of the principles of our representative system is to assure within each council appropriate representation of all social organizations of some importance active in its territory. If somebody distinguishes himself by his work with an important social organization, he may be selected as a candidate.

Here we may also speak of promotion—but in another sense. Not always does the person selected gain in social prestige—even though that is the usual case. Not always does the mandate appear to him as enlarging his authority: his status within the organization may offer him a position of eminence, and sufficient opportunities for social influence. But in every case the mandate opens to the candidate the possibility of a new channel of influence and of a new field of social and political activity. To some, the selection offers promotion in every respect; to some, only in the sense just mentioned.

The third question considered everywhere when selecting candidates is to assure proper representation to every particular social group. Within each social group, many factors influence the social status of its members.

It would be impossible to discuss here how some people get to be known and respected within the group to which they belong, and are accepted as those able to represent a profession or any particular human community. If somebody is selected as a candidate, we may speak again of promotion—but again in another meaning. Here a selection may appear either as an upward step in social esteem, or as the consolidation and formal recognition of some social eminence. At the same time, this recognition may serve to enhance the personal position of the representative, and open to him new opportunities of direct influence on state activity.

The process of drawing up tentative lists of prospective candidates appears thus as a chain of consultations with social organizations, representatives of professions, enterprises and other institutions, aiming both at selecting candidates and at ascertaining that they are acceptable to those groups which they have to represent. After the list is established, it is presented in rural communities and in small towns at mass meetings. In this way opinions presented by the people directly at public gatherings may correct the process of tentative selection.

For the higher levels, this procedure would be unacceptable: there is no sufficient social homogeneity to accept public gatherings as proper means of popular supervision over the selection of candidates. For larger territories and bigger towns, the tentative lists are discussed and accepted at specially organized meetings of party-delegates and also of delegates of other political organizations. These have to accept the lists, as they form the core of the Front of National Unity and must accept responsibility for the lists which are formally lodged with the appropriate electoral commissions to serve for the general elections.

DIFFERENCES IN INFLUENCE AT VARIOUS LEVELS

If participation in the work of People's Councils and their committees allows many thousands of men and women to exert some influence on the activity of the state apparatus, it is quite clear that the scope of their influence and the real impact of their activity on public and state life are not uniform.

There is no doubt that some differences are to be attributed to the position of the council to which they were elected. The councils situated higher in the hierarchy of the territorial division of the state are equipped with larger competences and may offer greater scope for active participation in influencing the economic, social, and cultural development of the territory.

The differences in authority appear also between representatives active on the same structural level and are to be seen in each of the

People's Councils. It would be interesting to ascertain how a representative arrives at a position of authority and what factors cause the development of his influence.

To approach this extremely complex problem, and to present some observations and hypotheses in that respect, it is necessary to distinguish first between the authority with institutional foundations, resulting from the office to which a deputy is elected, and the influence which he exerts as a representative.

It would be misleading to speak of the influence of the members of Parliament without distinguishing between back-benchers, members of the Council of State, members of the Government, and so on. The same applies to territorial and local levels. It would be misleading to speak of the influence of the deputies without distinguishing among those who are elected to specific offices, and particularly the offices of the chairman, the deputy-chairman, and the secretary of the presidium and others.

In fact the situation appears even more complex. Not every office to which a deputy may be elected enhances his position in such a way as to make his influence certain, and sets him clearly in a different category of political authority from the rest. To an intermediate group there belong the chairmanships and deputy-chairmanships of the council committees and even the membership of the presidium if not connected with permanent employment and treated simply as a social function.

Special considerations apply to the election to the most important offices within the presidia of the councils. Men elected to these functions exert large powers connected with the organization supervision and management of the work of all offices, executing the competences of the council and helping in the organization of the work of the council itself. It is necessary to select for these offices the people most appropriate from political, social, and administrative points of view. It is quite clear that besides the standing attained in the exercise of a representative mandate, many other factors influence the choice. But among many channels which may serve as opportunities for election, one runs through personal authority and influence gained by work done within the council and its committees.

This progress to a position of authority—if it has to be attained, among other factors, in consideration of achievements and distinction gained through activity within the council—leads usually in a gradual way, through positions of influence.

The functions of chairmen and deputy-chairmen of committees, and also in some respects the functions of members of the presidia exercised as social activity, may best be reckoned as positions of influence. These functions give no power to make decisions in the name of state authority or to organize and coordinate directly the activity of state institutions. But these functions—as an institution—offer enlarged opportunities for exerting influence and leaving the imprint of personal work, initiative, and opinions on decisions reached by the council, its presidium and committees. With this group of functions we reach a borderline of institutional and personal influence.

Among the chairmen of committees it is possible to discern at least three groups. Those belonging to one of these groups discharge their functions as means to promote and lead in common work. They are ready to guide and take personal initiative, but at the same time are willing to make use of the initiative, thought, experience, and work of others. Their aim is to organize the common effort for the best performance of duties pertaining to the committees. Committees acting under such chairmanship are usually the most efficient and exert the greatest influence. This position gives to their chairmen high authority and esteem and may lead them, if opportunity arises, to positions of authority.

Another group includes those who use their functions to enhance their personal influence. They guide the bodies acting under their chairmanship by their own initiative and opinions. If they act in a reasonable way and have the gift to make others agree with their views, they may leave a strong imprint of their personality on the work of their committee; and speaking in its name, they may exert strong influence. But if these traits of their character appear in a strong form, their personality creates some vacuum around them. As they do not allow members of their committee to have personal views and to develop too much activity and influence, they appear very useful and not easily replaceable. But at the same time they may cause some apprehensions and therefore they are but seldom selected for functions within the presidium.

It is possible also to discern a third group, that of the chairmen who have no real personal standing and no real personal influence.

They do not direct the work of their committees but act under impulses received from others. If they have to express some opinion or motion in the name of their committee, they act as spokesman of the others.

On the other side, in almost every council it is possible to find a large or small group of deputies who have authority and influence without any particular functions giving them institutional standing. These are mostly active in those committees in which the chairman sees his duty in organizing the common work. They also run, in fact, the committees in which the chairman is not able to be more than their spokesman. They use their personal rights to promote reasonable motions and resolutions and take hand in carrying out useful initiatives. Sometimes their outside work does not allow them to accept more time-absorbing functions, and they concentrate on some particular line of activity. Sometimes their activity has a larger scope; and as they consolidate their position, they are chosen either as chairmen of committees or as members of the presidium of the council. But even without being elected to these functions of influence they do exert real influence and authority. What allows these deputies to distinguish themselves from the rest?

It is understood sometimes that here again institutional factors are of no small influence. It is possible to argue that persons with authority in important political and social organizations, directors of offices and enterprises having some weight in social and economic life, people occupying positions of authority as experts in professions connected with the council competences, etc., gain in esteem and authority within the council, by the fact of their outside functions. It would be false to minimize the influence of this factor, but it would be false to attribute to it a determining quality. The outside institutional position may help a lot in building the authority and influence within the council, but it is not reflected directly in the influence exercised. Mostly it is not simply the office or position which gives authority to a representative, but the experience, wisdom, and information gained in his outside occupation, and the qualities of mind, character, and social attitude which have contributed to make him gain the post which he occupies. If he does not apply himself to the duties of his mandate, if he has no time or will to take an active part in inspiring the work of the council and its committees, in shaping motions, opinions, and resolutions, he exerts no real influence and in fact somehow fades in the background.

It may be argued also that large activity in different social and political organizations plays an important part in shaping the position of a deputy. In fact social activity may play no small part in arriving at positions of influence within the council. This activity may allow a deputy to serve as a link between the social organizations and the council. His participation in organized social work helps him to know the people, to understand social needs, and to take an appropriate stand in the exercise of his mandate. On the other hand, his mandate helps him to take initiatives and to exercise influence in ways serving the aims of the social organizations to which he belongs and helping to achieve their aims. But again it would be misleading to reach the conclusion that the authority and influence of a deputy are in direct and proportionate relation to his outside social activities. We see many illustrations that an excessive involvement in different social activities leaves a representative no time to perform properly the duties pertaining to his mandate. He may fade into the background, emerging only from time to time when he has to speak in the name of one of the organizations to which he belongs. In this case he exerts no real authority, and on the contrary wastes those opportunities of influence which he is able to reach.

Judicious activity within the council and its committees appears thus the most fundamental factor determining the use which a deputy makes of his opportunities. His eminence in the outside world, his engagement in different social activities, and his expert knowledge may contribute to his authority and influence. But all these assets are only potential factors of an influence which may become real only if he applies thought, energy, and time to the real work which is expected of him.

OTHER REPRESENTATIVE INSTITUTIONS

The representative organs of state power are not the only bodies provided to represent the people and to allow them to exert their influence on public life. In every village, meetings are assembled to discuss all topics of local importance, in which all adult villagers take part. To the competence of these gatherings belong the decisions about all public works which are to be done by the free initiative of the people, by means provided by them with some help furnished by the state. At these meetings, the people elect their bailiff who serves as a link between the People's Council, its office, and the population. The meetings discuss also the ways and means of accomplishing the tasks put in the plans of development for their community, and may express opinions regarding the efficiency of the administration and of the institutions serving the community.

In every town, gatherings of inhabitants of the blocks of flats are organized. Their primary function is to elect a block-committee to supervise the administration of the apartment houses, the maintenance of the houses, streets, and open spaces. They may also organize social amenities necessary to the inhabitants, on the basis of work and means furnished by the free initiative of the people, with some help provided by the state. They may elect social judges to settle disputes between the neighbors, without intervention by the courts of justice, and to stimulate proper social behavior in neighborly relations.

In the larger public enterprises we find a rather elaborate structure of workers' representation, known as workers' self-government. Its primary duty is to serve as a link between the management and the workers. The workers' self-government has to help toward the development of the enterprise and its proper functioning, both in public interest and for the benefit of the people employed. A special statute grants to the bodies representing workers' self-government powers to supervise the plans of production, to intervene on behalf of the workers regarding the conditions of work, to propose improvements in the process of production, and to control the economic effects of the activity of the enterprise.

There are also many different functions to which people are chosen to influence directly the working of public institutions. The people influence the administration of justice in many forms: as jurors, sitting on the courts of justice and participating on an equal footing with the judges in pronouncing sentences; as members of collegial bodies elected to punish minor misdemeanors and breaches of public peace. They sit on boards which decide on appeals in questions of public assistance. They are chosen to commissions provided to settle amicably disputes between workers and management regarding questions of work and pay in larger factories. They may be chosen to committees organized in some branches of administration to perform advisory functions.

We have enumerated some of the public functions open to active citizens, in order to substantiate the thesis that in the Polish People's Republic there are many channels open to the people to take active part in state activity; that representative authorities do not exhaust the forms of influence of the people over the exercise of state power.

We do not propose to enlarge on this topic, as it must be agreed that these forms are of limited significance, each having its particular use, each concerned with some particular and narrow task. On the other hand, the importance of these forms ought not to be underestimated. Even if each single one touches some limited area of action, taken jointly they provide an important link between the state apparatus and the population.

CHANNELS FOR EXPRESSING POPULAR OPINION

Returning to the main problem of popular influence over the process of implementation of state policy and of control over the exercise of the functions of the administration, which are the powers open to everybody?

For the average man, not himself a member of Parliament or a deputy to a People's Council, there are three principal channels of stating his views, presenting his complaints, and expressing his opinions.

The first is provided by administrative procedure established by law. Each citizen is empowered to present to every public institution, to every public authority and administrative body, his complaints and suggestions regarding the improvement of its activity. If he believes that his rights or legally protected interests have been infringed, he may present his case to the public prosecutor's office, so that appropriate steps may be taken to eliminate the transgression of legal order. Every public institution which has received a complaint or a suggestion is obliged to examine it and either take appropriate action or inform the author why his suggestion is considered ill-founded.

The second is provided by the obligation on the part of the representatives to maintain close relations with the population. Every member of the Sejm has days on which he receives visits by constituents who wish to present their cases or observations regarding some public question. This practice may serve many purposes, but is used primarily by the people desiring a deputy's intervention in their personal concerns. The practice of public gatherings is of much greater value for influencing the course of public activity. These meetings serve to achieve two interconnected aims. The speakers present to the people the political program of state activity; inform them of the activity of the representative bodies and other public authorities in their efforts to develop the life of our country, to improve living conditions, to provide better public services; tell of steps taken to perform the tasks set in the national plans of development. The people are encouraged to make their observations, to present their complaints, to inform the deputies about shortcomings in the working of public institutions and about the possibilities for improvement in developing the production or satisfying public needs.

We have passed the stage at which the desires expressed by the people were rare. We have also passed the stage at which they were accepted too easily, without means to satisfy them, causing waste by unfinished works and public disappointment. At present a very vast flow of desiderata appears at the time of elections, i.e., when the program of the Front of National Unity for the following term of the representative assemblies is presented and discussed; the list is steadily supplemented as a result of public meetings and other public gatherings. The deputies must not only take notice of the desiderata presented, but also take care of their proper treatment. First the unreasonable proposals must be eliminated, i.e., those for measures either without any real social value, or whose social benefit is not proportionate to the efforts necessary to provide it. The rest—the reasonable ones—must be compared in importance with the means necessary to accomplish them. In this way they are sorted out: some to be accomplished by means provided by the people themselves, with much or little help furnished by the state; others, to be undertaken by state authorities with means provided by the state. In all cases, it must be decided when, and under which conditions, it would be possible to accomplish them.

Each year each People's Council investigates the list of accepted desiderata belonging to its competence, to ascertain if their satisfaction is in accord with the priorities resolved.

If we accept as one of the directives of public action that, as far as possible, the reasonable wishes of the people must be fulfilled, we must use the resources to meet the demands of the people and we must develop public services according to their desires. That means that the desiderata must be taken in consideration when formulating the national plans of development, and that they influence their content. Naturally, the country's resources must be used primarily to assure the steady and balanced growth of our economy, to assure the functioning of all basic services without which the raising of the living conditions of the people would be in jeopardy. The desiderata may influence only in some degree the political priorities fixed for the development of particular fields of economic, social and cultural activity. They may influence the use made of reserves and surpluses, which may be directed according to more or less free choice. Even that is enough for us to accept the desiderata as one of the important channels of the people's influence.

The third and last channel of direct influence of the people lies outside the mechanism of state institutions. It is exercised through political and social organizations serving to express the will and the interests of the people. It is superfluous to remind political scientists that in our age organized political forces form the determining factor of all state activity.

Everyone is well aware that in the Polish People's Republic, the leading political force is the United Workers' Party, which directs state activity; that it collaborates with the United Peasants' Party and the Democratic Party as well as with other popular organizations, and in particular with professional unions, cooperatives, and other mass associations; that the means of coordination of their activity is a popular movement, the Front of National Unity.

It is quite clear that the most fundamental of all the means for influencing the activity of the state is, for active people, their participation in the United Workers' Party or in other organizations belonging to the party-system. I conclude with this statement because I believe that my task was not to describe the working of the party system, but those institutions established within the state mechanism to provide for close relation between the state and the people, as channels of the people's activity in influencing the state, as means to unite the political control of the state by the party with the initiative coming directly from the activity of the people.

19

NOTES FOR A THEORY OF NONDEMOCRATIC REPRESENTATION

DAVID E. APTER

INTRODUCTION

These notes are preliminary to a theory of nondemocratic representation. Need for such a theory has been apparent for some time, particularly in relation to the processes of development, which is a different context from that in which we are accustomed to consider representative institutions and their functions. In my view, most (although not all) nondemocratic representation is better seen as "predemocratic," rather than as alternative or hostile to it. Such representation is also functionally varied, depending for its relevance on the stage of development and the prevailing type of political system. Indeed, different political systems stress forms of political

This essay was written under the auspices of the Politics of Modernization Project of the Institute of International Studies, University of California, Berkeley.

participation relevant to the immediate context of their social situations. Because a political type is a means to solve problems, each type of system has its advantages and disadvantages. None is permanent any more than the context of social life is permanent. Representation is a variable thing, and its forms and consequences are different in each type of political system. I offer these remarks to challenge the more commonly accepted view which evaluates all representation as it approximates our own Western experience or some ideal type of it.

The analysis begins with an effort to describe the changing character of social life by focusing on the special relation between government and society formed through some form of representation. Three main types of representation are emphasized: *popular,* as associated with "one-man, one-vote," and a conciliar form of decision-making; *interest,* as with special corporate groupings seeking special and parochial attention; and *functional,* as with technicians, planners, civil servants, and so on. Each type represents a moral claim, so to speak. Popular representation is based on the rights of *citizenship.*[1] Interest representation is based on some presumed social significance or contribution to society from a particular type of group, primarily *occupational*—for example, trade unions or business or professional organizations. Functional representation is based on presumed or recognized expertise useful to society, primarily *professional.*[2]

This framework implies some main lines for research: (a) a

[1] Although an elaborate numbers game can be played with representation, particularly the form known as electoral geometry, we incorporate in this notion two main types of popular representation, which may or may not involve electoral machinery. In the first, direct representation, citizenship becomes a shared condition or a common property of the members of a community with defined obligations and rights requiring direct participation on a Rousseauean standard. In the second, because of size, numbers, and complexity, direct democracy is impossible; citizens cannot participate directly in the decision-making process, and some "representative" must do the job. Representation in this sense requires a manageable elite speaking on behalf of a wider public. This form of popular representation is most common, and is our primary concern.

[2] Functional representation derives from the more technical aspects of social life, opening up special access to decision-making on the basis of a particular utility. Administrators and civil servants, governors and soldiers, specialists of various kinds in public works, such as irrigation, public health, and even religious or ideological matters, gain key access in proportion to the need for their skills by government. See Harold Wilensky, *Organizational Intelligence* (New York: Basic Books, 1967), pp. 94–129.

developmental social context imposing conditions within which representation occurs; (b) a set of political types, each of which emphasizes alternative modes of representation; (c) a competitive relation between each type of representation—popular, interest, and functional—in terms of a set of functions which we call the functions of representation; and (d) the functions themselves, which are *goal specification, institutional coherence,* and *central control.* (We assume that representation has these three functions as a significant minimum.) Hence two models emerge. The first, a general one, specifies the relation between society and government in terms of stratification and political systems-type variables. The second, a model of representation, is based on types of claim to access and functions of a representational elite. This representational model is an intervening variable in the general model.

Although the concepts employed can be applied to any concrete system, our concern here is to elaborate them in the special context of predemocratic, developmental polities. Illustrations of their use will be suggested in a series of short synoptic descriptions. These are intended to be suggestive of some possible future lines of application. Although these illustrations are purely descriptive and impressionistic, it is possible to operationalize the entire approach by identifying the main groupings of social actors (clustered in the present stratification categories) and determining empirically and over time their type of claim to representation (popular, interest, and functional), the "weight" of that claim, and the elite functions they perform (goal specification, central control, and institutional coherence).[3]

THE ROLE OF REPRESENTATION

As already indicated, these comments are designed to refer to predemocratic, rather than "anti-" democratic, systems. Special attention is warranted because the association of representation with democracy is so close that to speak of nondemocratic forms of representation seems somehow a travesty. Certainly there is an "incompleteness" about predemocratic representation, as if somehow it waits for "fulfillment." Our Western conception of government

[3] Empirical work of this kind on Argentina, Chile, and Peru is presently under way in collaboration with Torcuato di Tella under the auspices of the Politics of Modernization Project of the Institute of International Studies, Berkeley, California.

implies an integrated political system in which needs (motives), access (participation), and goals (purposes) are balanced through representatives popularly elected and brought together in a conciliar decision-making body.

But, predemocratic systems of government are not simply imperfect forms of democracy. They imply a different pattern of integration, perhaps a more coercive one, in which needs are more arbitrarily defined, access is restricted, and goal priorities are realized within a public context. Public and private tend to be the same. But, representation exists here too, as we shall see. Discussion of it, however, requires us to assess both the political form of government and the general underlying complexity and structural characteristics of society by identifying groups which demand government recognition in many ways: expressing needs, demanding access, and identifying goals, which governments may or may not acknowledge.

In general we can say that representation implies a permanent relation between a government and its society. The limits of authority each can impose on the other change, however. Because these limits are in some measure determined by "social capabilities," they are best evaluated in a context of development and modernization. Analysis of the evolving bases of social life leads to identification of the particular representational claims that form the tension between society and government common in all systems, which is ultimately manifested in a changing equilibrium between discipline and freedom as follows:

a. Concretely, in order to identify the group representational basis of society in a developmental context, I use certain stratification categories that seem to correspond to a particular developmental stage. These categories are pre-class, e.g., caste and ethnicity; class in the sense of the formation of occupationally based classes; class in the sense of the emergence of multibonded forms of class; and finally, postclass, e.g., the growth of specialized functional status groupings. Generalizing, we obtain a picture of the developmental process in which multiple and overlapping claims to representation result from a mixture of traditional social clusters and contemporary innovative ones introduced from industrialized systems.[4]

[4] Interesting combinations of roles result, which affect permissible behavior, such as a Latin American economist (functional status membership)

b. Analytically, the relationship between discipline and freedom provides a more directly political concern. It makes a difference if society is the independent variable and government is dependent, or if government is the independent variable and society is dependent. In the first instance, the claims of the society become the boundaries within which a government needs to act; while in the second, society is to be molded and changed by governmental decision. To handle this set of political problems we have developed four types of political systems: two in which government is the independent variable, *mobilization systems* and *bureaucratic systems;* and two in which society is the independent variable, *theocratic* and *reconciliation systems*. None of these systems needs to be "democratic" in the sense of Western representative government, which is excluded from this discussion.[5]

It should be clear from the discussion so far that the representational variables that link stratification to political system are central for this analysis. We are able to treat the relations between society and government in terms of those elite formations that compete for priority performance of three main functions: *goal specification, central control,* and *institutional coherence*. The general proposition emerges that, where society is the dependent variable and government the independent one, these three functions are more likely to be performed by government-sponsored elite formations, such as party leaders in a single-party system. In contrast, where society is the independent variable, competition between private and public bodies for the performance of these functions is likely. In both cases, however, the ability of particular groups to take a priority position vis-à-vis these functions will be seen to depend upon the stage of development in terms of the prevailing group structure. How these elite functions are distributed determines the participant basis of the society. Today, when these functions are seen in the context of modernization and development, we describe the result as a "participation explosion." This "explosion" includes greater access to roles in the modernized sectors of society as well as the spread of

living in an upper middle-class community (multibonded class) descended from an aristocratic family of landowners (caste origin changed into occupational class). Such a role is likely to be linked with planners and economists from the United Nations and other international bodies, yet it is associated in a reasonably comfortable manner with all other social groups in the system.

[5] For a more detailed discussion of these types, see my *The Politics of Modernization* (Chicago: The University of Chicago Press, 1965).

such roles in the society itself. Hence the wheel comes full circle. Greater proliferation in the modernized role sector means more modernization. This, in turn, changes the pattern of prevailing needs in the system.

THE DEVELOPMENT PROCESS AND THE GENESIS OF NEEDS

So far we have referred to the concept of *need* derivatively in terms of modernization and made visible in the form of political demands. It is obvious that needs in traditional societies will differ in many important respects from those in industrial societies. During modernization, however, old needs will continue long after new ones appear. Need seen in developmental terms becomes progressively more complex. It has two aspects: concrete demands and the mechanisms by which these demands are represented. The first is a series of events of a day-to-day sort. The second is a set of institutional arrangements. This latter aspect concerns us at the moment.

Representative institutions are based on claims to representation by interest, functional utility, or equality of right. They derive their complexity from the overlapping qualities of traditionalism, modernism, and industrialism.[6] We can describe the systemic aspects of development in terms of the continuum shown in Figure 1.[7]

Each general stage of development corresponds to a particular cluster of defined needs arising from social displacement and the formation of new tasks and objectives in the society, in combination with an overlay of "obsolete" ones. The result is cumulative and

[6] The contrast between modernizing and industrializing in social terms is that modernization is a process in which roles appropriate to (integrated with) an industrial society are established in the absence of an industrial infrastructure. Industrialization, on the other hand, means that the economy has passed beyond the stage where resources are used directly to produce technically simple products for export or direct consumption and has reached a stage of complex application of resources and technology—all within "a pattern of inter-sectoral flows involving capital and intermediate products." See R. H. Green's review of Szereszewski's "Structural Changes in the Economy of Ghana, 1891–1911," *The Journal of Modern African Studies,* 4: 1 (May 1966), 126.

[7] The continuum is a common one. It is often used in comparing modernizing countries. There are some special problems here, however. If we set the continuum on an axis, we find that, while traditionalism can give way to modernization, it is a contradiction in terms to say that modernization gives way to industrialization. The point is that modernization does not end in industrialization but is, rather, continuously defined by it.

determines which roles are appropriate. However, a set appropriate to one developmental stage is never completely abandoned. It continues to remain significant in the next stage—sometimes serving a useful purpose and sometimes producing negative consequences. More important, the combination of need with role creates an integrative problem of the greatest importance, both in terms of the stratification system as well as effective decision-making. If the institutional arrangements for linking them are seen in the particular combination of representational claims prevailing in the society in question, then the opportunities these provide for competitive elites to perform elite functions become a central empirical concern, be-

	Traditionalism	Modernization	Industrialization
Claims to Representation	interest	interest	interest
	function	function	function
	right	right	right

FIGURE I: *Developmental Continuum and Representation*

cause such competition creates information for government and, more generally, results in participation in decision-making precisely in the most sensitive areas of developmental change—for example, the alteration in the hierarchy of power and prestige in a system. We can now turn from the concept of need to the analysis of stratification.

THE STRATIFICATION CATEGORIES

Each stage of development has been described in terms of social mobility. The most limited pre-class case is caste (or caste-like), in which portions of a population are separated into distinct and separate groupings (whether religious, ethnic, or racial). Boundaries here emphasize primordial attachments or an exclusivism which goes beyond ordinary prejudice.[8]

[8] Such exclusivism extends this concept well beyond its ordinary usage in India to include ethnic and all other exclusivist boundaries difficult to penetrate except through kinship. Hence intratribal relationships in Africa, even in the same contemporary political framework, can be regarded as a form of

More complex stages of development enlarge *class* access. Mobility is greater than with caste but still clearly bounded (as in a Marxian sense). It includes a subjective awareness of membership in a semipermeable group, the life chances of whose members are similar and primarily determined by occupation. This notion (similar also to the one held by Weber) makes class dependent on the relation to the means of production. Much less restrictive than caste, it is not "primordial" in identification, although it tends to transform its class interests into general values for a whole society. Its boundaries are fixed when opportunities for occupational mobility are limited. With this type of class one can also speak of the formation of class "consciousness." Demands for class representation here include seeking redress for grievances arising from limited access to mobility. We refer to this as class *A*.

At a more advanced stage of development, class is a more multibonded affair and attributes of membership derive from many factors: religion, occupation, income, residence, family background, style of leisure, and so on. Class in this more Marshallian sense, which we refer to as type *B,* puts forward claims which, also based on interests, *transform issues of value into negotiable interests.* The result is opposite to class type *A*. It breaks up rather than creates solidarity.[9]

Finally, we have postclass status differentiation based on types of status clusters, particularly those associated with industrial skills and embodying a degree of professionality. These create claims for functional representation and include private as well as public bureaucratic status groups and technocratic groups. The latter are specially characteristic of highly industrialized countries.

We can restate the argument so far by combining the developmental and stratification variables in the structural model shown in Figure 2.

During industrialization the multibonded class type (class *B*) comes to predominate, as do the new types of status elites based on a functional role in industrialization or its related activities. These

---

caste relationship as the term is employed here. Caste may, of course, vary independently of hierarchy. See Clifford Geertz, "The Integrative Revolution," *Old Societies and New States* (New York: The Free Press of Glencoe, 1963) for a discussion of "primordial" attachments.

[9] See T. H. Marshall, *Class, Citizenship, and Social Development* (New York: Doubleday, 1964), pp. 138–143. See also S. Ossowski, *Class Structure in the Social Consciousness* (London: Routledge & Kegan Paul, 1963), Part 2.

groups form an organizational elite. Using highly germane functional criteria (education, training, professional skill), such groups represent an intellectual "class" in the limited sense that they create information and knowledge which becomes the basis for innovation within industrial societies. Innovating status groups are found not only in industrialized societies, where they occupy central power and prestige roles, but also, more derivatively, in late-stage modernizing societies. Indeed, such groups are part of the modernizing process linked, too, to their counterparts in industrial systems.

	Traditional	Modern	Industrial
Caste			
Class A			
Class B			
Functional status			

FIGURE 2: *Development Sequence*

Hence, while we speak of development as a process along a continuum from traditionalism to industrialization (from left to right), in practice modernization is a process which moves from right to left—that is, from roles originating in an industrial society, which we recreated in a nonindustrial setting. The consequence of this "reverse" overlapping of roles leads to the "embourgeoisement" hypothesis.

THE "EMBOURGEOISEMENT" HYPOTHESIS

If this analysis is correct, this reverse formation of roles (reverse in a historical sense) describes both a process and a tendency, which at the most general level can be called the "production of pluralism"—that is, the proliferation of roles and role sets organized around primarily instrumental ends. Class *B* and status relations are thus common even in early stages of modernization. This has the effect of converting conflicts over values into conflicts over interests. It allows us to suggest that the behavioral consequence of the growth of functional representation is the instrumentalization of need, which results in preferences for immediate gains rather than postponed gratifications. This consequence produces a predicament in nondemocratic systems precisely because, in varying degrees, they operate on the basis of a higher component of "postponed" satisfactions than do representative democratic systems. Modernization, then, produces "embourgeoisement," which in turn creates a plurality of instrumental ends, located unevenly in the stratification system and creating a tug-of-war among popular, interest, and functional claims.

This leads to a central proposition underlying the present analysis. We have already suggested that the greater the degree of modernization, the more the modernized roles in the society gain predominance, proliferate, and expand. These roles are predominantly instrumentalist in consequence. In the absence of an industrial infrastructure, however, such roles are not integrated around some central allocating focus; hence they create a severe "management" problem for government. The reason follows from the explanation suggested above: while representation on the basis of modernized roles may take the form of demands for popular representation, remnants of traditional roles may outnumber them. Popular representation then leads to a struggle for power. Those leading demands for a genuine popular representational system are the traditionals or near-traditionals, while the modernized section supports a doctrine of the "weightier part." More often, "populism" is the result, with popular participation channeled into purely formal conciliar bodies lacking functional substance, as in most "single-party" systems. Claims may be made on the basis of interest groups formed in the modern sector. Also functional claims may arise. Whatever the form of representational need, however, the proliferation of modernized roles creates such ambiguity, coalitional possibilities, and competition between principles of representation by various elites that not only does the management problem become great but also the possibilities both of conflict and of stagnation tend to grow. The greater the problem of such role conflict, the likelier is a drastic nondemocratic political solution. *Hence, the greater the degree of modernization, the greater the possibility of multiple claims to representation, and the greater the possibility of restrictive and authoritarian political solutions.* We can explore this proposition a bit more fully.

In the period of traditionalism (despite the variation in political types), the relations between systems were both horizontal and vertical caste, or caste-like (ethnic), involving a high degree of exclusiveness. In Africa, Europeans were virtually a caste group at first (cultural, racial, and religious primacy), imposed vertically on hitherto horizontally related ethnic caste groups (tribes). Subsequently, in most territories, the Europeans became a class group. In Latin America, vertical caste-caste relationships tended to harden in terms of Spaniards and Indians. In the African case, the dominant caste-status group was expatriate; in Latin America, it was first Spanish, then creole, and eventually aristocratic and nationalistic. The typical form it took in the latter case was the patron-client relationship to sustain rural power. (Conflicts over federal or unitarian rule commonly erupted with this relationship.) Methods of cutting across such exclusiveness could also be found. Empire was one practical way whereby a dominant ethnic group could create political links and, by imposing hegemony, change caste into status —slave, warrior, and so on. Perhaps the most common links, which in varying degrees reflected traditional social organization, were based on kinship.[10]

In the early stage of the transition from traditionalism to modernization these caste-class or caste-status relations change. Caste tends to remain primarily in rural areas (especially in the form of patron-client relations, as with the *haciendados* and *campesinos* in Peru or Chile), while in urban areas a "middle class" of the *A* type emerges, sandwiched between the caste or caste-like status groups. (Such a middle class also represents the commercial and mercantile development characteristic of modernization.)

This second-stage phenomenon shows similar characteristics in many parts of the world. In Africa it included occupational groups, such as clerks, teachers, and others related particularly to commercial life. At this point political factions representing class interests arise. Caste and status groups may also form into factions with restrictive but primordial ideologies of primitive nationalism. (In Africa the former were usually concerned with widening the possibilities of representation in local and, more particularly, municipal councils.)

[10] Tribal or ethnic-ethnic forms of caste, as in precontact Africa, can be described as horizontal linkages. Caste in terms of political and culturally defined groups can be described as a form of vertical linkage.

At a still more advanced stage of development, status groups may survive as a sector of an aristocratic class. The most rapidly growing group is a middle class of the multibonded type, lacking class consciousness, but aware of the self-rewarding characteristics of modernization, and very much preoccupied with social mobility.[11] During the transition to industrialization, this multibonded class begins to draw in both upper and lower class groups of the *A* type (as when *campesinos* move toward and into *barriadas* to become lower-middle-class groups).[12] Toward the end of the modernization period the *A* type class disappears. Modernization thus favors a class structure similar to urban middle-class life in industrial societies, the characteristics of which are increasingly accessible to all. In addition, because modernization today takes place through links with highly industrialized societies, the transposition of key roles creates salient points for the spread of "middle-classness." Hence modernization brings about the "embourgeoisement" of developing societies.

This "embourgeoisement" accounts for the fact that even under conditions of high modernization with extreme inequality, as in Latin America, radical working class activity of the class *A* variety is slight. Even peasant movements succumb to the lure of the cities. The multibonded notion of class does not lead to polarization of groups into ideological extremes showing ideological propensities. Instead, issues of values are translated into issues of interest. Issues of interest result in demands for representation on the basis of corporate groupings, including well-entrenched interest groups which can function best within the context of the formal pattern of "one-man, one-vote" while using special advantages to rig elections and sustain group representation. True, frustrations of some of the middle class of the type *B* variety, especially the intellectuals, may take the form of a radicalization, especially among youth or university students; but it is the middle class which shows these radical

[11] This is essentially what has already happened in Latin America. The broad public remained a residual caste (for example, Indians in Peru) or a peasant class. In Africa, on the other hand, in few areas has an aristocracy emerged. The old caste (ethnic) groupings have been rendered increasingly obsolete. No status elite has emerged aristocratic in quality, but rather a new type of elite, based on universalistic criteria: civil servant, technocrat, i.e., professional, trained abroad, but with strong middle-class associations.

[12] The aristocratic class becomes obsolete, some of its members becoming members of the technocratic elite, others gradually becoming submerged in the elite section of the middle class.

offshoots, not the working class.[13] Indeed, when a country reaches the final stage of advanced industrialization, it is characterized by such a proliferation of multibonded class roles that it is difficult to speak about class at all; and it is preferable to refer to interest groups and competing (popular and functional) status roles.

The point is that if one sees development in structural terms, one can define a functional pattern of increasing need differentiation. The "embourgeoisement" phenomenon changes the demand for access from collective caste or class claims to personal status advantages by means of multiple organizational groupings. Thus conditions are created for competitive elites, which cater to increasingly fractionalized interests.

As suggested earlier, each stratification category—caste, class *A*, class *B*, and functional status—indicates a type of need and demand. We have emphasized that these needs and demands will overlap and reinforce each other, just as the different stratification groups themselves will overlap. Hence the "symposium of needs" and the coalitional linkages possible in the society, which become more complex and differentiated as a society moves from a more traditional to a more industrial footing, create the "pluralistic" problem for government. The key question about representation with nondemocratic governments is how they will confront and manage this problem.

TYPES OF POLITICAL SYSTEMS AND THE FORMS OF ACCESS

Public need has been discussed in terms of developmental patterns of stratification. Before going on to a discussion of representation itself, we must first examine the problem of *access*. Access is a function of the political system. The political system as used here is formed as the result of a relation between the norms of a society and the prevailing patterns of authority. On the first axis, norms may be expressed symbolically in ideological or religious terms, in ethical precepts, or in terms of concrete goals of society.

[13] Some of the late-stage countries in Latin America have more in common with the highest stage of industrialized countries than with early-stage industrializing ones, with the exception that many of the former tend to have the atmosphere of industrial societies during depression. Of primary concern in both is distribution in the face of frustrated production.

The most effective political systems combine in a linked system both intermediate and ultimate ends with powerful motivational results, such as Calvinism in the seventeenth and eighteenth centuries or socialism in modern China. By "authority," the second axis of the relation defining a political system, we refer to the degree of accountability of leaders to those led. *In theory, perfect accountability exists where there is perfect representation.* The two sets of variables define four possible political types, each involving different types of access. Systems emphasizing ethical (consummatory) values and hierarchical authority result in "mobilization" systems. Those emphasizing concrete (instrumental) values and pyramidal authority are "reconciliation" systems. Systems with instrumental values and hierarchical authority can be called "bureaucratic" systems. Those with consummatory values and pyramidal authority can be called "theocratic" systems. We can diagram these as shown in Figure 3.

Concrete applications of each type are:

1. *Mobilization systems,* such as Communist China, have a universalizing political ideology in which issues of interest are concerted into issues of value. A command system of control comes closest to the pure type.[14]

2. *Reconciliation systems* are not necessarily democratic, although they are representative. Examples include democratic countries, as we know them, as well as "single-party" states, such as Senegal and some socialist countries, such as Yugoslavia. Consummatory values exist; but they are essentially privatized, inhering in the individual. Public behavior is seen in instrumental ends.[15]

[14] Mobilization systems do not need to be of the "left." They may be of any political persuasion. Peron's Argentina began with an effort to create a mobilization system combining both "left" and "right" characteristics. It failed, especially in the second half of its tenure. Guinea, Ghana, and Mali attempted to establish mobilization systems around a universalized political ethic (African socialism); but they had limited developmental capacities. Characteristics include a charismatic or prophetic leader, looking outward and employing a proselytizing ideology. The main problem, as Weber first pointed out in terms of charismatic authority, is the ritualization of leadership and decline in belief leading to self-interest rather than community interest, which proves inimical to the latter.

[15] The problem is that the instrumental ends are in danger of becoming completely separated from consummatory ones so that the latter are randomized. The resulting conflicts strain the legal framework or mechanism of bargaining by affecting the sanctity of their rules. A high degree of self-restraint

3. *Bureaucratic systems* tend to result from a change from one of the other systems. For example, the military subtype of the bureaucratic system would be of a "Kemalist" or possibly "Nasserist"

		Authority	
		Hierarchical	Pyramidal
Norms	Consummatory Values	Mobilization Systems	Theocratic Systems
	Instrumental Values	Bureaucratic Systems	Reconciliation Systems

FIGURE 3: *Political System-Types*

type in which the main problem would be the accessibility of the elite. Here the danger of institutional formalism would arise in the fashion described by Crozier. The advantage of this type of system is that it sustains specialized instruments of political control in order to maintain integration. Examples include Egypt, Argentina, and post-Nkrumah Ghana. Subtypes other than the military form are also common.[16]

4. *Theocratic systems* were seen classically in feudalism, when, by virtue of the local pattern of government based on proprietary and memorial rights as well as local and reciprocal allegiances, they were held together through lines of unstable kinship. The whole system was infused by devotional extremism and a religious ideology. The problem was that the system's stability depended heavily on ideological or religious unity; this dependence contradicted the realities of local power with consequent conflicts over the proper roles of church and state. However, more stable theocracies have existed, as in the small New England religious communities.[17]

---

in behavior is required. The emphasis on instrumental ends tends to erode this self-restraint, and a loss of generalized meaning ensues.

[16] One we have called the "neo-mercantilist" subtype, with civilian bureaucratic control; the other a modernizing autocracy, which (like Afghanistan, Thailand, or Morocco) employs monarchical leadership and components of a military, party, or army bureaucracy for political rule.

[17] To reject the publicly defined consummatory norms would normally

It should be pointed out that these types of political systems are not real or concrete in the sense of a membership group; but instead, they must be seen as analytical and applied as ideal types (although they are not ideal types in the Weberian sense). More important, each system tends to give priority access to different kinds of claims to representation.[18] Mobilization systems, although as suggested earlier they may be populist in character, tend to favor functional claims to representation. Such functional claims, however, may not be restricted to purely development functions, but may also include catering to party organization. Bureaucratic systems will tend to favor claims to representation based on interest and regulate these according to recognized and institutionalized standards. Theocratic systems (and here we have in mind only historical, not contemporary, cases) tended to favor popular claims to representation in the context of a widespread religious reform or messianic movement, yet allowed scope for interest claims by means of which the more instrumental qualities of social life were realized. In reconciliation systems all three claims to representation—popular, interest, and functional—tend to compete with industrial subtypes showing considerable conflict between the first and third. We can diagram these propositions as shown in Figure 4.

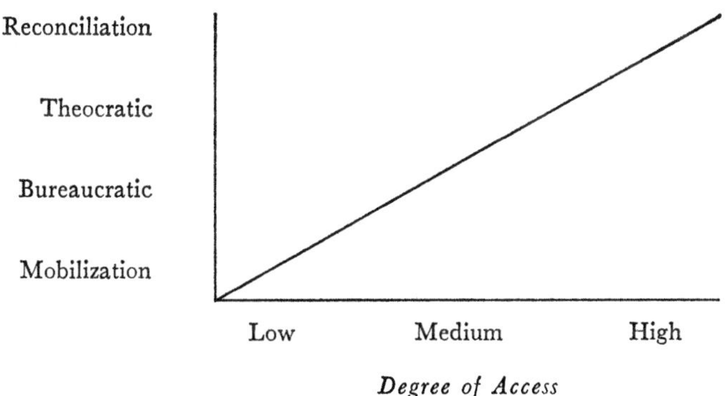

FIGURE 4: *Representational Access by System-Type*

mean expulsion from the community, or constitute grounds for terminating any meaningful participation. Control in the system is in the hands of those claiming a special quality of religious or devotional inspiration.

[18] It must be pointed out that the variable of access and type of claim is a function not merely of the type of political system which prevails but also

SOME PROPOSITIONS

1. Mobilization systems respond to pluralism and "embourgeoisement" by restructuring society along political lines in which popular representation becomes a symbolic gesture of unity; interest group representation is made public; and functional representation is bureaucratized.

2. Reconciliation systems respond to pluralism and "embourgeoisement" by oligarchical manipulations, corruption, and the use of economic advantage to restrict popular representation and expand interest group representation with subordinate functional representation.

3. Theocratic systems respond to pluralism and "embourgeoisement," ensuring a good fit between consummatory religious values and popular belief, by allowing popular representation, interest representation, and functional representation to occur as long as none threatens the sanctity of the religious values.

4. Bureaucratic systems respond to pluralism and "embourgeoisement" by manipulating interest group representation and functional representation and restricting popular representation.

To translate these propositions into more operational terms would require ranking the type of claim and the degree of significance within that claim of various concrete groupings in the system. Hence we could rank representative groupings from the various sectors of the stratification system in terms of their significant access on the basis of right, function, and interest. A number of interesting hypotheses would emerge almost immediately. For example, in the case of Argentina it is possible to show over time how various groups, such as landowners or trade unionists, shifted from popular representational significance to interest representational significance as the system of government changed from one type to another, when the bureaucratic government of Peron changed, eventually becoming a reconciliation system under Frondizi. Hence differential

of the degree of development. Hence early-stage reconciliation systems may show some popular representation, but this tends to be limited to "citizens" who represent only a small part of a total population, excluding slaves and other categories of "noncitizens" from participation, as in the Greek city-states.

access on the basis of claims, although it may occur for a variety of reasons, needs to be seen in the context of changing patterns of stratification on the one hand and alternative model types of government on the other. As we have already suggested, both "systems" are linked by representation.

The result is a sequence of differentiation reflecting the proliferation of need and the instrumentalization of ends embodied in the development process as it moves from a state of traditionalism to industrialism. Each stage of the process presents a problem for each type of government; namely, its response, by virtue of its own "systems-properties," to the problem of managing and controlling pluralism and "embourgeoisement." To summarize, the variables can be arrayed in diagrammatic form as shown in Figure 5.

Stage of Development	*Stratification Relationships*	*Nondemocratic Political System-Types*			
		Theócratic	Bureaucratic	Mobilization	Reconciliation
Industrial	Class B Functional Status Residual Class A	Representational Claims (popular, interest, and functional)			
Modern	Class A Class B Residual caste	Representational Claims			
Traditional	Caste Ethnic	Representational Claims			

FIGURE 5: *The Developmental Typology as a General Model and Representational Claims*

FUNCTIONS OF ELITE REPRESENTATION AND THE GENERAL MODEL

So far, we have concentrated on the evolving relations between changes in stratification resulting from development and government according to system-type. These have been linked by representational access on the basis of access claims. The precise nature of these claims and the rights and proprieties they imply form an important part of the normative dimension of politics. Moreover, they define what kind of information government should have at its disposal by recognizing the legitimacy of the claims implied. Much political struggle has been precisely over the degree of access each type of representation can be allowed in a political system.

However, this analysis says nothing about the various types of participation in decision-making by virtue of these claims. For this we must turn to the analysis of elites and the competition among them. Elites, as used here, constitute a set of variables intervening between society and government, which have their own significant subsystem properties. Representational elites are those with special access to power and prestige by virtue of the wider grouping they represent in society or the functional significance of the roles they perform for some object of government.[19]

We can now define the functions themselves:

1. *Central control:* the ordered maintenance of discipline in a political system on a day-to-day basis.

2. *Goal specification:* the identification and priority ranking of policies; hence, a sharing in policy formulation on the basis of a longer term.

3. *Institutional coherence:* the continuous review, reformulation, and adaptation of the fit between boundaries of subsystems, including both the regulation of overlapping jurisdictions and ideological adjustment.

With such a formulation it is possible to determine in each case whether the concrete organizational elites are specialized vis-à-vis

[19] By organizational elites we include a wide variety of roles, including administrators, chiefs, army officers, civil servants, priests, businessmen, etc., behind which stand particular organizational groupings, administrative bodies, clans or castes, armies, bureaucracies, churches, and industrial enterprises. How elite functions are distributed is the key not only to nondemocratic representation; it is in conflicts over which groups shall monopolize these functions that the case of nondemocratic policies can be isolated. In bureaucratic systems (with government the independent variable) priority is given to functional elites relating to discipline and administration, i.e., armies and civil servants. In mobilization systems (where government is the independent variable) popular representation cannot be expected to be restricted only within a single-party framework (in which party serves to distribute the elite functions and allocate access at the request of government); it is also nonfunctional. In theocratic systems (where society is the independent variable) popular representation needs to be managed by religiously organized functional elites, who thereby restrict and shape government policy.

these functions or whether they are engaged in a constant conflict to extend their degree of access.[20]

By combining these categories with those already employed we obtain the diagram in Figure 6.

Just as it was possible to operationalize the access claim of various groups in terms of their claim to representation, so it is possible to evaluate the significance of the elite in terms of its degree of access in decision-making by functional significance. Particular elites, such as landowners, members of government, civil servants, businessmen and merchants, trade union officials, and the like, can be seen in the context of their access to decision-making by means of their ability to perform functions of central control, goal specification, and institutional coherence. For example, it is quite possible for businessmen in the United States, with claims to access based on interests, to take part in goal specification and institutional coherence to a very high degree. Their degree of access, however, will be limited by competing claims based on popular and functional claims from other elite representatives of the system. Since the United States is a democratic subtype of a reconciliation system, the general pattern of competition is built into the political system and quite acceptable. In a quite different situation, as in a mobilization system such as Guinea's, not only would the claim to representation from the same group (whether public or private) be far less acceptable; but even if it were accepted, the group's share in functional access to decision-making would still be smaller than it would be in a democratic reconciliation system.

Assuming we could find numerical values for these rankings, what would we be able to identify as significant but derived theories from the data? One answer is that we should be able to account for many specific structural relations within society and between society and government. Moreover, since this is a predominantly structural model, we should be able to determine the major sources and gains and losses of information in a system. This has far-reaching theoretical significance, because the general efficiency of a type of political system can be related to various levels of development. If the

---

In reconciliation systems, the manipulation of popular, interest, and functional elites is a basis of political bargaining and negotiation.

[20] In the first instance, the claim to legitimate access is likely to be on the basis of functional expertise. In the latter instance, functional expertise and representation by virtue of public participation are likely to be employed.

Stage of Development	*Types of Stratification and "Embourgeoisement"*	*Types of Political Systems*											
		Theocratic			Reconciliation			Bureaucratic			Mobilization		
		Functions of Elite			Functions of Elite			Functions of Elite			Functions of Elite		
		C.C.	G.S.	I.C.	C.C.	G.S.	I.C.	C.C.	G.S.	I.C.	C.C.	G.S.	I.C.
Industrializing	Class B Functional Status Residual Class A												
Modernizing	Class A Class B Residual Caste												
Traditional	Caste Ethnic												

FIGURE 6: *The General Structural Model and Representational Functions*

(Shaded boxes refer to illustrative cases discussed previously.)

theory is correct, we should be able to make some predictions about the capacity of different political systems to handle integrative and developmental tasks at different stages of development—a useful object in its own right, which also sets the stage for further studies concentrating on behavior within the structural context.

We can now review the dimensions of this model:

1. The traditional-industrializing continuum is a statement of the growth in complexity of social need leading to demands.

2. The differentiation in stratification indicates the group basis of competitive claims to access—popular, interest, and functional—which arise from social need.

3. The degree of hierarchy in a system indicates the differential pattern of access which government will allow in terms of the functions of the elite.

4. The degree to which ends are consummatory and nonempirical, or instrumental and empirical, will determine the quality of political response.[21]

We can now restate the central proposition: *The greater the degree of hierarchy, the narrower the participation in central control, goal specification, and institutional coherence.* To which we can add *"the lower will be the supply of information available to government."* In other words, we use the functions of the organizational elite to indicate how much information the government is able to obtain. This leads to another proposition: *Where the amount of information available to government is small, coercion will be applied in order to maintain the balance between government and society. Coercion is a substitute for uncertainty.*[22]

Coercion, which we define as the application of violence or the threat of violence by the state, in turn causes a loss of information. It does so by using the organization elites as a coordinating and punitive arm of government. Hence the following proposition: The more advanced the system in developmental terms and the greater the degree of hierarchy, the more the organizational elites will be used to *control* the sectors of society. The greater the degree of

[21] These four propositions suggest a relation in which empirical patterns emerge from the analysis of real or concrete units through developmental-time and between types of systems. It is thus possible to use them for heuristic comparative purposes.

[22] On the variables of coercion and information, see the discussion in *The Politics of Modernization*, p. 40.

development, but the less the degree of hierarchy, the more the organizational elites will be used to *coordinate* the sectors of society. The first implies coercion through the elites. The second implies a sharing in power through the application of information.

The main points should now be clear. When representation is viewed as the link between social need and government decision-making, it defines the relation of public need to access in government. The pattern of representation will vary with system-type, in terms of both participation and function.[23]

In mobilization systems, where government is the independent variable and society the dependent variable, representation is therefore a control device "representing" government to society through the organizational elites. Minimum information and maximum coercion are the results. In a reconciliation system, where society is the independent variable and government dependent, the organizational elites share in power, provide information to government, and help coordinate society through participation in decision-making. Information is at a maximum, coercion at a minimum. In both cases the intervening variable is representation. Thus, by determining how well social need combines with political effectiveness, representation is the most sensitive general indicator of structural balance in a system.

THE REPRESENTATIONAL MODEL

We have attempted a development approach using stratification to indicate the formation of group needs and interests by means of which representative elites can be identified in a general model and organized separately in a representational model. Such needs have been seen to produce three types of representation: popular, interest, and functional. Access has been defined in terms of legitimate claims (popular, interest and functional), operating within each governmental type: mobilization, reconciliation, theocratic, and bureaucratic. The role function of the representative

[23] It would be possible to devise a scale of participation and a scale of functional access in each general type of political system at each stage of development (including the variable access between those who claim technical knowledge, i.e., technocrats, and those who claim information about public needs). We can ask how effective is the role of the expert in monopolizing the functions of the elite, and how competitive with popular representation.

elites varies in each. These functions are: central control, goal specification, and institutional coherence. Since we have treated representation as an intervening variable, the three types of representation and the three functions will result in very different consequences and purposes of representation in each political system as well as in each stage of development. Operationalizing representation in these terms thus emphasizes its multiple purposes, its many different aspects, rather than the habitual, although often implicit, one of assuming that a particular combination of representational forms or functions leads to a particular political type of pattern of balance.

My emphasis has been entirely conceptual, and it is so primarily so as to enable us to develop a true theory of representation. To do this we should be able, first, to correlate certain types of representation with certain functions; second, to universalize the correlations; and third, to find a generalized explanation of why the correlations appear. It would then be possible to make representation the independent variable with political system and developmental stage as intervening or dependent. Hence, my object has been to specify the conditions under which a theory of representation is possible, even though this is perhaps only the first step; namely, the establishment of the matrix for empirical correlations, as seen in Figure 7.

Types of Representational Access Claims	*Functions of a Representational Elite* Central Control	Goal Specification	Institutional Coherence
Popular			
Interest			
Functional			

FIGURE 7: *A Matrix for a Theory of Representation*

At the present stage, however, we can see only the variable consequences of each "box" in Figure 6, rather than correlations or syndromes. These remain entirely problematical. Still, the possibilities are interesting; and we can speculate, as I will now attempt to do, about which relations are significant. To do that properly would require much more systematic work. The applications that follow are merely "trial runs" on a purely descriptive and impressionistic basis for illustrative purposes.

A PRELIMINARY APPLICATION OF THE TWO MODELS

Applying so many variables represents severe problems of language. Not only is it difficult to handle the simultaneous relations involved without distortions imposed by our ordinary notions of sequences, but we are dealing with two "sets." In one, society seen from the standpoint of the development process is the independent variable. The functions of the elite and government are intervening variables, with "political balance" or the stable relations between rulers and ruled as the dependent variable. Here we want to know how, in the absence of freely representative relations in a political system, governments manage the growing complexity of need and provide suitable satisfactions to the members of a society. In the second "set," government is the independent variable. The functions of the representative elite are intervening. The development process is the dependent variable. In the first "set" we find concrete systems which fall predominantly in the pattern of theocratic and reconciliation system. In the second are those which fall mainly in the pattern of bureaucratic and mobilization systems.

Using these differences as our guide, we can now discuss the dimensions of the model employed in terms of its implications for nondemocratic representation as well as different stages of development. We will not discuss all the possible types but use several for illustrative purposes.

A Traditional Theocratic System and Change to a Traditional Bureaucratic Type. Stratification in traditional theocratic systems was based on caste relations determined by kinship, i.e., tribal ethnicity. Such systems tend to link kinship with ancestors; in which case, ancestral obligation is a form of shared central control between the living and the dead. Conflicts between ethnic groups define the central poltical problem; elites emerge from kin groups. Institutional coherence derives from priests and others, such as elders, to ensure the propriety of religious beliefs. Representation thus combines lineage and kin or clan leaders with ancestors in the form of kin "interest" and client "function." Government is not separate or distinct from the kinship elites; but rather, the central figure. Indeed, priest, king, and lineage merge. The combination results in the performance of the central control function by government.

What keeps the balance of the system is stability in the stratification sphere and the harmonization of social relations with sustained belief in imminent practices by a kinship elite with popular links through clans or other familial units. Emphasis on functional representation is at a minimum. Popular forms of pluralism are managed on the basis of reciprocal kinship or ethnic relations. This arrangement is accepted as a divine expression. The problem of control is, therefore, to sustain the relation between consummatory and instrumental values. Kinship representation combined with priestly authority is the general method employed.

We have chosen the case of the Arab caliphate as an illustration, because it was in our terms "traditional" in its developmental stage; i.e., organized on caste-ethnic lines (Semitic tribes), which originated in a theocracy (founded by the Prophet), and transformed itself first into an expansionist mobilization system (the Arab conquest), and then into a bureaucratic system (the Arab Empire). Our primary purpose here is to use the typology first in a dramatic, historical way to illustrate some of the categories suggested above. The Arab caliphate was organized for war in order to spread the faith. Its first phase was purely religious. After the death of Mohammed a military organization developed that represented hierarchical authority but with instrumental values subordinate to religious ones. This combination has frequently been a compelling force in history. Ibn Khaldūn notes that "religious propaganda gives a dynasty at its beginning another power in addition to that of the group feeling it possessed as the result of the number of its [supporters]."[24] (The quotation notes the temporary quality of this form of religious power.) Bernard Lewis, commenting on the caliphate after the death of the Prophet, suggests that those who elected Khalifa (the deputy of the Prophet) "can have had no idea of the later functions and development of the office. At the time they made no attempt to delimit his duties or powers. The sole condition of his appointment was the maintenance intact of the heritage of

[24] See Ibn Khaldūn, *The Muqaddimah,* trans. Franz Rosenthal (New York: Pantheon Books, 1958), Vol. 1, p. 320.

the Prophet."[25] So established, the Arabs, organized along military lines, began the twin tasks of conversion and conquest.[26] If the early caliphate was hierarchical in its system of authority, its very imperial successes meant that military commanders and governors could exercise increasing autonomy and control. The principle of election to the caliphate by powerful governors was followed. In theory at any rate, the Muslim community as such was represented.

The forms of representation during the early expansion period of the Arab Empire were extremely limited. Important family dynasties exercised influence in court. Administrators, tax collectors, and other officials associated with the organization of public lands and rents occupied central decision-making positions. The key to representation was military, administrative, or familial power, with each serving as a claim to wealth. In Mecca a wealthy class of patricians dominated the elections to the caliphate. Their representation, based on political skill supported by great wealth, quickly turned them into an oligarchy, which in turn led to a decline in religious commitment. Conflicts arose between civil administrators and the oligarchy. Competition for support from non-Arab converts to Islam, who were anxious to obtain advantages as well as the financial success of the empire, shifted the priority away from consummatory and toward instrumental values. "The assumptions of this system were the identity of Arab and Muslim and the maintenance of the religious prestige by which the Caliph exercised his authority. Its breakdown became inevitable when these assumptions ceased to be valid."[27] The result was a growth in oligarchical corruption, nepotism, and eventually civil war.

"The administration of the Empire was decentralized and in disorder and the resurgence of nomad anarchism and indiscipline, no longer restrained by a religious or moral tie, led to general instability and lack of unity. The theocratic bond which had held together the early caliphate had been irrevocably destroyed by the murder of 'Uthman, the civil war that followed it, and the removal of the capital from Medina. The oligarchy in Mecca was defeated and discredited. Mu'awiya's problem was to find a new basis for the cohesion of the Empire. His answer was to start the transformation

[25] Bernard Lewis, *The Arabs in History* (New York: Harper & Row, 1960), p. 51.
[26] *Ibid.*, p. 52.
[27] *Ibid.*, p. 59.

from the theoretical Islamic theocracy to an Arab secular state, based on the dominant Arab caste."[28]

What were the dominant groupings to be represented? They were first organized around war and administration by means of appointed chiefs who came to have territorial jurisdictions. Their importance to the caliphate was so critical that they formed a "court" in which intrigue was a key characteristic, particularly against the Mecca castes. Functional "representation" based on administration was thus arrayed against group "representation" based upon caste. The former prevailed and the secular, bureaucratic Arab state resulted.

The case emphasizes forces that tend to limit the effectiveness of a mobilization system and lead to its demise. Its success is likely to produce limited accountability but many claimants to power. Representation as such barely exists and is more likely to result in intrigue than in responsible actions. The reason there is virtually no representation is that the leader personifies the total community, and any publicly defined pattern of accountability is seen by him as a division in that community. Harmony and devotion, not division and conflict, are the aims. When the consummatory values associated with such devotion begin to decline, then de facto representation leads to civil war between rival chieftains and the rise, first, of a bureaucratic system.

A Traditional Reconciliation System and Its Consequences. Traditional reconciliation systems are organized in stratification terms around kinship. Kin groupings clustered into caste-like relations are entered by marriage, adoption, or co-optation. Coalitions of caste relations hover somewhere between caste and class *A* and are characteristic of ancient European reconciliation systems about which we have some knowledge, such as Athens, the Roman Republic, or the Florentine city-state. In each of these cases and within the general category of caste-type relations, a dynastic pattern of stratification could be found. However, such general characteristics hold for more than antique European protoypes and would even include those age-grade segmentary systems in Africa, in which entry is based on generation. Central control in such reconciliation systems is normally through a king in council dominated by senior castes, coalitions of castes, or age-grades. These may vary in type

[28] *Ibid.*, p. 64.

from dynastic familial organizations and other groups which maintain stewardship over land and possess other property rights not easily attainable by the ordinary public. Goal specification consists primarily in special protection for the major economic and ethnic groupings. Institutional coherence rests with the consultative and conciliar procedures, including courts and councils, magistrates and priests, and shared participation of overlapping caste-like groupings in the reconciliation of conflicting interests. The traditional reconciliation system thus emphasizes representation on the basis of familial seniority. To illustrate this more fully we can analyze the case of the Roman Republic.

The Arab case demonstrates how systems change from theocracy to mobilization to bureaucratic representation. Another case of a traditional system is better known because historically it is closer to the European experience; namely, the traditional reconciliation system of the Roman Republic, particularly during the attempted reforms of the Gracchi. Government had been primarily aristocratic with the domination of the burgesses by the old senatorial families. During the expansionist phase of the Roman Empire this worked reasonably well. But, at the height of Rome's glory, as Mommsen suggests: "The government of the aristocracy was in full train to destroy its own work. Not that the sons and grandsons of the vanquished at Cannae and of the victors at Zama had so utterly degenerated from their fathers and grandfathers; the difference was not so much in the men who now sat in the senate, as in the times. Where a limited number of old families of established wealth and hereditary political importance conducts the government it will display in seasons of danger an incomparable tenacity of purpose and power of heroic self-sacrifice, just as in seasons of tranquility it will be short-sighted, selfish, and negligent—the germs of both results are essentially involved in its hereditary and collegiate character."[29] The Roman case would indicate a shift from claims to popular representation on the basis of a narrowly limited definition of citizenship to rural interest representation on the basis of clanship estates. Struggles over access to decision-making resulted in a corresponding decline in institutional coherence (and the formation of a religious vacuum that prepared the ground for the successful entry

[29] Theodore Mommsen, *The History of Rome* (New York: The Free Press, n.d.), Vol. III, pp. 297–98.

of Christianity at a later stage), leading to struggles over central control and goal specification among various clans, and, as well, to the development of different classes.

Attempts to prevent the senate aristocrats from plundering the system and to recognize the needs of the public gave rise to conflict between "optimates," who wished the rule of the best, and "populares," who favored the will of the community. The result was conflict over and struggles between rival "classes" as well as between "estates." Attempts to create major reforms, first by Tiberius and subsequently Gaius Gracchus ended, in each case, with their deaths.

The Roman illustration is interesting because it demonstrates the difficulties as well as the typical problems of reconciliation systems that are not democratic; i.e., they exclude part of the community from effective representation. The Roman case excluded slaves, foreign burgesses, and effectively the urban poor; yet, nevertheless, considered them part of the society. The civic community was thus only a part of the whole. The magistrates were chosen from a relatively small number of families. Nevertheless, the citizens could record a vote on important issues. Politicians, in order to be elected, needed to have a faction behind them. The basis of faction was in the *gens,* the family. Hence, family connection and political marriage was extremely important.

In addition to family, personal obligation and the resulting patron-client stratification system was important. Faction, intrigue, personal connection are all characteristics of representation in reconciliation systems that provide for accountability in conciliar bodies representing the "weightier part" of the community but not necessarily the most functionally significant. What H. H. Soullard suggests for Rome is certainly true of reconciliation systems more generally. "It is this far-reaching nexus of personal and family relationships and obligations that underlies the basis of Roman public life, a fact which the nobles themselves may have sought to obscure. Its form naturally will have varied at different periods of Rome's history. Thus in the early days the tie of the clan was probably the predominant factor; families would group themselves around such leading patrician clans as the Fabii, Aemilii, and Claudii."[30] The Roman case merely illustrates in a historically familiar context a general phenomenon found in many modernizing societies today. If

[30] H. H. Soullard, *Roman Politics 220–150* B.C. (Oxford: The Clarendon Press, 1951), p. 3.

we take the same characteristics, the separation of society from effective civic community, and put them in the context of modernizing nations—whether old ones, as in Latin America, or new ones, as in Africa—we see many of the same problems. In the Latin American case the result has been the growth of class *A* conflict and class *B* coalitions, thereby providing manipulative control over representative organs by various oligarchies. Representation has been on the basis of family. Although such representation was originally based primarily on rural landowning wealth, it has expanded latterly in the form of controlling dynastic commercial and industrial oligarchies. Hence, overrepresentation of a "weightier part" has developed and the patron-client relationship has extended into every aspect of political life. Precisely to change this system, many of the modern "democrats" in Latin America, such as Frei in Chile, have turned their attention and have attempted to create a theocratic modernizing society by means of land reform and more effective representation.

The Modernizing Reconciliation System. Modernizing reconciliation systems are likely to be extremely unstable in the primary stages of modernization because of the survival of many traditional practices. Overlapping caste, class *A*, and class *B* relations provide the basis of competing coalitions. Interest representation predominates; central control is weak and bureaucratic; goal specification of the developmental variety is manipulated by politicians with only marginal participation by technocrats; and institutional coherence is based on corruption, mobility, and payoff. If popular representation occurs, it militates against developmental planning. Uneven access to power accentuates inequality and social discrimination. Many Latin American countries fall in this category.

In later stages of modernization, with the growth of class of the *B* type and its intermediary status clusters between class *A* structures, central control tends to become more organized around a bureaucracy; goal specification is shared by competing class and status groupings; while institutional coherence is sustained through multiple and overlapping institutional groupings. The pattern is likely to lead to organized plunder, with repeated interventions by the military. The combination of political and economic stagnation, popular representation in voting, and functional representation through the bureaucracy, army, and developmental agencies creates conflict between popular and functional principles of representation.

As we have suggested, reconciliation systems are not necessarily democratic in the Western sense of the term. Caste, class *A*, and class *B* relations are linked to familial and personalistic ties. Such overlapping role sets combine within a single community elements of caste opportunism and class conflicts (as in *campesino* movements), so that the development of multibonded class and status relations uses the structure of representative government as an umbrella to protect its interests from demands produced by caste and class *A* types of conflict. Moreover, when such conflict gets out of hand, representing a management problem for the class *B* elites, the latter tend to favor military intervention leading to a new constitutional framework.[31] Such efforts attempt to link, by political means, the structure of social relations and roles established in each sector of the stratification system with government on the basis of interest representation. A new round of corruption occurs as well as a new tendency to plunder the system in the absence of more positive representational links and associations. The crisis in central control soon repeats itself; hence the predicament. Sharing power through popular representation by means of the proliferation of voluntary associations, committees, local governments, and general participation in assemblies and councils throughout the structure of pyramidal authority only intensifies the conflict between popular and interest claims to representation. But in the exercise of their functions, the elites emphasize distribution rather than development. This exaggerates a "plunder" psychology with few possibilities for managed and enforced savings in the community. Representational access in terms of any organized interest—whether based on class or function—becomes dominant at the expense of the others.

The problem of the nondemocratic reconciliation system is thus accountability without constraint and political participation for short-term gains. The result is likely to be political and social stalemate, punctuated by periods of conflict.

An Industrializing Reconciliation System. The third type of reconciliation system, that occurring in industrialized countries,

[31] See the interesting theory of military intervention advanced by José Nun in "América Latina: La crisis hegemónica y el golpe militar," *Desarrollo Económico,* 6 (July-December 1966), 22–23.

represents the most acute stage of the "crisis of meaning"—inherent in the model itself. Class conflicts have given way to status coalitions, each supporting popular representation and interest representation in competition with functional representation. Central control has become a function of conflict among bureaucrats, technocrats, and politicians. Goal specification is a tug-of-war between interest and functional representation. Institutional coherence is based upon popular representation. Here lie many of the familiar problems confronting pseudo-democratic societies, including the inadequacy of representative mechanisms and restricted access. Yugoslavia and Poland might serve as examples of industrialized reconciliation systems, with even the USSR moving in that direction. A few Latin American countries, such as Brazil and Argentina, might also fall into that category, despite their military regimes, but for the fact that they are not yet sufficiently industrialized. In any case, representation is much the same as in the modernizing society, except that either a party, a bureaucracy, or a military group is responsible for both central control and goal specification, while institutional coherence is left to whatever class and associational groupings are found available, perhaps surviving from the previous system. In other words, nondemocratic reconciliation systems in industrial societies tend to be "tolerant" of the social system and to allow institutional coherence to be handled locally by the community itself, while functional access is increasingly prominent.

Modernizing Mobilization Systems. Characteristic cases of modernizing mobilization systems would include Guinea, Ghana, and Mali immediately after their independence. The stratification relations of modernizing systems are of both the caste and the class *A* types. One finds a typical traditional caste/colonial, or expatriate, caste stratification system alongside of a "middle class" conscious of its position and performing modern tasks.[32] A mobilization system tries to eliminate the colonial caste, root and branch, and to integrate class and remaining traditional caste relations around new political clusters—a political "class" of the *A* type which embodies the community, such as attempted by the Parti Démocratique de Guinée, the Union Soudannaise in Mali, or the Convention People's Party in

[32] In this usage I would reject the notion advanced by those who claimed that there was no "class" in Africa. Vertical caste (European/African) was followed by class *A*/caste (African elites versus tribal groups) and class *A*/class *B* relationships relatively quickly.

Ghana, while manipulating populism as a substitute for popular representation. Party organization creates representative clusters and attempts to define participation in functional terms: the socialization function (youth movements); the production function (trade unions and corporations); the rural innovation function (cooperatives and farmers associations); and the ideological function (ideological institutes). Interest representation is likely to be suspect and regarded as "neo-colonialist" or imperialist. Attempts to alter caste relations are made by changing the principles of representation and by modifying sources of mobility—both politically, through a "single party," and by bureaucratic co-optation. Central control is likely to be in the hands of a party-government coalition in which the key posts in each are occupied by the same individuals. Goal specification is in terms of planning based on a combination of ideological and technical goals, in which technocrats, engineers, economists, statisticians, and the like, play a large part, normally in some conflict with political leaders. Institutional coherence is based on increasing bureaucratization, again with a high ideological component. Two characteristic conflicts of principle exist between government-sponsored elites and the remnants of traditional elites, and between ideological specialists in the party and civil servants and technocrats. Here we find representation on the basis of function ideologically linked with relevant groupings in the society. Counter-elites are excluded; but even these may not necessarily be restricted in terms of social mobility within the system.

The main differences between traditional and modern forms of mobilization systems are (1) that populism is used to support functional representation in the modern forms; and (2) that populism requires a consultative base, while functional representation requires a special access to functional elites. Populist and functional elites contend with each other for power. Popular representation is limited to being of the testimonial variety of populism. Access to central control and goal specification is restricted to those concerned with development or maintenance of support. The institutional coherence function is restricted to programmatic ideology, with organizations modified according to the degree to which they fit the ideological pattern.[33]

In general, we can say that, even where popular representation

[33] See Aristide R. Zolberg, *Creating Political Order* (Chicago: Rand McNally, 1966), pp. 93–125.

is minimal, growing competition between populist and functional elites for access to central control and goal specification produces considerable accountability. Even the functional elites seek to expand their competitive access by broadening their recruitment base in society. The tendency is to move downward through the restratification of the public into corporate functional groupings relevant to development and systems-maintenance. Not class, but *corporate* grouping is characteristic; hence, a kind of "corporate representation" in primary stage modernizing mobilization systems is seen as the means of reconciling populism with functional expertise.

The solution just mentioned is rarely achieved, however, because of the appearance of the "embourgeoisement" phenomenon, which breaks up the stratification pattern into too many complex coalitional multiples for restratification along corporate-functional lines. Moreover, even caste elements prove difficult to eradicate, not to speak of class *A* type groupings. The middle class of the type *B*, growing as modernization proceeds, makes demands based on wider needs. Thus, central control needs to be even more tightly organized in a military or paramilitary type of formation. The result is government versus the elites. Goal specification then relies more heavily on systems-maintenance than on development. Institutional coherence tends to be a combination of ideological orthodoxy and coercion. Government-monopolized central control is allocated on an appointive basis to administrators. Goal specification is toward a future objective. An elite of ideological specialists is required both to create such goals and to ensure their status as consummatory values. Institutional coherence is handled by administrative magistrates or tribunals dedicated to the preservation of ideological uniformity. The functions of an elite are joined within a narrow circle, closely associated with government and hostile to other groupings, particularly other caste groupings in the system. When there is weakness or failure in the performance of any of the elite functions, government is likely to apply coercion. Hence, "embourgeoisement" creates the conditions for mobilization and also prevents the mobilization system from working.[34] Under such paradoxical conditions, popular representation, in the form of a party elite, would collide with the governmental functionaries or technocrats over an increasingly restricted access to elite functions.

[34] *Ibid.*, p. 127.

The Industrializing Mobilization Systems. During industrialization the problem of the decline of consummatory values in combination with the primacy of instrumental ones tends to fit directly with a structural pattern of differentiation, in which class conflict gives way to multibonded class with coalitions and groups forming on the basis of functional significance. Party leaders and technocratic elite are likely to compete for central control, as in the modernizing case; but party leaders and bureaucrats are likely to handle goal specification by means of consultative instruments; while institutional coherence is similarly dealt with by party leaders and plant managers. The industrial system injects new and mutually opposing elements into the picture: on the one hand, the need for decentralization of command units (as the complexity of the system grows); and on the other, the increasing bureaucratization occasioned by the effort to retain command over a decentralized decision system. Representation is thus likely to be functional on the basis of the productive system and consultative on the basis of the hierarchy. We can call the resulting subtype *consultative* (as distinct from popular) representation, as exemplified in China by the direct contact between cadres and the masses.[35] Even in China, however, the emerging stratification pattern creates an interesting problem; namely, the "embourgeoisement" phenomenon, which breaks up society into competitive status groupings, making it difficult to treat the population in terms of any given class or corporate interest, but rather as representative of elaborately distributed needs.

Breaking up the class pattern into multibonded class emphasizes competitive claims to popular representation under the guise of consumer interests. If new technocratic elites, crucial to the developmental process, gain supremacy over the party elite, central control would be shared by administrators, civil servants, and managers. Goal specification would be decentralized with a corresponding depoliticization of many aspects of social life. Institutional coherence would be provided by the shared and overlapping organizational pluralism associated not only with production and distribution but also with local government. At this point consultative representation may be transformed into popular representation. If that should occur, then the political system could become democratic.

[35] James K. Townsend, *Political Participation in Communist China* (Berkeley and Los Angeles: The University of California Press, 1967), *passim.*

The industrializing mobilization system is of great importance because it seems to produce a contradiction between political and economic needs. In highly industrialized societies the multibonded pattern of class spreads throughout the system. It becomes virtually meaningless to speak of classes in the Marxist or Weberian sense.[36] The new types of status groupings, each with special claims to representation and power, are competitive in terms of the function of the elite and their type of claim to representation. Most important is the role of the new technocrats, whose functional value is based upon knowledge or innovation. They are opposed by the bureaucrats, whose claim is based upon continuity and efficiency; and by the politicians, whose claim is based on instrumental or consummatory values of a populist variety. This conflict arises because of the role of information. The modernizing society has a model and a goal—industrialization. It can afford to be imitative. The main difference between modernization and industrialization is that the latter creates a revolution in innovation and technique. In industrial systems it is necessary to reconcile representation of interests and function with new knowledge (innovation). Each of these types of representation involves a form of information which govermnent requires during industrialization. Hence the effect of high industrialization is to diversify need as a basis of information, setting up the following causal chain: *The need of information results in more diverse representation on the basis of complex interests. This emphasizes instrumental values. As consummatory values decline and the need for information grows, the mobilizing industrial system will move toward a reconciliation system.*

SOME TENTATIVE GENERALIZATIONS

By putting so much emphasis on development, we have related system-type to representation in terms of changing needs and information. Our formulation does not deal with democratic systems, but it could include them. In modern predemocratic developing societies, and in some industrial ones as well, democracy is a goal based on developmental priorities rather than an independent normative aim, based on a prior, if implicit, agreement on popular

[36] The concept of false consciousness seems merely a presumptuous convenience, adopted by messianic intellectuals as a warrant of superiority in a world which otherwise largely ignores them.

representation. The maintenance of representative government in democracies is partly a function of an ability to convert potential conflicts over values into conflicts over interests *without, nevertheless, allowing interest representation to become dominant. This implies an effective blend of consummatory and instrumental values and high accountability on the basis of popular representation, both of which imply agreement over the balance of representational claims with regulated competition of functional access by elites.* Such a system is subtle, complex, and delicate.

In a mobilization system, on the other hand, consummatory values clearly dominate. Overt challenges to hierarchical authority are uncommon and popular representation is minimal. Indeed, pluralism is the enemy. The corporate community is, at least formally, highly unified; and dissidents are silent. However, a tendency toward functional representation manifests itself. During the early stages of development, particularly in premodern systems, these functional representatives include military and administrative figures in bureaucratic roles.[37] In mobilization systems at the highest stage of development, industrialization, these roles tend to become more specialized around those most germane to generating information and technique; and the clusters of functional roles facilitates central control and goal specification.

We conclude with the following propositions:

1. Both mobilization and bureaucratic polities are limited accountability systems, with government the independent variable and society dependent. Emphasis in the former is on functional representation. In the latter, functional representation is mixed with various forms of patron-client interest relationships.

2. Both reconciliation and theocratic polities are high accountability systems in which society is the independent variable and government dependent. Emphasis in the former is on a mixture of interest, functional, and popular representation; and in the latter on popular and interest representation personified in a religious/ethical authority.

Although representation is treated here as an intervening variable, it does have several generalized subsystem characteristics. First,

[37] It is important to stress that quite often the role is created by the individual, i.e., a trusted lieutenant is made an administrator. If he, as occupant, can be replaced, but the role is retained, then role institutionalization has occurred and it is possible to consider the role independently of the occupant.

information is created through the functions of the elites. The greater the access to central control, goal specification, and institutional coherence by the elites, the more broadly is power distributed, the more likely are the elites to engage in competition to represent diverse groups, and the greater is the degree of information available to decision-making. When the system begins as a mobilization system, the competition among cities constitutes a disciplinary problem for government; elite functions are reduced and information is lost. The proposition that then emerges is: *When a society of the mobilization type is at the stage of late modernization or industrialization on the development continuum, it develops a multibonded/status social system. The competition for access by elites leads to decentralization of power but to no change in the principle of hierarchy, thus posing an authority problem for government likely to lead to coercion on the one hand and intrigue on the other.* Intrigue will be the main activity of the elites competing for access to central control, goal specification, and institutional coherence. In the absence of good information, coercion will be applied by government.

In reconciliation systems such competition among elites is likely to lead toward a greater degree of elite participation by wider sectors of the public, with two main tendencies emerging: representation on the basis of multibonded class, or *popular* representation; and representation on the basis of modern status, or *functional* representation. Competition among elites consists of conflicts over the role of experts versus politicians, with civil servants and technocrats among the former and elected representation among the latter. Such competition profoundly affects the effectiveness of participation by the public. Under conditions of high industrialization, a sense of powerlessness can lead to public feelings of alienation as well as to a decline in the overarching shared consummatory values of the system; so that the conversion of issues of value into conflicts of interest produces an excessive fractionalization of power which renders effective decision-makers impossible. Under the circumstances, free available information becomes unusable. *The proposition that emerges is that in reconciliation systems if the competition among elites for access to the elite functions and the differing claims to representation produce an excessive fractionalization of power, resulting in the privatization of wants and randomization of ends, then the rules of the system themselves become vulnerable. Such systems produce increasing amounts of information and little co-*

ercion; but the communications net is so overloaded, and the claims to participate in central control, goal specification, and institutional coherence are so competitive that the systems tend to be ineffective.

The conclusion to these notes is really to state a problem; namely, that the long-term process of industrialization polarizes social structure into groups that are counterposed against each other in a competition for representation that is imposed by the need for information. Although I believe this produces a long-run tendency toward a reconciliation system, the likely possibility is a "dialectic" between a modern form of the corporate state, with a high emphasis on functional representation, and a democratic state, with a high emphasis on popular and interest representation.

In sum, we have attempted to identify the types of representation that are functionally distributed to particular elites under conditions of variable access and growing need.